Comrade
Sisters

Women of the
Black Panther Party

The family we choose, a bond that defies location, time and biology, a life well-lived

Jackie Hood
Carol Houston
Donna Howell
Peggy Hudgins
Lulla Hudson
Audry Hudson
Ericka Huggins
Adrienne Shankari Humphrey
Rosalyn Ikedife
Phyllis Jackson
Patti Solomon Byrd Jenkins
Diane Jenkins-Aubry
Regina Jennings
Ann Johnson
Carolyn Johnson
Marolyn Johnson
Nancy Johnson
Rosa "Malikia" Johnson
Pat Jones
Audrea Jones
Kathy Jones
Judy Juanita
Joan Kelley-Williams
Isabella Kelly
Mabel Kennon
Kathy Kimbrough
Yvonne King
Melanie King
Tamara Lacey
Joyce Lee
J. Tarika Lewis
Mary Luddy
Vanessa Mac Arthur
Hazel Mack-HIlliard
Yasmeen Majid
Cookie Marsha
Jeanie Marsha
Erlene Marsha
Charla Marsha
Carolyn Martin
Ila Mason
Dora Matthews
Connie Matthews-Tabor
Christina May
Mary McIntosh
Vivian McMillan
Rosemari Mealy
Joyce Means
Agnes Minatee
Maryann Mitchell
Jo Ann Mitchell-Stringer
Vanetta Molson

Mere Meanata Montgomery
Frances Moore
Renee Moore
Ruby Morgan
Olive Morris
Claire Muhammad
Falomi A Muhammad.el
Pauline Napier
Millicent Nelson
Miriama Rauhihi Ness
Sandra Netter
Fredrika Newton
Akua Njere
Lenora Noble
Cynthia Norwood
Njinga Onyame Nyameke(Patti
Byrd) Kiilu Nyasha
Denise Oliver Velez
Ethel Paris
Paula Peebles
Barbara Pelson
Dianne Pequese
Sylvia (Reenie) Perez
Pamela Perkins
Tamisha Wendie Peterson
Gussie Pheanious
Dorothy Phillips
Sandra Pratt
Brenda Presley
Evelyn Proctor
Donna Quiett
Dale Rascoe
"Bootsie" Annette Reaves
Sylvia Rivera
Beverly Robinson
Candi (Thelma) Robinson
Billie Robinson
Pat Rogers
Marsha Rogers
Marie Roper
Johnnie Marie Ross
Wanda Ross
Madalynn Carol Rucker
Lillie P. Rushin
Osa Russell-White
Leslie Salley
Barbara Sankey
Leslie Johnson Seale
Artie Seale
Afeni Shakur
Assata Shakur
Cleo Silvers

Pamela Hooks Simmons
Carlotta Simon
Betty Sio
Cyndi Smallwood
Gloria Smith
Rose Smith
Joy Smith
Majeeda Smith
Pauline Smith
Yolanda "Yo-Yo" Smith
Alease Stallworth
Marva Strickland
Veronica Sumpter
Aliya Sutton
Marcia Taylor
Ella Jo Taylor
Shirley Taylor
Elaine Thomas
Rosita Thomas
Debra Thomas
Cynthia Anderson Thompson
Eva Thompson
Jan Thompson
Nkenge Toure
Betty Powell Toussaint
Valerie Trahan
Agnes Tuisamoa
Celia Turner
Marsha Turner Tayor
Ruth Wakabayashi-Kondo
Pamela Ward Pious
Brenda Washington
Mary Lou Watson
Joceiter Weaver
Jackie Web
Diane Webster
Geraldine Williams
Karen Williams
Tommye Williams
Naomi Williams
Ora Williams
Mary Williams
Sharon Williams
Saundra Williams
Lauryn Williams-Jackson
Jeannie Wilson
Lola Wilson
Ukali Linda Bethea Wilson Joy
Wooley
Delores V. Wright
Elaine Young X

Comrade Sisters

Women of the Black Panther Party

Stephen Shames
Ericka Huggins

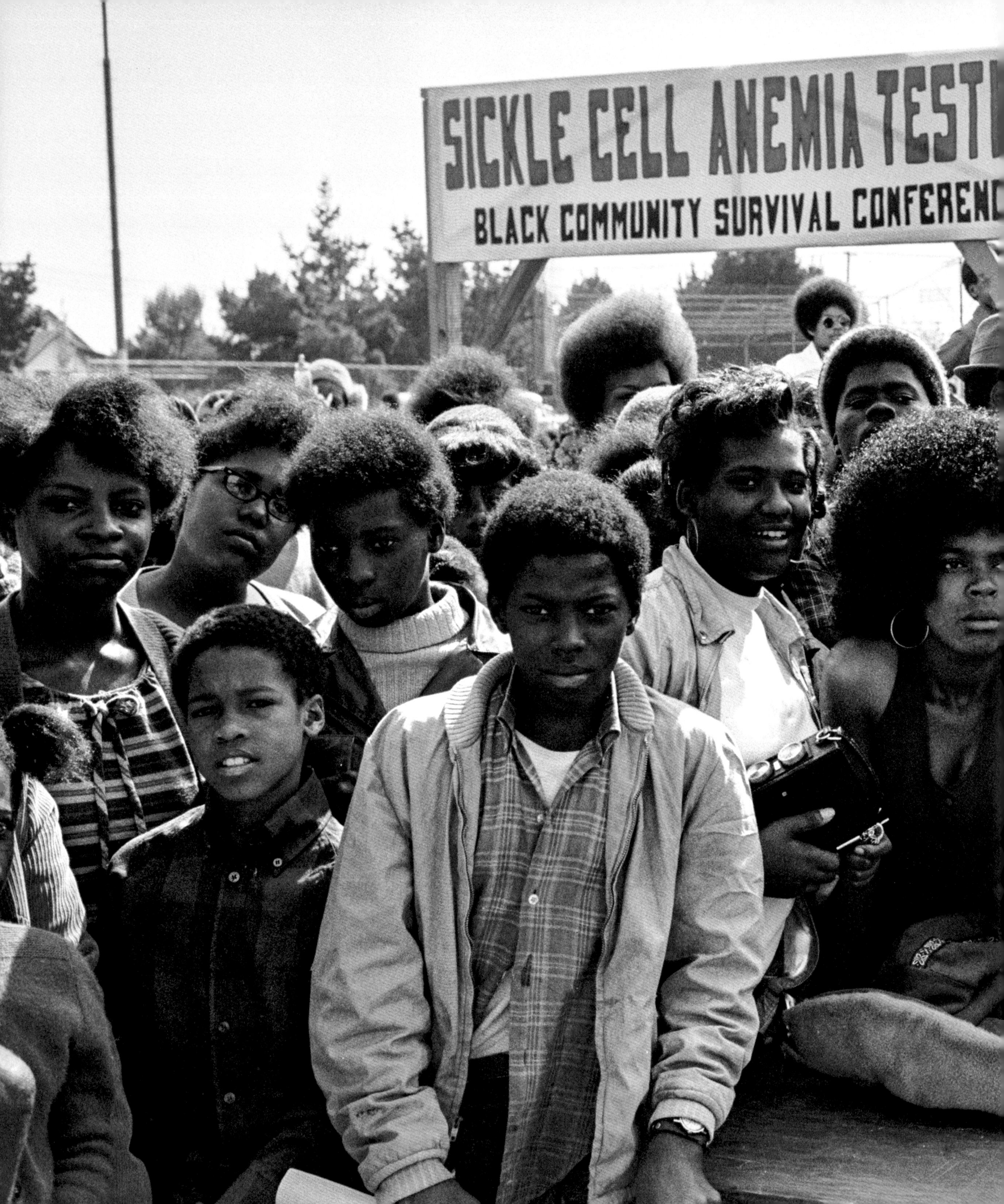

SICKLE CELL ANEMIA TESTI
BLACK COMMUNITY SURVIVAL CONFERENC

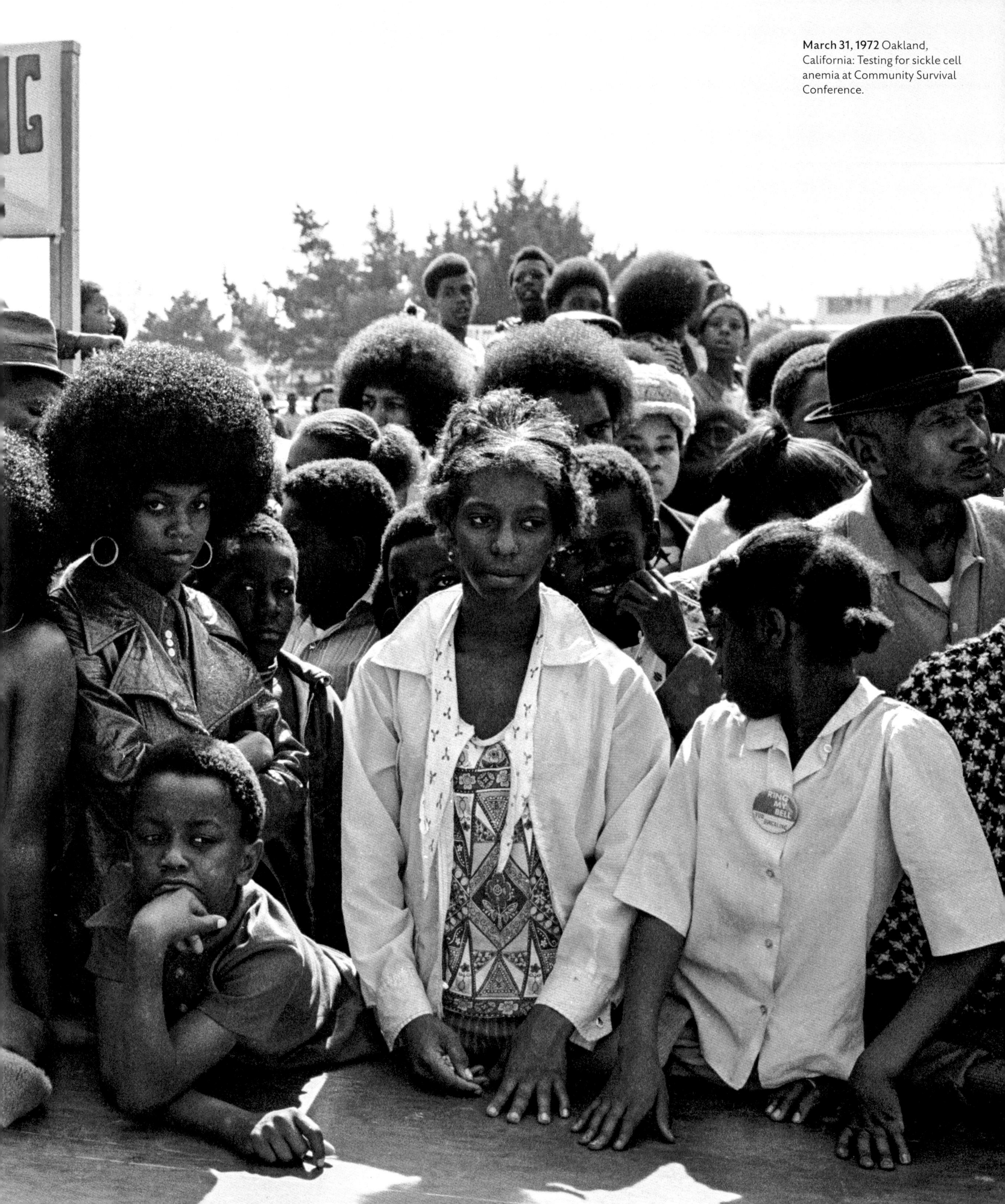

March 31, 1972 Oakland, California: Testing for sickle cell anemia at Community Survival Conference.

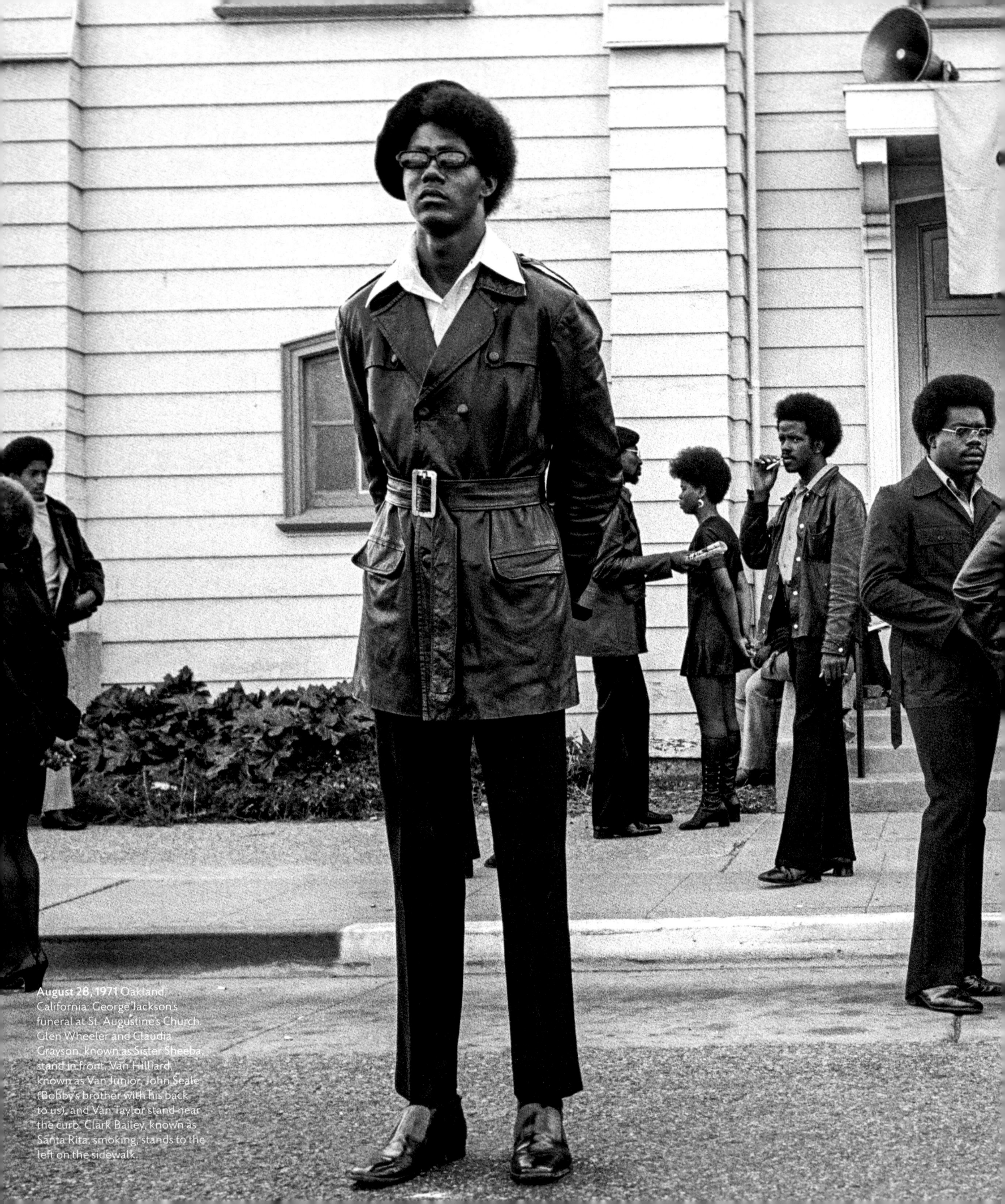

August 28, 1971 Oakland, California: George Jackson's funeral at St. Augustine's Church. Glen Wheeler and Claudia Grayson, known as Sister Sheeba, stand in front. Van Hilliard, known as Van Junior, John Seale (Bobby's brother with his back to us), and Van Taylor stand near the curb. Clark Bailey, known as Santa Rita, smoking, stands to the left on the sidewalk.

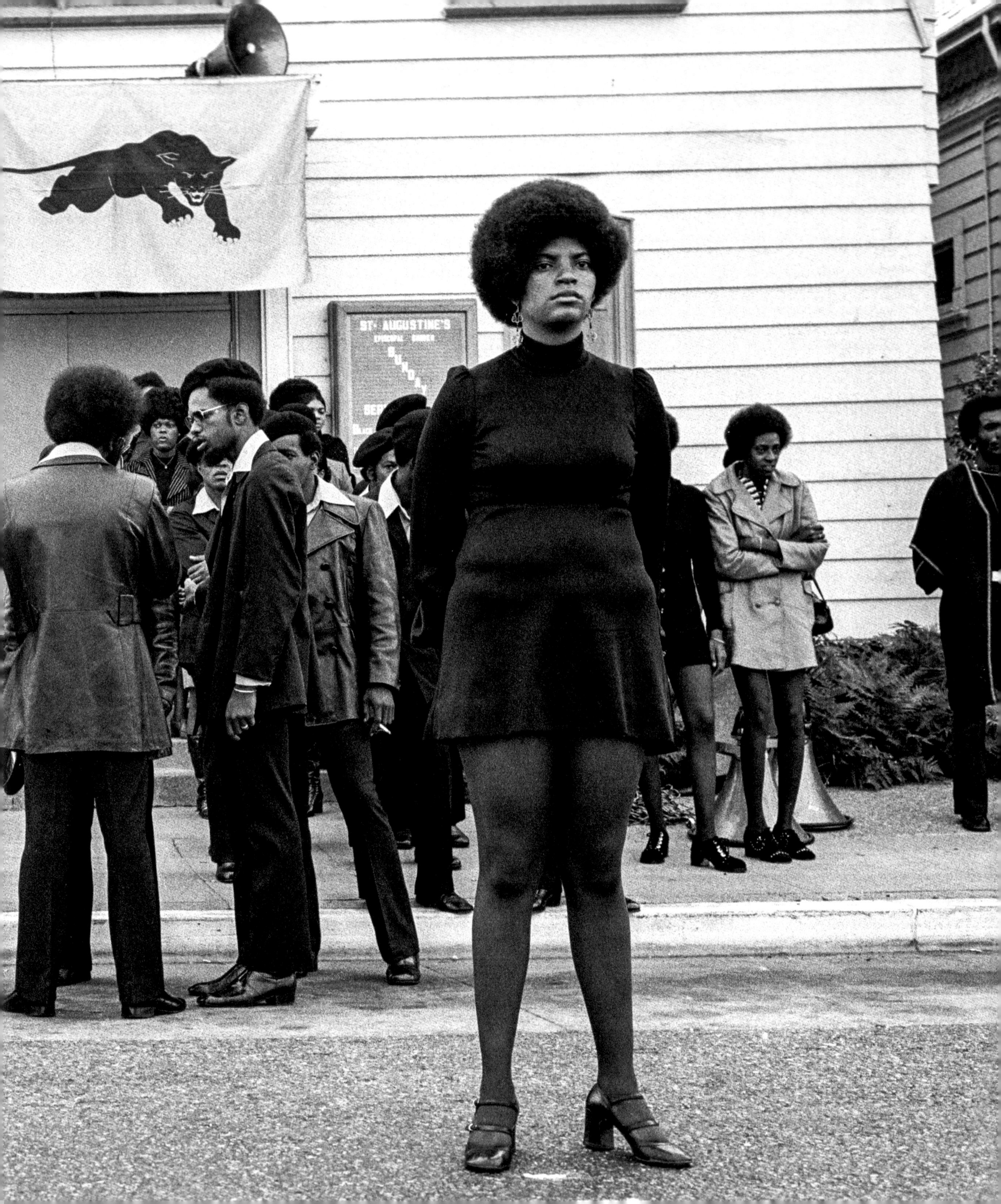

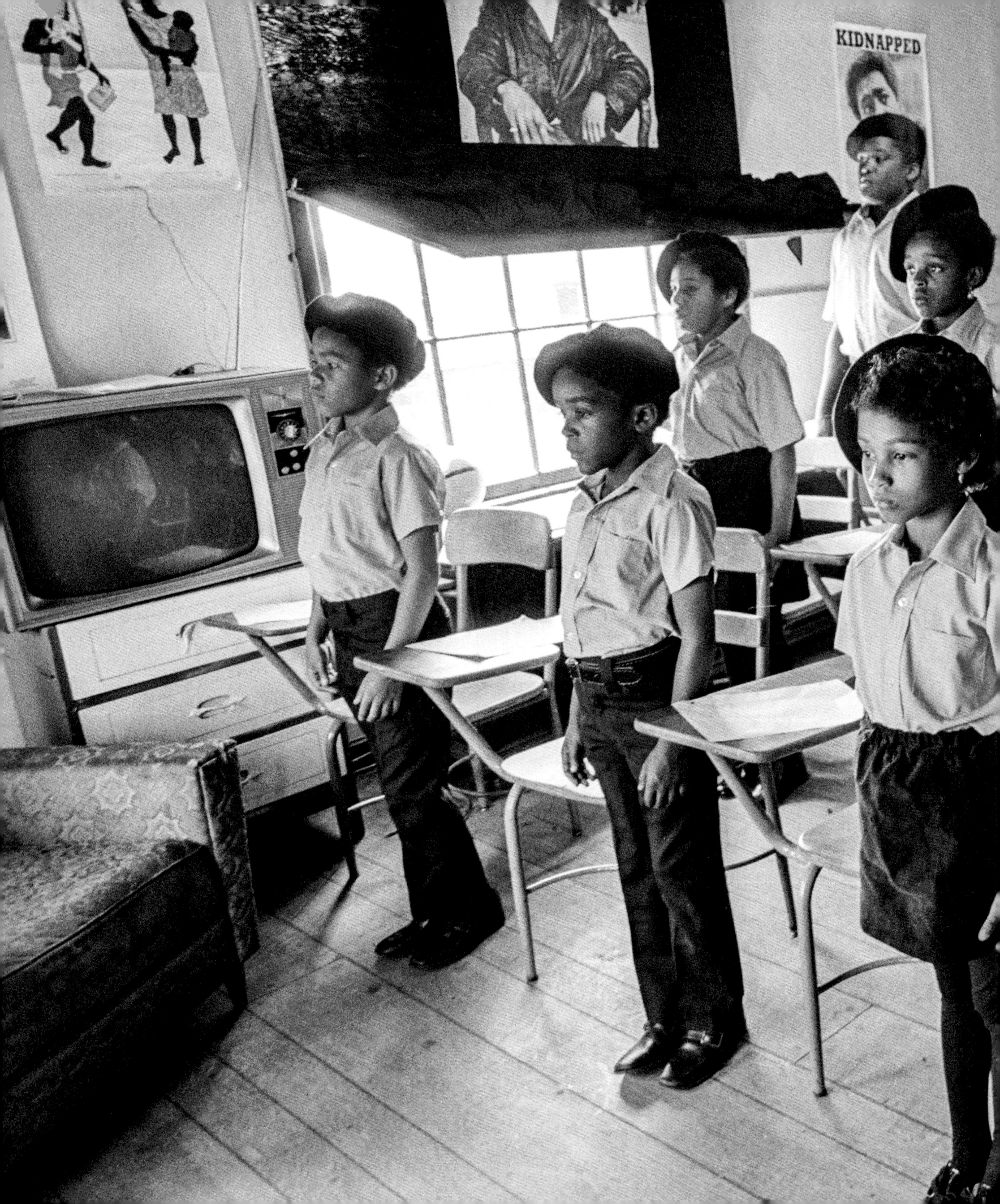
KIDNAPPED

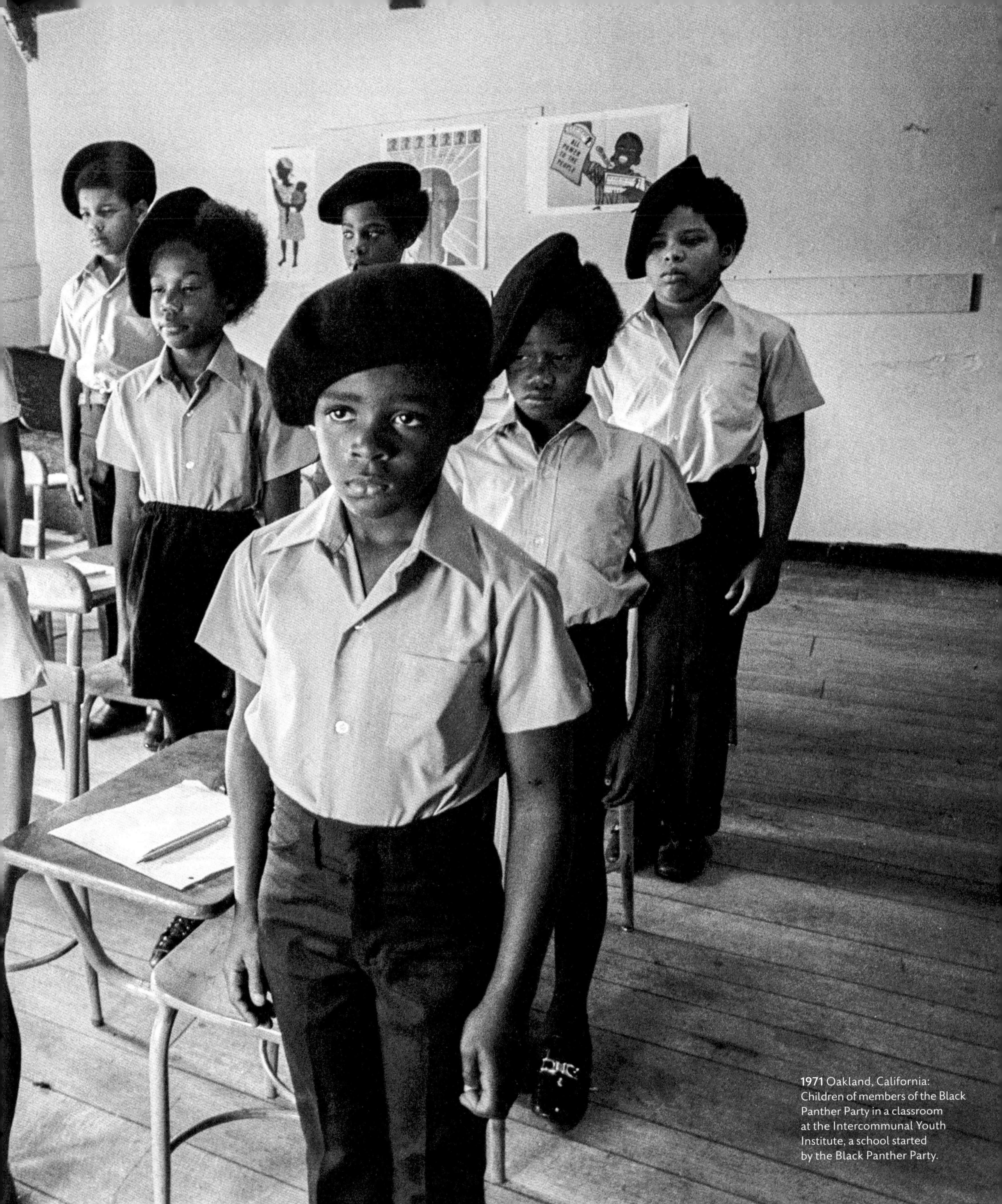

1971 Oakland, California: Children of members of the Black Panther Party in a classroom at the Intercommunal Youth Institute, a school started by the Black Panther Party.

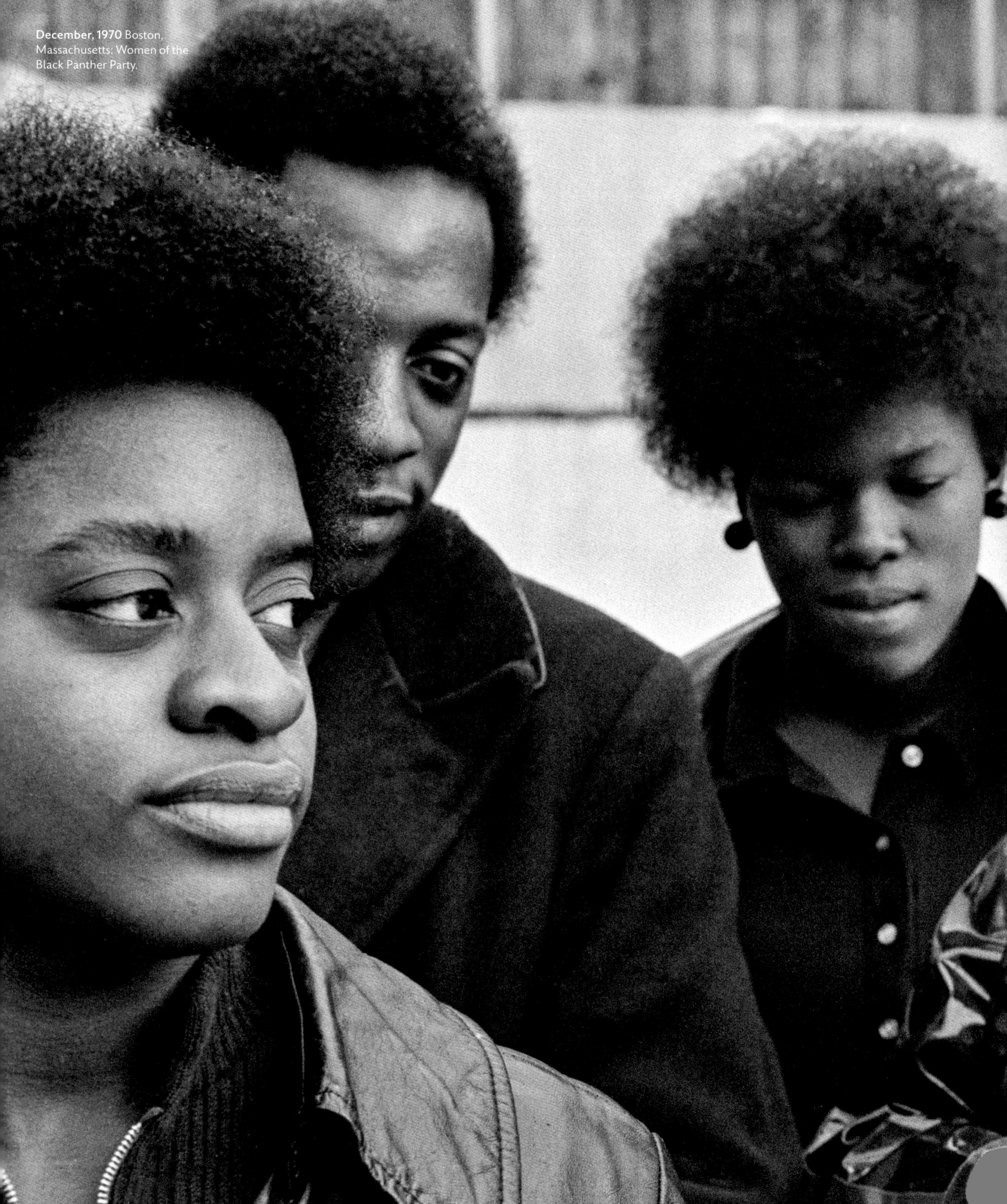

December, 1970 Boston, Massachusetts: Women of the Black Panther Party.

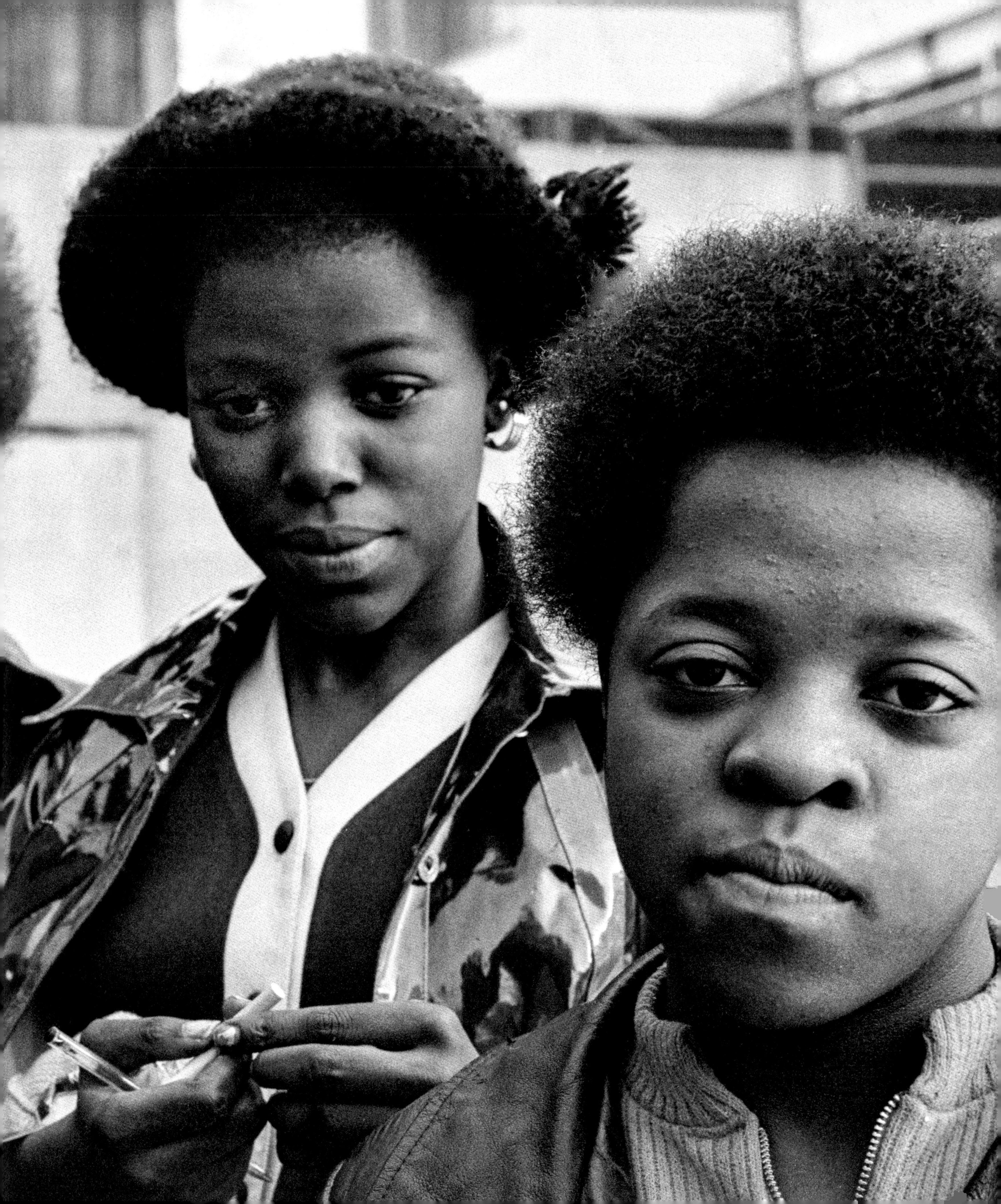

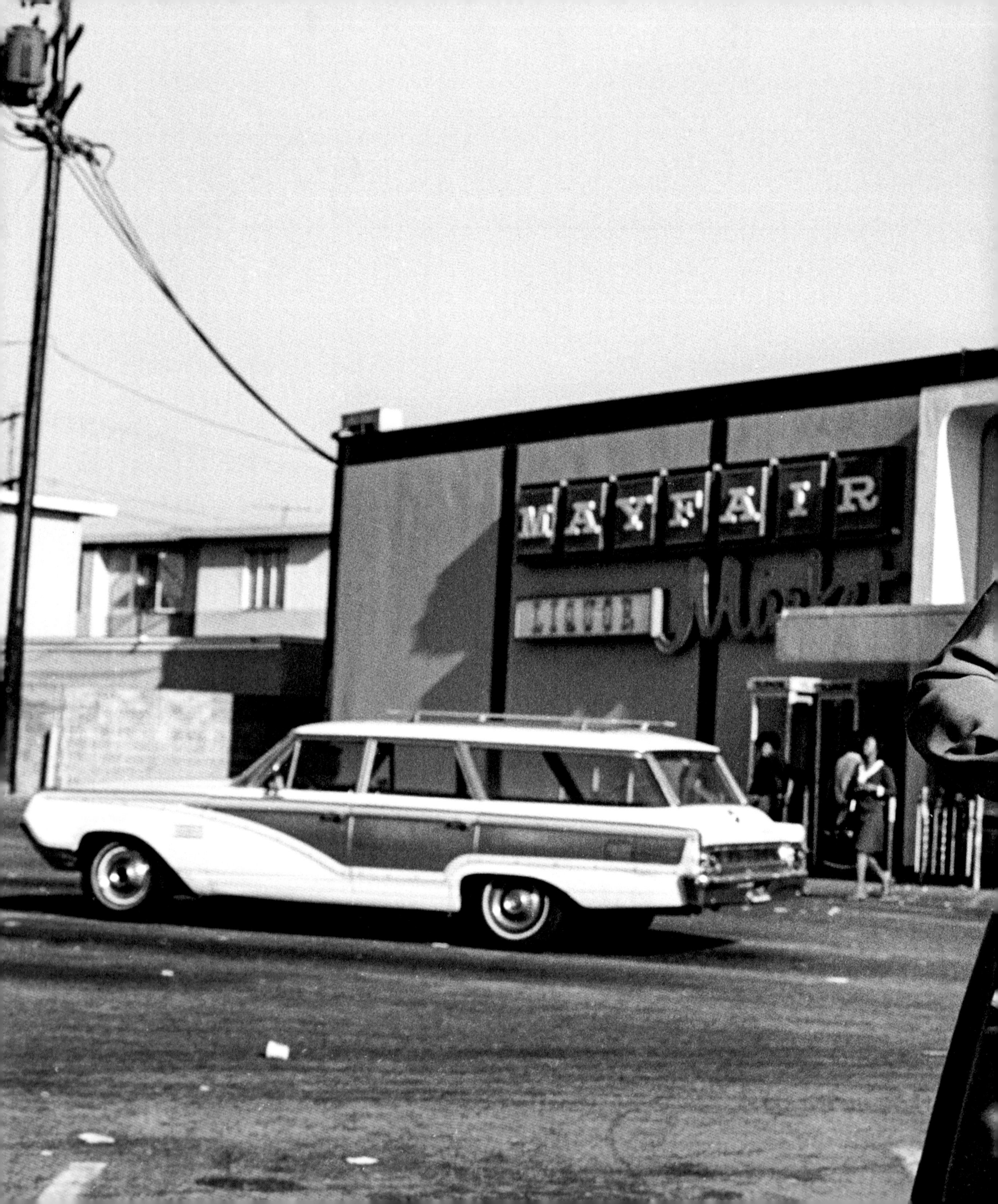
MAYFAIR
LITTLE Market

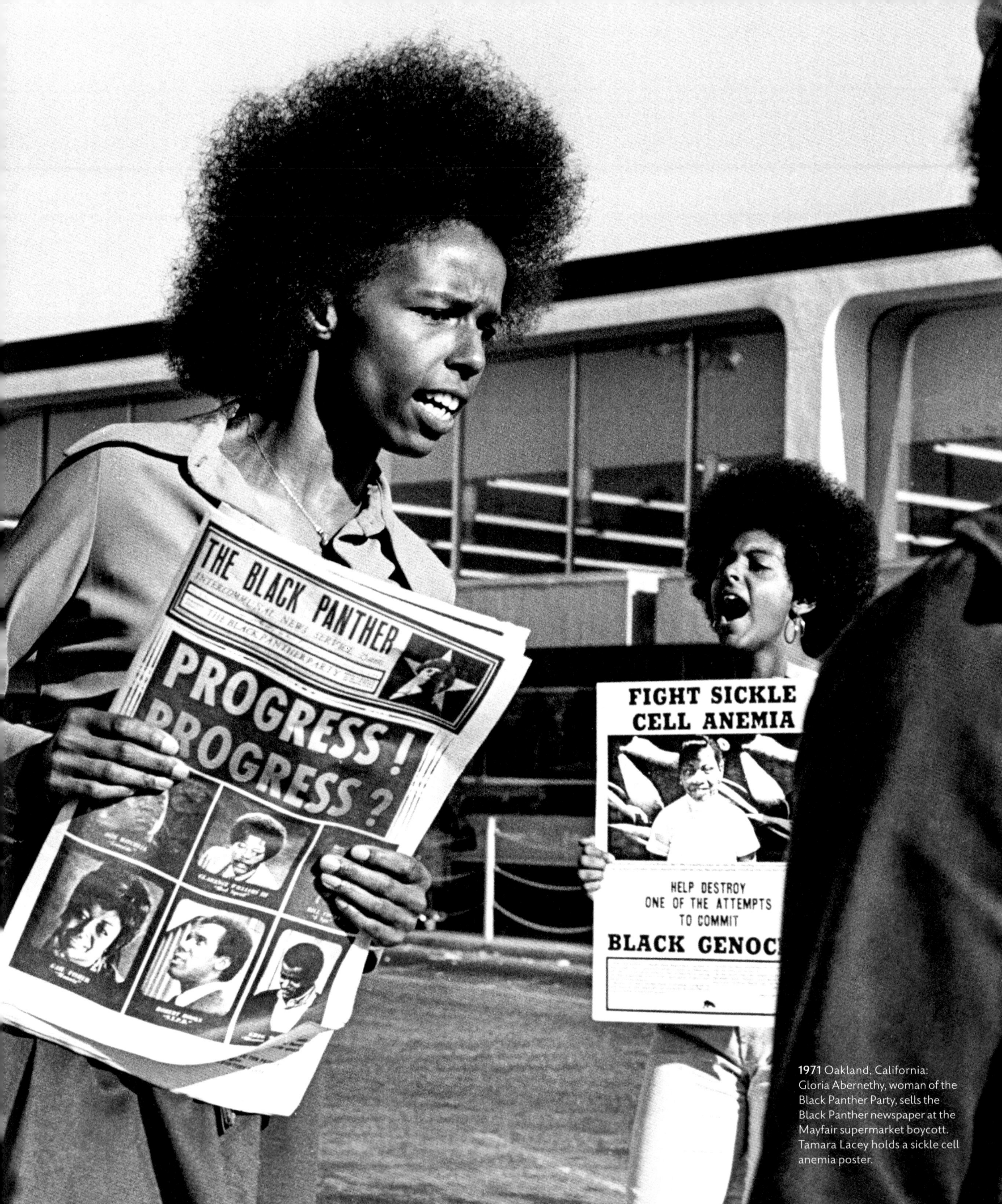

1971 Oakland, California: Gloria Abernethy, woman of the Black Panther Party, sells the Black Panther newspaper at the Mayfair supermarket boycott. Tamara Lacey holds a sickle cell anemia poster.

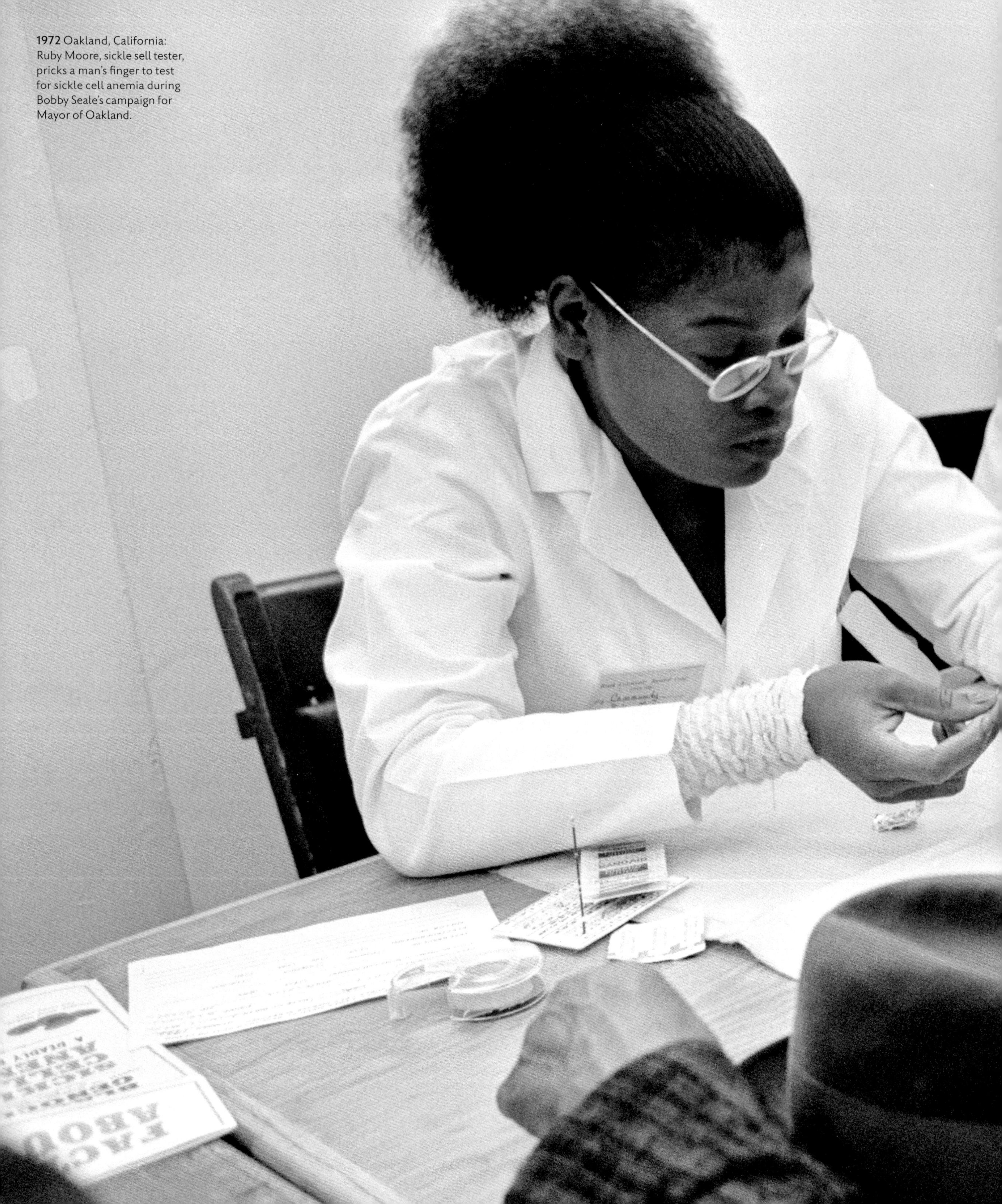

1972 Oakland, California:
Ruby Moore, sickle sell tester,
pricks a man's finger to test
for sickle cell anemia during
Bobby Seale's campaign for
Mayor of Oakland.

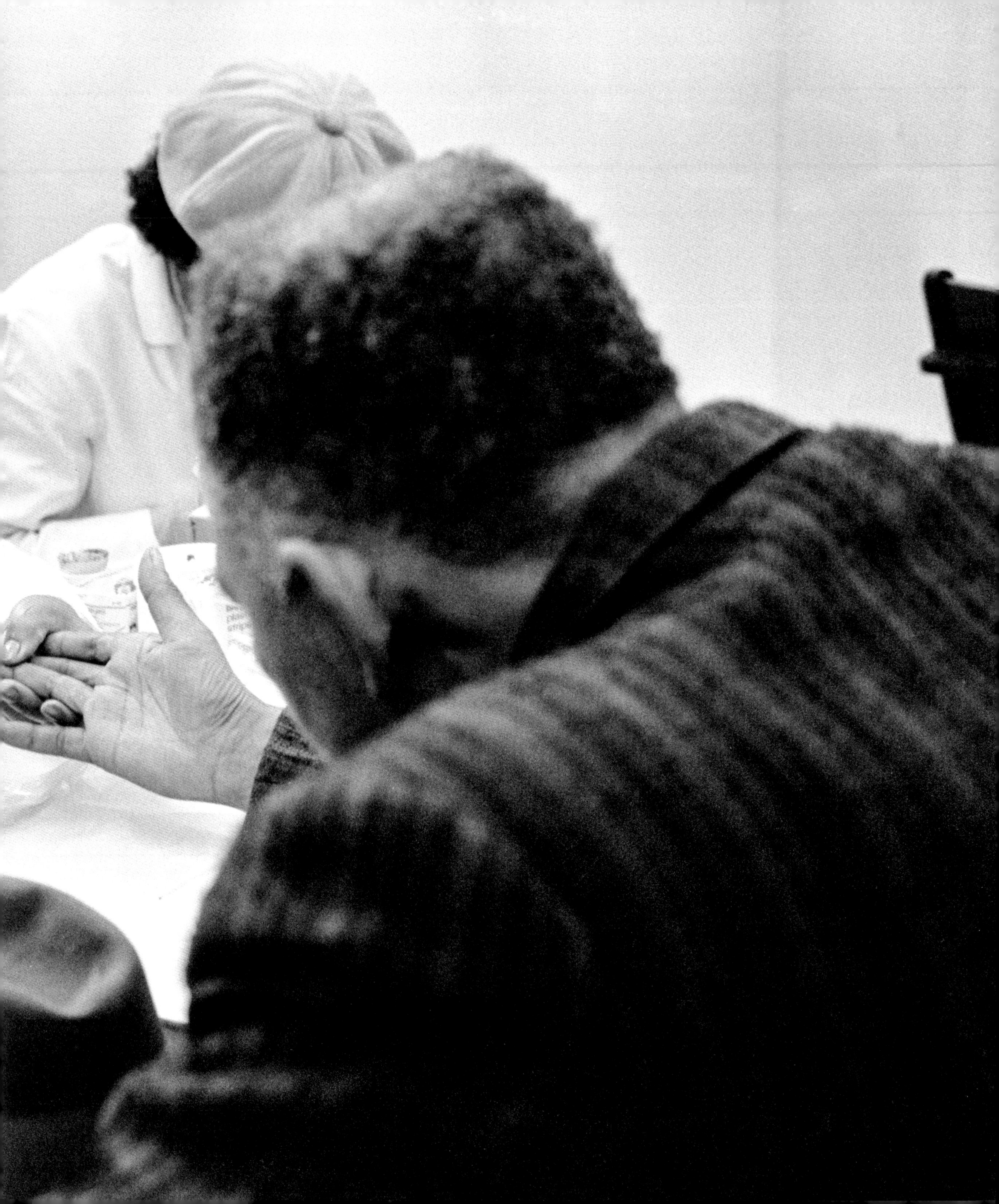

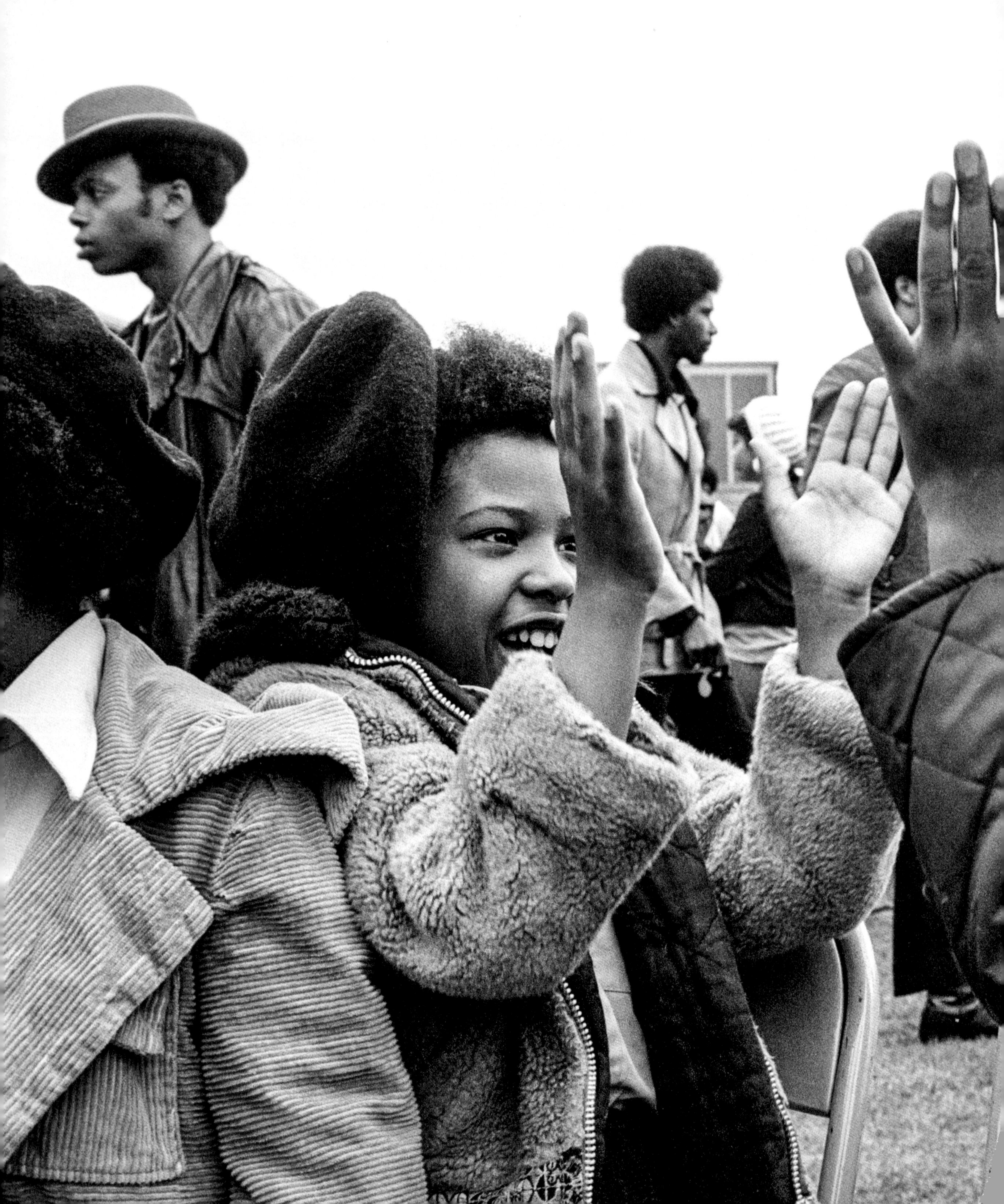

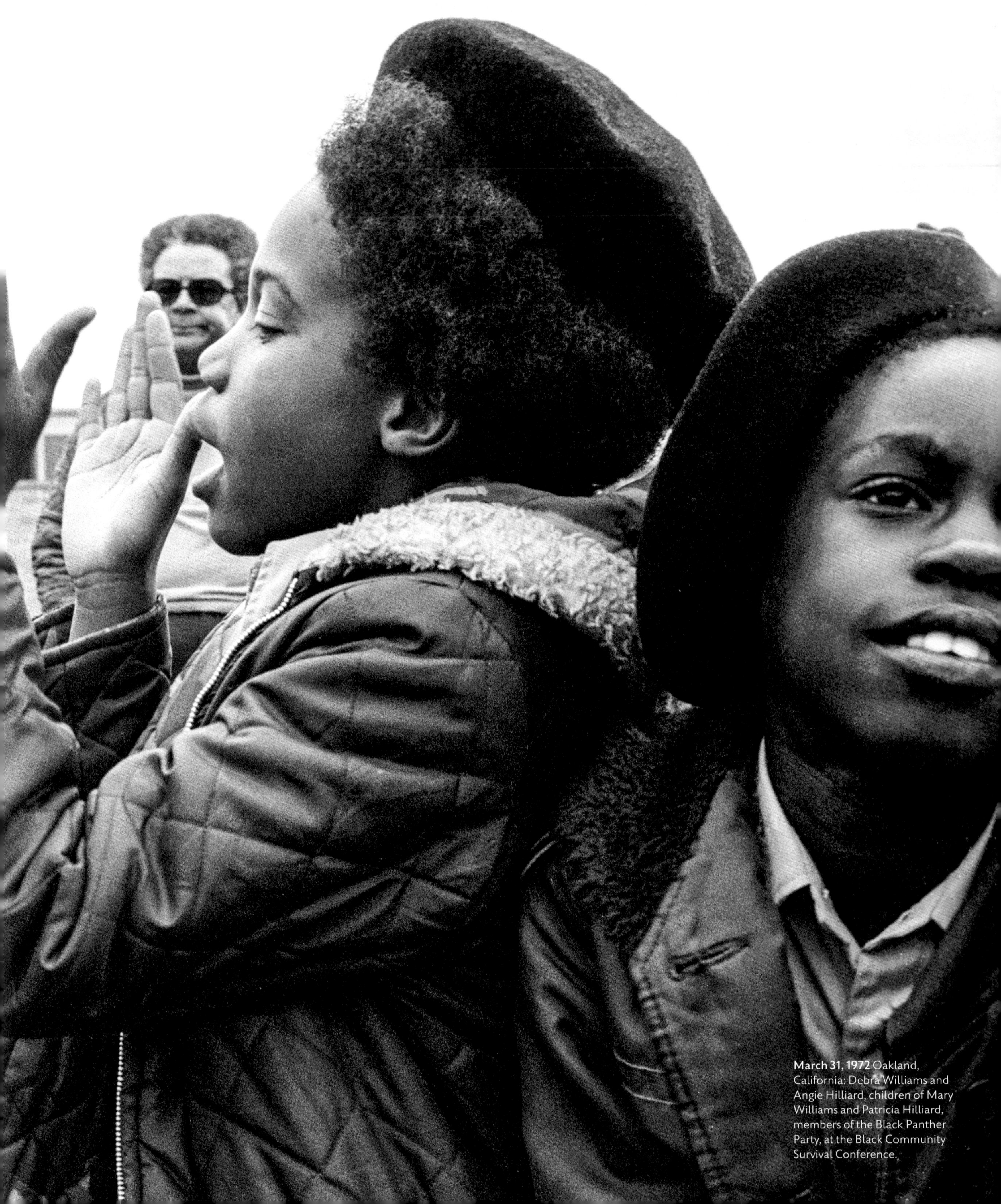

March 31, 1972 Oakland, California: Debra Williams and Angie Hilliard, children of Mary Williams and Patricia Hilliard, members of the Black Panther Party, at the Black Community Survival Conference.

Foreword

By Angela
Davis

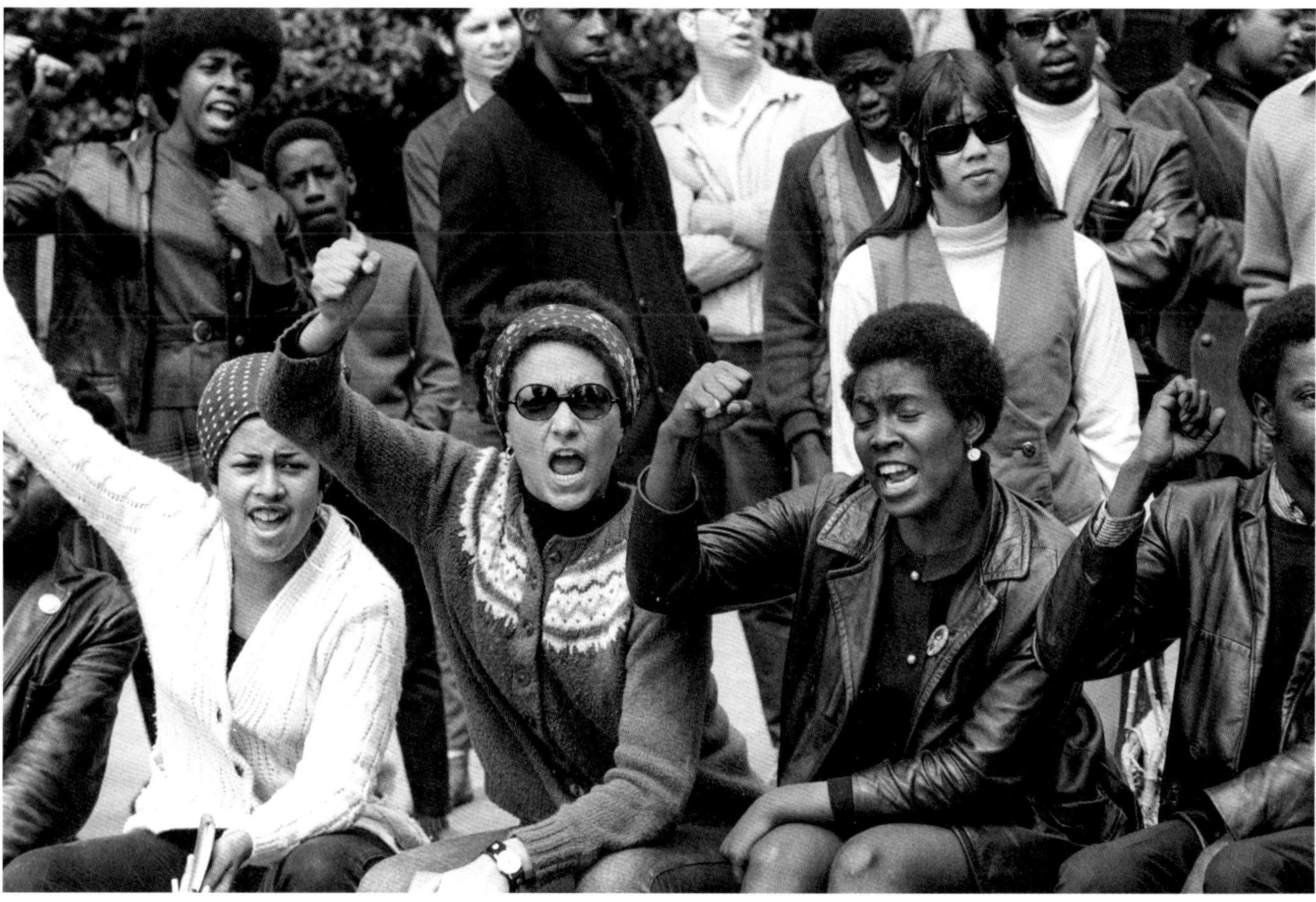

1969 Berkeley, California: Women of the Black Panther Party give a clenched fist salute at the "Free Huey" rally in Provo Park.

Over the years, I have encountered many people who consider themselves knowledgeable about the history of the Black Liberation Movement. They can quote Frederick Douglass ("If there is no struggle, there is no progress…"). They are aware that even though Frederick Douglass praised the work of anti-lynching and woman suffrage leader Ida B. Wells-Barnett, her radicalism (combined with the fact that she was a woman) rendered her a controversial figure for most of her life. They may even be aware of the significant, yet still largely unacknowledged role women played during the era of civil rights activism. However, when they discover that at least 66% of the membership of the Black Panther Party consisted of women, they find it difficult to incorporate this historical fact into the patriarchal frame and masculinist premises that tend to define the most well-known Black radical organization of the 1960s. This compelling book, co-authored by Ericka Huggins, a shining star of the BPP, and social justice documentarian Stephen Shames, dramatically changes those terms.

As a previous rank-and-file member, longtime supporter, and life-long friend of the Black Panther Party, I am honored to offer a few words of introduction to this book that documents the immense contributions of women members. I thank Stephen Shames, who I first met at a 1969 rally held in Oakland's DeFremery Park, unofficially renamed Bobby Hutton Park in 1998. I have known Ericka Huggins since 1968—we met shortly after she and her husband John Huggins arrived from New Haven to work with the Black Panther Party in Los Angeles. The following year I was a part of a group within the Party that came together to protect Ericka and her infant daughter, Mai, after John was killed on the UCLA campus and the Los Angeles Police decided to arrest her on charges of plotting a revenge attack. When we both found ourselves in jail at the same time on two different coasts, we wrote letters to one another. We each rejoiced when the other was released. And so, it feels like we have been sister comrades for several lifetimes. I have also known other women who are recognized by their affiliation with the BPP—Kathleen Cleaver, Elaine Brown, Assata Shakur, Fredrika Newton, and Tarika Lewis, for example. Today I join them in paying tribute to the many women of the Black Panther Party who have left indelible marks on our history.

Multiple generations now separate us from the era defined both by the legendary activism of the Black Panther Party and by the severe, often lethal police repression in virtually every major city in the U.S. As important as the work against police repression may have been—and indeed, it laid the foundation for Black Lives Matter and for contemporary abolitionist theories and practice—we must also bear in mind that the new radical linking of anti-racism with anti-capitalism that characterized the Party's approach to Black Liberation was matched by a

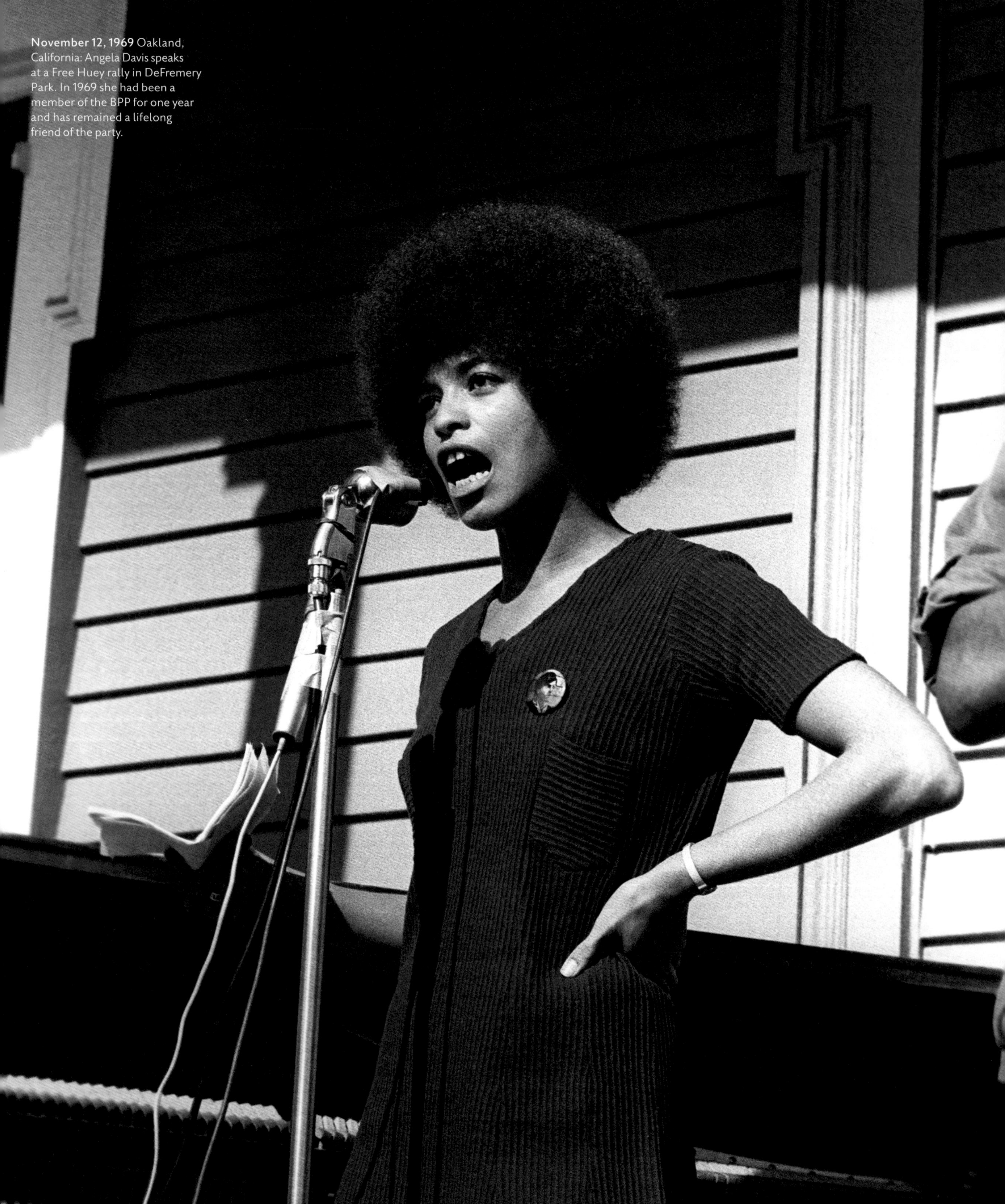

November 12, 1969 Oakland, California: Angela Davis speaks at a Free Huey rally in DeFremery Park. In 1969 she had been a member of the BPP for one year and has remained a lifelong friend of the party.

tenacious dedication to Community Survival Programs. These programs demonstrated that freedom is far more than a checklist of formal rights. Freedom involves free breakfast for children, free groceries, free education, free health care, free transportation to visit incarcerated loved ones. Altogether there were over 60 Community Survival Programs, and they were primarily run by women.

Because the media tended to focus on what could be easily sensationalized, and because the most well-known targets of police and government repression were male—from Huey P. Newton and Bobby Seale to Romaine Fitzgerald and Veronza Bowers—there has been a tendency to forget that the organizing work that truly made the BPP relevant to a new era of struggle for liberation was largely carried out by women. That women in the Winston-Salem, North Carolina Chapter of the BPP organized a committee in the early 1970s to free Joan Little is, unfortunately, a little-known fact. This stunning collection of historical photographs, complemented by contemporary conversations with women members of the Black Panther Party, reminds us that women were literally *the heart* of this new political approach to Black freedom.

It is often difficult to rectify historical errors that are so deeply engrained that the prospect of restoring accurate representation seems an entirely marginal concern. So, we are very fortunate that archival evidence of the centrality of women to the work of the BPP exists and that many of the women who engaged in that work can attest to their own lived experiences. During an era when women are at the forefront of Black Lives Matter and so many other major social justice struggles, including global campaigns against racism, against gender violence and for climate justice, and at a time when we are finally rescuing women's legacies from the ashes of history, it is essential to recognize women of the Black Panther Party for their invaluable leadership. Their roles in this organization persuaded people all over the world—from Brazil and Palestine to New Zealand and South Africa—that radical change was both necessary and possible. They served the people, body, and soul.

As this book demonstrates, the style of leadership offered by women of the Black Panther Party was down-to-earth and profoundly collective. This was leadership designed to serve the people, to ensure their survival, and, ultimately, to radically transform social institutions by prefiguring what life might be like if people of all racial, religious, and class backgrounds could claim substantive access to education, healthcare, and nutrition. For 55 years, these phenomenal programs and this radical vision have comprised the legacy of the Black Panther Party.

Oakland, California
January 12, 2022

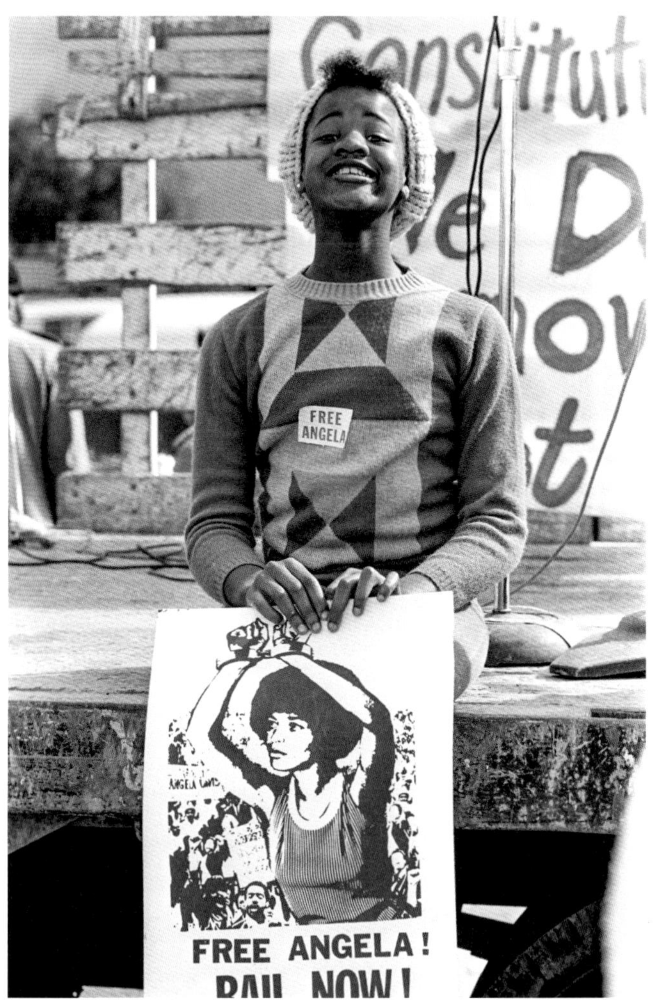

1972 Oakland, California: Girl holds a "Free Angela" poster at the Black Panther Party's Constitutional Convention rally in DeFremery Park.

Preface

By Stephen Shames

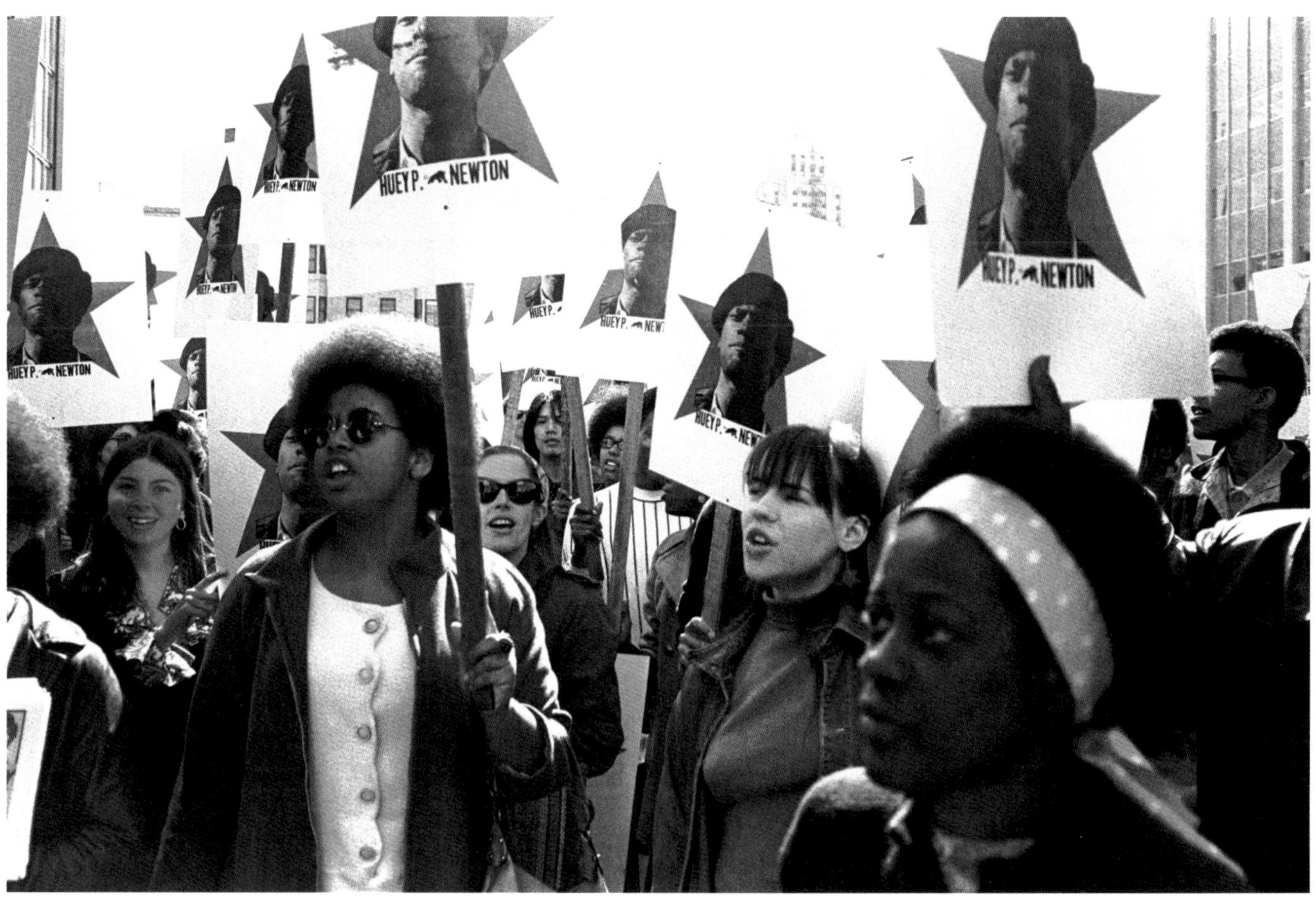

Comrade Sisters: Women of the Black Panther Party is my third Black Panther photo book. It is a project that is long overdue. Most media on the Black Panther Party focuses on the men—yet nearly two thirds of Party members were women, and women ran most of the 60-plus Survival Programs that are the legacy of the Party. I am proud to be part of this book about women, by women, because the stories of the Comrade Sisters resonate with my mother's life struggles and transformation.

My mom, Priscilla, was a brilliant, creative person. She attended Radcliffe (Harvard University). She was a gifted reporter and writer who served as editor of the student newspaper. Upon graduation in 1948, the *New York Times* offered her a correspondent's job. However, she had a one-year-old son and, as was the custom in those days, she decided her role was to stay at home, raise the kids, and support my dad's legal and political career.

Two and a half decades later, after her children were mostly grown—inspired in part by the women of the Black Panther Party and the growing woman's movement—Priscilla earned her PhD and became a professor in the English Department at Cal State Fullerton. Her field of study was "The Portrayal of Cowboys and Indians in American Literature." She became a passionate supporter of Native American rights, as well as woman's liberation. In 1970, she visited Alcatraz Island in solidarity with the Alcatraz Indian Occupation. In 1977, she was a delegate to the National Women's Conference in Houston.

As a child growing up in the 1950s, I was not aware that anything was wrong with our society. However, by 1968, as I entered adulthood, I saw with new eyes how my mother's dreams and potential had been throttled before they had a chance to blossom. My understanding was re-enforced by the experiences of my women friends—including the women of the Black Panther Party—as they struggled for equality.

I photographed the Black Panther Party from 1967 to 1973. I witnessed and my camera documented the positive power of the women of the Black Panther Party as they served the people—body and soul—feeding and teaching children, providing medical care, clothing, and hope. I am in awe of the Comrade Sisters. The names of these women are on the inside cover of this book. As you look at their photographs and read their words, you will be in awe of them too.

As we navigate this dark period of creeping authoritarianism, climate disasters, income inequality, and pandemics, the women of the Black Panther Party have so much to teach us. Perhaps if we follow their example—and work to secure economic, political, racial, and gender justice—we will weather the storm and create a better world for our children, and their children, and their children's children.

It's about time.

May 1, 1969 San Francisco, California: Men and women at a May Day "Free Huey" rally in front of the Federal Building.

Comrade Sisters

By Ericka Huggins

Comrade: com.rade/pr. 'käm'rad,
    a familiar spirit, a team mate,
    a friend in struggle,
    an intimate, fellow traveler
Sister: sis.ter / pr. 'sist'r
    family, sibling, friend, partner, member
Comrade Sisters: the family we choose,
    a bond that defies location, time and biology,
    a life well-lived

Many of us have heard these three words: *Black Panther Party*. Some know its history as a movement for the social, political, economic and spiritual upliftment of Black and Indigenous people of color.

What is the Black Panther Party and how was it conceived? In late 1966, two young men, Bobby Seale and Huey P. Newton, then students at Merritt College in Oakland, California, discussed their concerns about the historic dismissal of the human rights of Black and oppressed people in the United States. Torn by their vision of freedom and the reality of the routine deaths of men and women due to systems that furthered conditions of poverty for millions—limited healthcare, inadequate housing, food insecurity, police abuse and over-incarceration—they agreed to form an organization to defend and redefine their communities. In October 1966, Bobby and Huey conceived the Black Panther Party for Self Defense. Its brave Ten Point Program, written in 1966 and revised in 1972, remains relevant to this day.

Beginning with community police patrols and Free Breakfast for School Children Programs, the BPP expanded out of Oakland to open offices in over 40 states in the U.S. Sixty Community Survival Programs sprung up in big cities and rural towns across the country, north, south, east, and west. Their goal was to meet basic human needs—to provide land, bread, housing, education, clothing, justice, and peace. In addition, the party continued the Lowndes County Freedom Organization's tradition of ensuring that thousands of people in Lowndes County, Alabama, were free to register to vote. We were also one of the first young Black movements to speak out against the Vietnam War. The party became well-known and loved for its recipe for change: *All Power to the People.*

This book, through its photographs, words, and art, focuses on the vast contribution of women members of the Black Panther Party (BPP). By 1969, women accounted for more than half of the party membership. Women from every state in the U.S.—and internationally, across the world—were drawn to the possibility of a transformative movement for freedom. These women, *Comrade Sisters,* were mothers, sisters, aunties, cooks, housecleaners, churchgoers, middle and high school students, students at Historical Black Colleges and Universities (HBCU), teachers, artists, factory and retail workers, poets, dancers, writers, and musicians, all called by the model of the BPP. We were young and full of love for all people. If the government won't take care

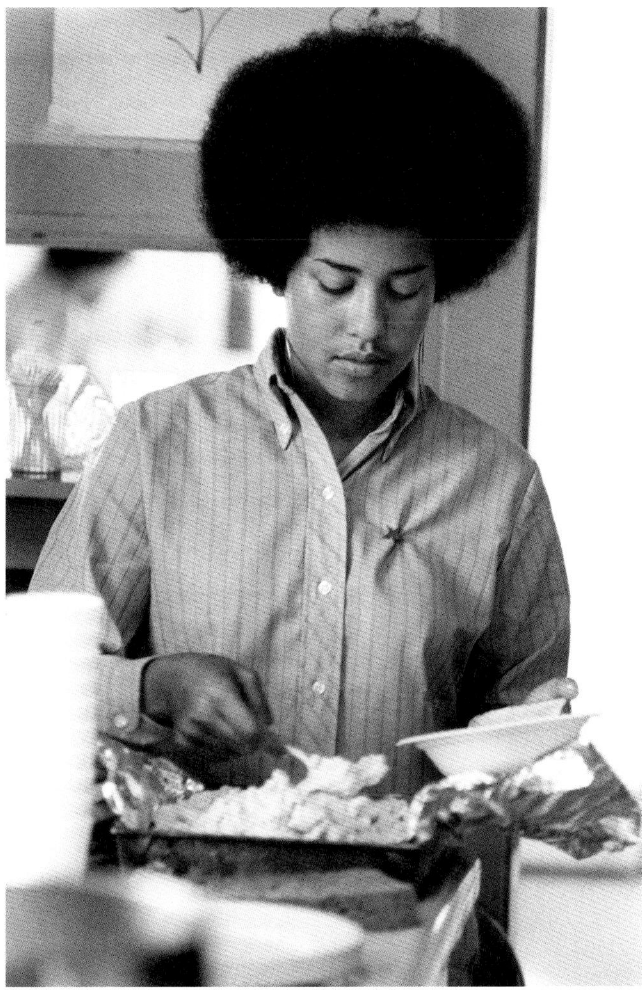

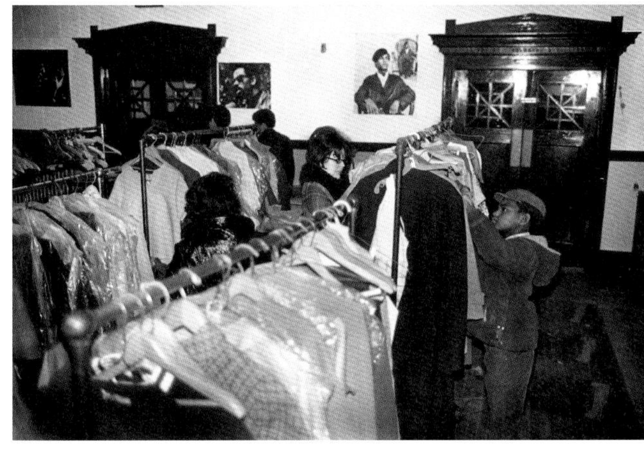

Top: **1969** San Francisco, California: Black Panther Marsha Turner/Taylor prepares food. Children eat a nutritious meal at the Black Panther Free Breakfast for School Children program at Ridge Point Methodist Church.

Bottom: **March, 1970** Oakland, California: Black Panther Free Clothing Program.

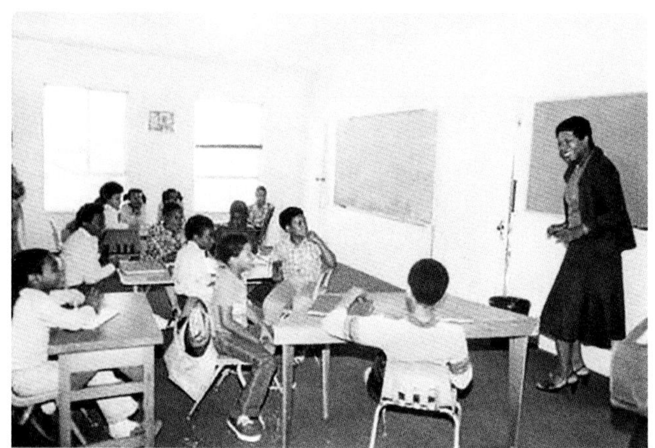

of its people, we will do it ourselves. We will serve the people, body and soul.

The women of the Black Panther Party are not special in some way that separates them from others. They are simply women who, whether at age 12, 14, 16, 18, or 21, decided that there had to be 'a way out of no way' for Black and poor people. Given the opportunity to step forward and give, they spoke up and grew their innate skills to create brilliant models for community leadership.

What motivated them? Love.

This love was demonstrated through their work in the BPP, especially the Community Survival Programs. The Free Breakfast for School Children Programs spread across the country, feeding children in recreation centers and church basements every morning before school for many years. Recognizing the needs of their community, women led the BPP to create the People's Free Medical Clinics, which offered family healthcare and sickle cell anemia testing. This led to the idea for the Free Ambulance Program. This program was created to make sure that people without money or proof of insurance received needed emergency transportation to the nearest hospital. In some cities, people were left to die, having been refused ambulance service. In the BPP Chapter in Winston-Salem, NC, women and men of the BPP were trained and licensed as Emergency Medical Technicians to staff the van of the Free Ambulance Program and provide this lifesaving service.

How did the women and men of the party know what to offer? People spoke and we listened. We created free clinics, community food programs, programs for seniors and teens, the Busing to Prison program, liberation schools, after-school programs and childcare centers. Every Community Survival Program was fully replicable in locations and cultures around the world.

In Auckland, New Zealand, in 1979, a group of young Fijian, Samoan, Tongan, and mixed-roots women and men read Bobby Seale's book, *Seize The Time* (1970). They formed the Polynesian Panthers, based on the community service model of the BPP. Why? They recognized the similarities between the conditions in which African-Americans, Latine and Indigenous people of the U.S. lived, and the inequities in the basic human rights of Pacific Island people. Programs for housing and the provision of food and services for incarcerated women and men were just the beginning.

Similarly, in South India in 1975, young men and women formed the Dalit Panthers, taking cues from the Black Panther Party. They organized themselves to fight against caste oppression and oppressors.

Today in Brazil, in Africa, and in the U.S. Community Survival Programs have re-appeared in housing projects, favelas, community centers, and churches to support the lives of generations now and to come. The simple statement at the end of the Black Panther's Ten Point Program has inspired millions to serve their communities.

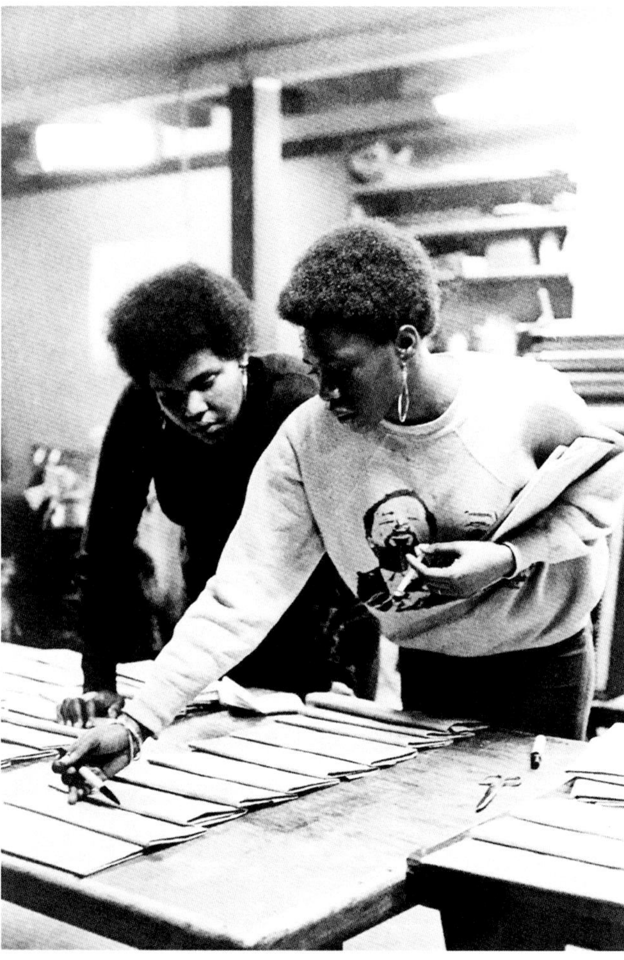

Top: **1979** Oakland, California: Maya Angelou sharing her poetry with children in a classroom at the Oakland Community School, on one of her many visits.

Bottom: Two women preparing the Black Panther Intercommunal News Service for mailing at the National Distribution office in San Francisco.

We want land, bread, housing, clothing, justice, and peace.

How did we sustain these programs then, and how can they be sustained now? Love.

The Intercommunal Youth Institute, 1969–1973, was open to sons and daughters of members of the BPP and a few families from the local neighborhood. When one of the grandmothers spoke to us about the need for a larger and dedicated site for the children, we listened. When the community pleaded with us to open the school to all families with children in the community, we listened. Then we created a model elementary school, The Oakland Community School (OCS). It opened its doors in the 1973-74 school year and remained open until 1982. It was community based, tuition free, child centered, and parent friendly. We served three meals a day and took care of every child's health needs through an arrangement with the Oakland Children's Hospital. The OCS motto was "the world is a child's classroom," and we were dedicated to helping children learn *how*, not *what*, to think.

This book features Stephen Shames' poignant photographs of women at work in many locations throughout the U.S. The book will also lift up the names, the words, the art, and the lives of women of the Black Panther Party. Many of the women mentioned in these pages are being seen and heard for the very first time.

One book is not large enough to tell all of their stories—their tales of compassion and solidarity in the face of oppression could fill volumes. Yet, represented here is the organized, coordinated and sustained effort made by those who managed the multi-layered community services of the BPP, including grassroots campaigns to seat mayors, assemblypersons, judges, and neighborhood councils. I am honored to be the weaver who brings this tapestry of stories to the printed page.

This book is a very late, very humble shout of gratitude to those who have been unknown and unsung for so many years. You have acted with courage, and have carried so many important memories with you, throughout your lives and careers. Comrade Sisters: we thank you for coordinating the rides and assisting those served by the Seniors Against A Fearful Environment Program (S.A.F.E.), which ensured the elders of our community always arrived home safely. Thank you for testing hundreds of women, men, and children for sickle cell anemia. You registered hundreds of people in the south, north, east, and west to vote; you organized and delivered thousands of bags of groceries, and you sold thousands of Black Panther Party newspapers. Thank you to the women of the Polynesian Panthers for contributing your voices to this book, and for speaking up on behalf of men, women, and children of Pacific Island communities in New Zealand, Samoa, Fiji, and Tonga. Thank you to the sons and daughters of Comrade Sisters who have passed, for contributing the stories of love, discipline, and courage that your mothers left with you. You came to represent!

Though the BPP ended in 1982, its legacy continues.

Though not every voice of every woman of the Black Panther Party is included in this book, you will find between the front and back cover as many names as we could collect. So many women who joined the party 40 to 55 years ago have since transitioned from this life. Many remembrances, written by their children or by their Comrade Sisters, are gathered here to celebrate their commitment to their party and their people.

As you reflect on the beauty and the messages in each of these photographs, we encourage you to hold in your hearts the experiences of each of these women, memorialized here in their own words and the words of their loved ones.

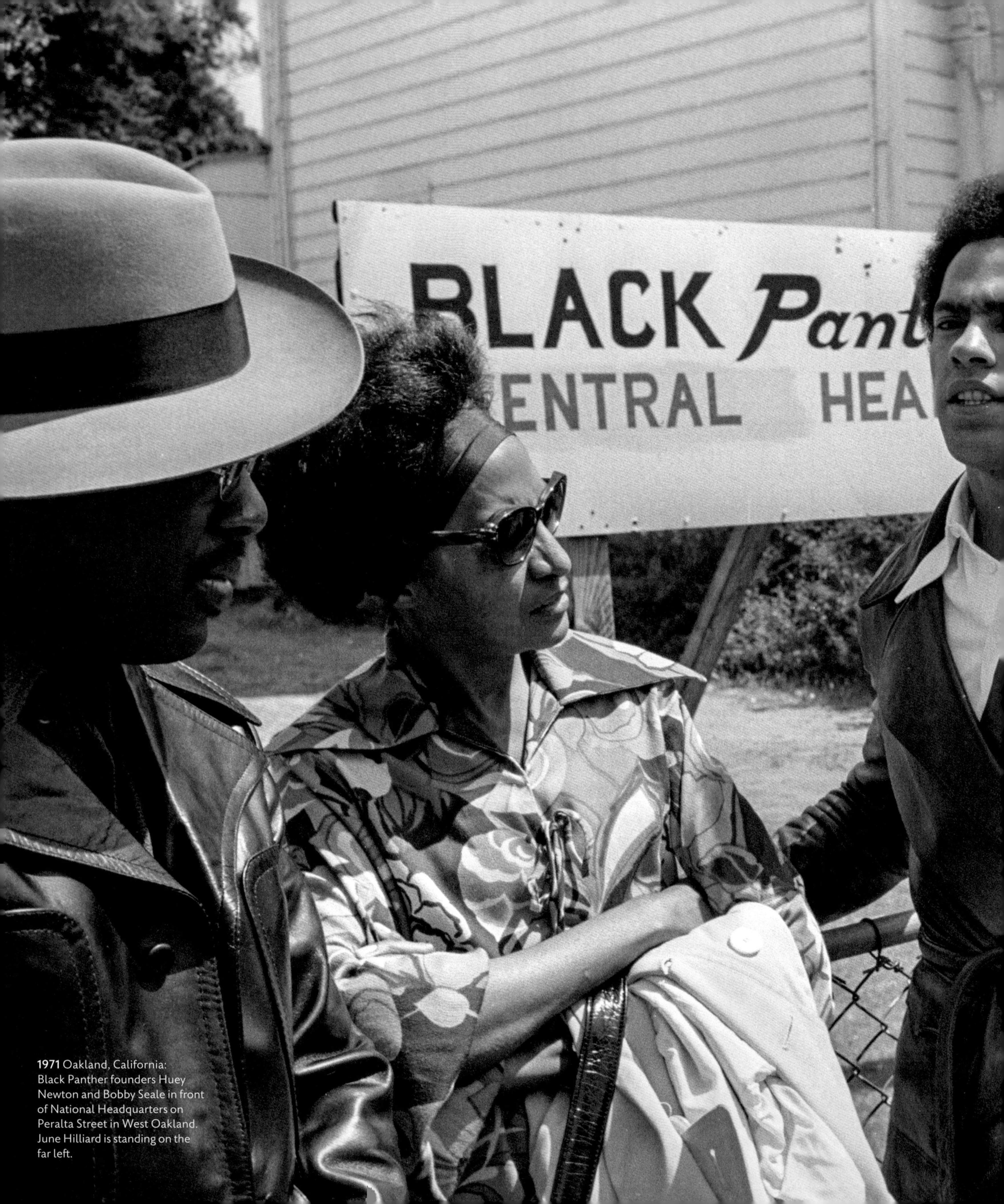

1971 Oakland, California: Black Panther founders Huey Newton and Bobby Seale in front of National Headquarters on Peralta Street in West Oakland. June Hilliard is standing on the far left.

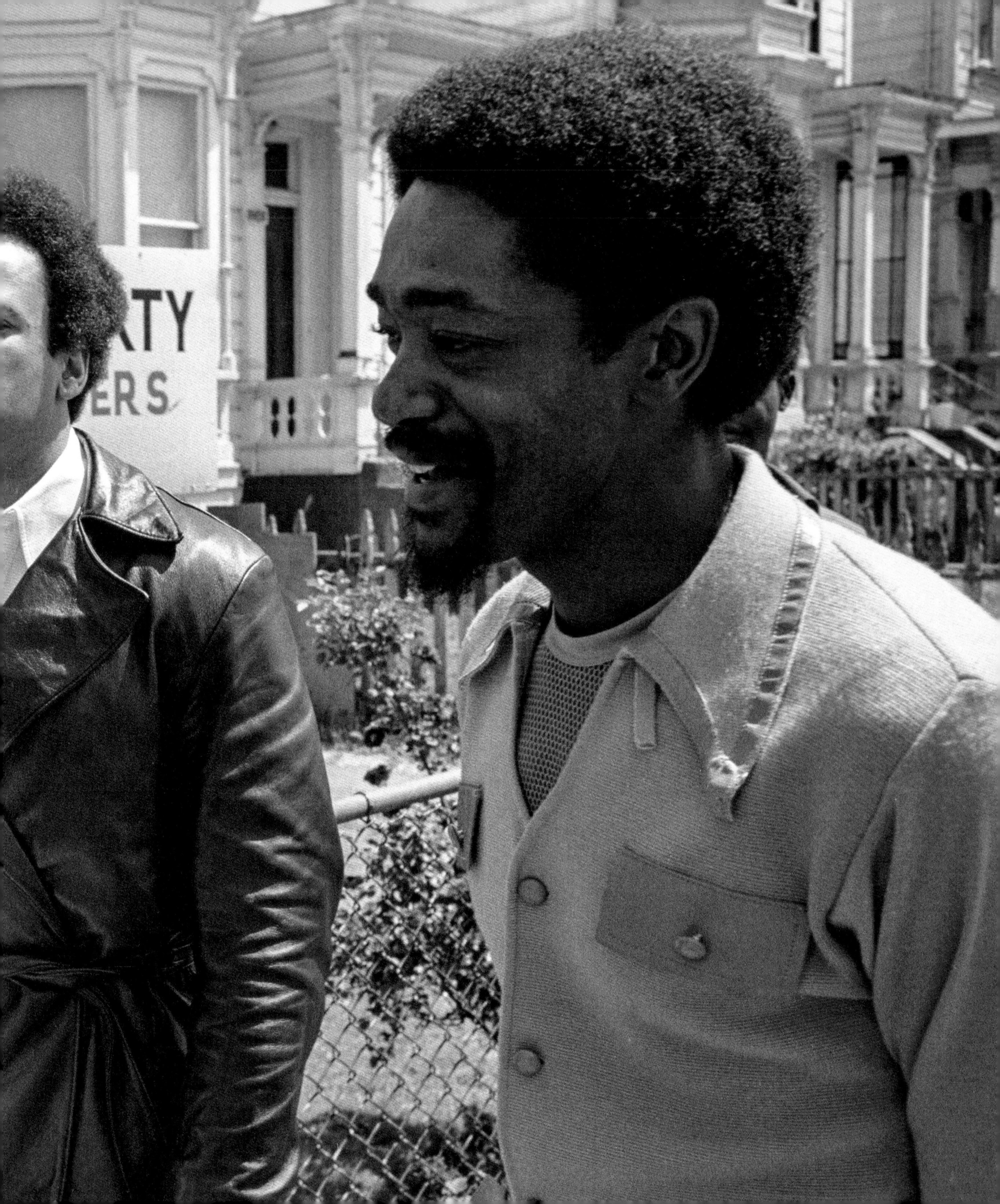
ATY
ERS

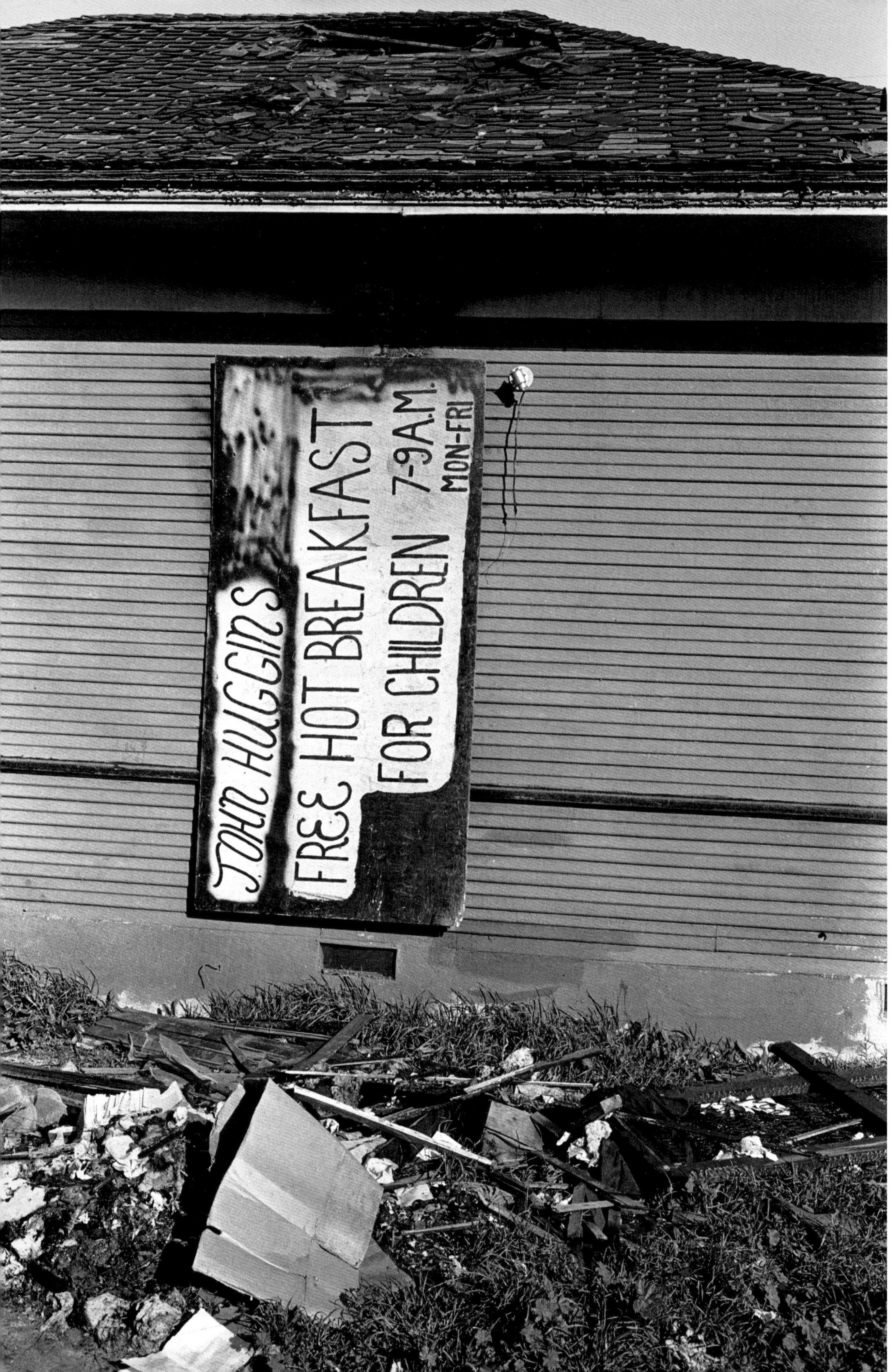

JOHN HUGGINS
FREE HOT BREAKFAST
FOR CHILDREN
7-9 A.M.
MON-FRI

Hello, sisters. My name is Cheryl Dawson. I was born and raised in Berkeley. I served in the party in Berkeley. I joined the Black Panther Party because my soul was on fire: a serious burn-down, because when I was about 15, my mother started giving me books by Frank Yerby.

I found out that he was a mixed-roots man, which allowed him to understand both sides, and the middle, of chattel slavery in America. This is when I began to understand the plight of my people. This is when I began to understand why the school counselor told me, "Don't ask for college prep classes; take vocational classes like the rest of your people."

I didn't know what the word 'vocational' meant. When I asked the counselor, he said it meant cooking and cleaning. That didn't work. I just kept reading and I kept working. And when I was a freshman at Cal State University, Hayward…

My brother Bob was two years younger than me. He's gone to glory now. Bob had a condition where he was intermittently paralyzed. He used to sit out on his porch in San Francisco. He'd drink because my father drank. It was a hard thing in our family, this drinking. I loved my brother.

One night, the San Francisco Police Department pulled up. They passed by his house, saw him sitting there with somebody. They decided to hunt him that night. They went to his front porch and beat the absolute *I don't know what,* out of my little brother. When they finished beating him, they threw him on the porch steps, got in their car, and drove off.

I was so angry. I was also frightened, because of all that I knew had happened to our people. I saw what was happening, with the Oakland Police Department shooting us like birds on a fence.

So, I was at Cal State, and it was time to choose what my social life was going to be, which sorority I was going to join. I had to figure out where I fit. It was a debacle. One day someone said, "Why don't you come with me to a meeting and check out the Black Panther Party?" So, I went to Merritt College—Oakland City College, at that time—and I heard Bobby Seale and Huey P. Newton speak.

I thought, "This isn't really a choice at all. Either I'm going to go back to school and deal with the sorority thing, or I'm going to serve my people." Well, I chose to serve the people.

1970 Los Angeles, California: Panther community center and Free Breakfast location after a police raid.

I left the university. There were no questions asked. I was unapologetic. I told my family. They thought I had lost my mind. I explained, "I'm going to fight for our people because we're going to die if we don't fight." I was unrepentant, and I didn't have sense enough to be afraid of anything. I mean, whatever came my way, I was like, "All right, you're here. I'm here, I'm watching you. You're watching me." So, I just continued to do the work.

I love the community. I love the people. I took care of elders. There wasn't a night that went by that I didn't go knock on every door I could find. When I had made my way through the community, then I was done.

I started the day by serving children at the Free Breakfast for School Children Program. Every morning, I packed a big diaper bag with bottles, diapers, and baby food. I got that ready and bundled my little baby up—she was about as big as the bag. She was three months old, a precious, beautiful little doll. I wrapped her up and then she and I would go to the car in the dark. I'd look down the street and see this car that I recognized. I knew it was the FBI. I'd tuck my daughter in the car and I'd say to her, "Well, here we go. We're going."

We drove by the FBI in the dark, every morning. As soon as I passed them, the lights came on in their car, they eased out and they started tailing me. That's how they spent their day, tailing me. I think about that; I used to talk about it. I was afraid for my baby. I was afraid that something would happen to her, but I couldn't envision stopping the work. I felt if I stopped, we were going to be washed away, like water down the drain. That fire would be extinguished: that slow fire that I had burning, from learning my history and from living here in Berkeley—which is not so New Age and not so liberal.

Finally, I found a vehicle for change in the party. I want young people like my grandchildren, my granddaughters, to know: Serve the people. Serve your people. Get your education. Love your parents. Have a relationship with God as you understand God. Rise to the level of your gift. Rise to the depth and the dimension of your dream. Capture it, bring it close, name it, and give it to the people. Give to the people. Go there. Use your gift. God gave you this ability. Reach for your dream. Keep your core centered in your faith. And bring it back. Turn it around and point it towards your community.

In this way, we can all rise together. We all share the glow of the accumulated risk, gifts, and blessings that we encounter as a people. That is how we will rise. That is how we will continue to stand. This is what I believe.

Cheryl Dawson
Berkeley Chapter, CA

Summer, 1970 Oakland, California: Mother and child listen to speakers at a pre-rally in DeFremery Park for the Constitutional Convention, which was to be held that September in Philadelphia.

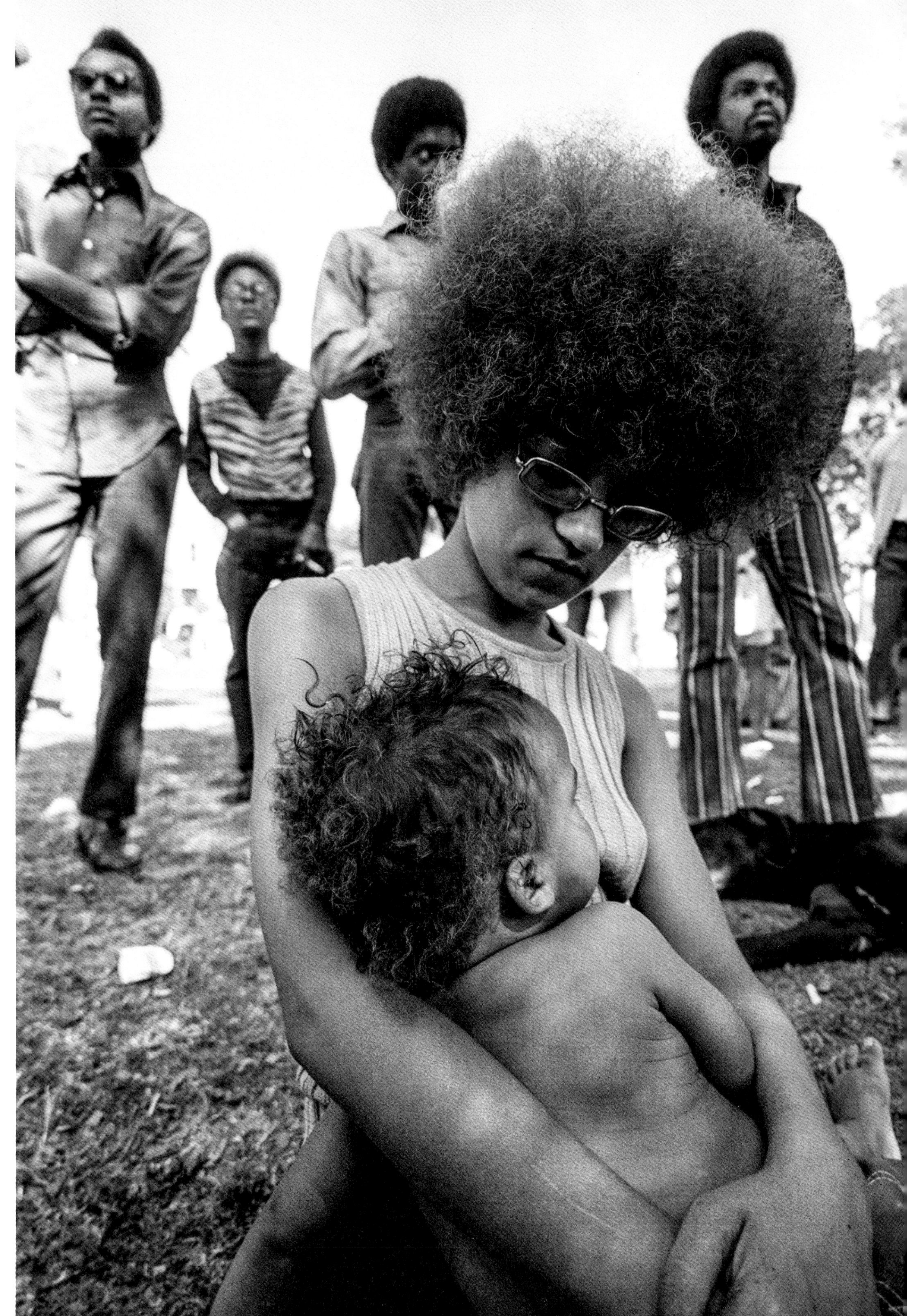

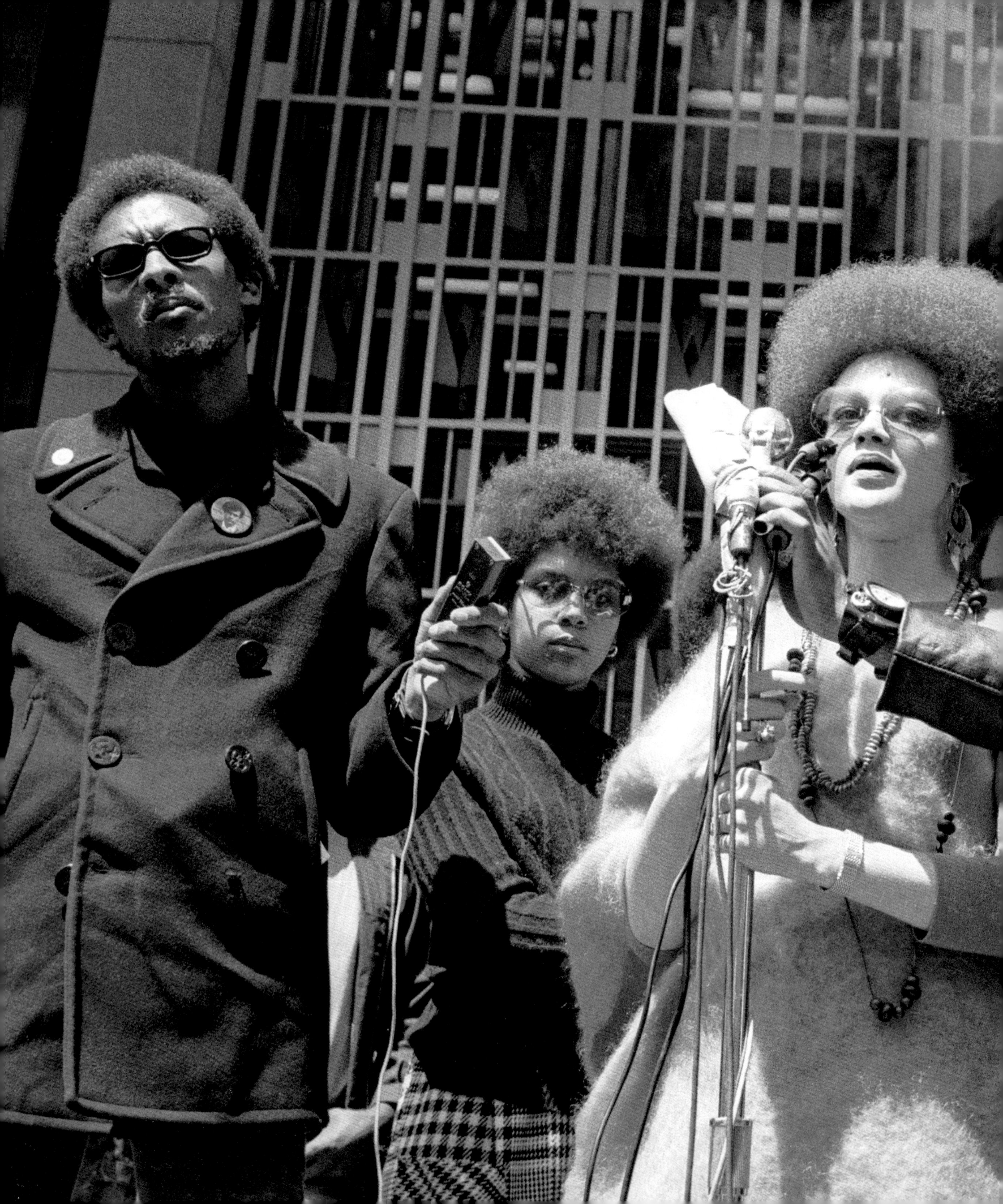

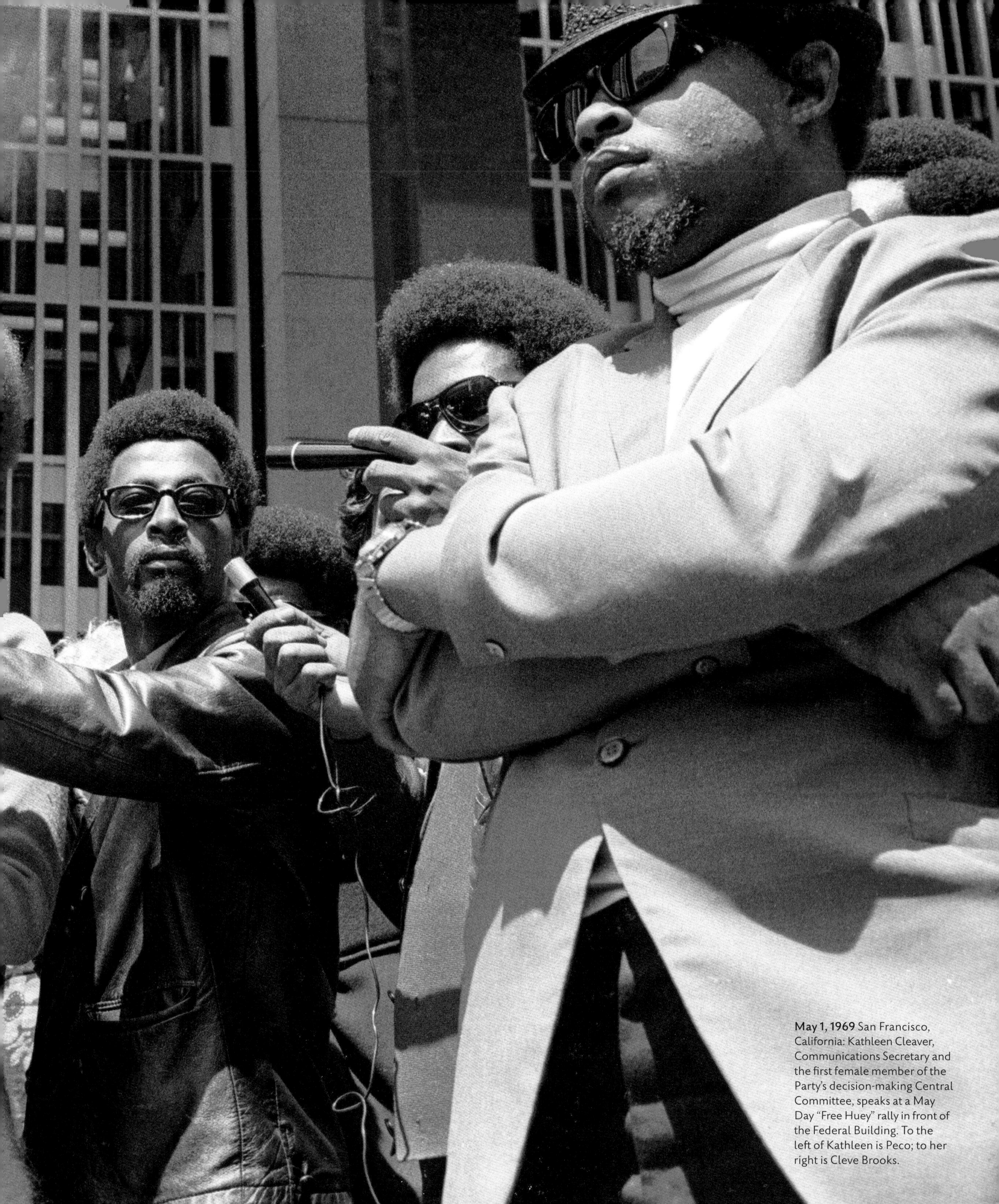

May 1, 1969 San Francisco, California: Kathleen Cleaver, Communications Secretary and the first female member of the Party's decision-making Central Committee, speaks at a May Day "Free Huey" rally in front of the Federal Building. To the left of Kathleen is Peco; to her right is Cleve Brooks.

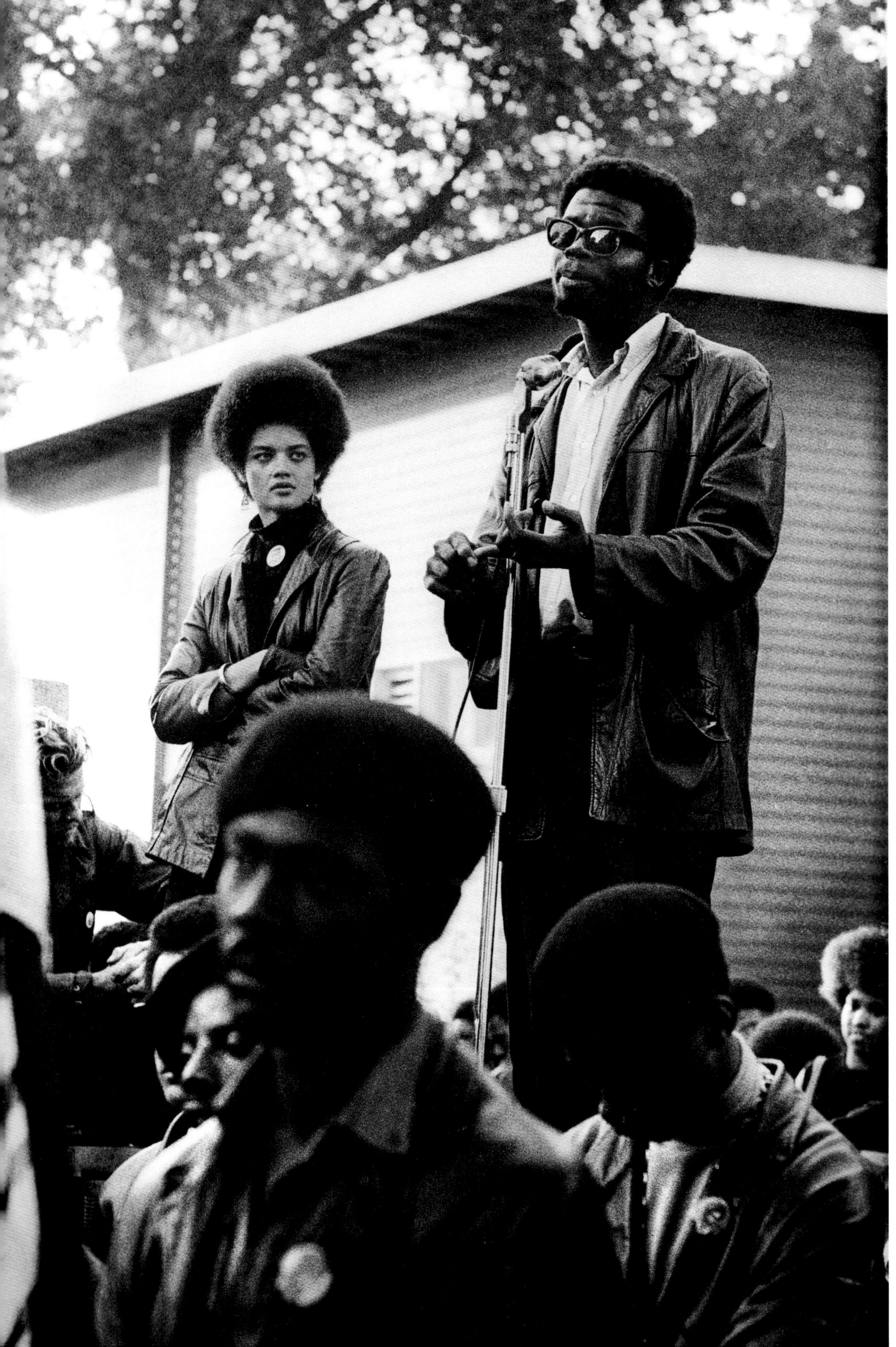

In 2016, I waited backstage at the legendary Apollo Theatre in Harlem with a group of party members. We had gathered as a panel to follow the New York premiere of the documentary film *The Black Panthers: Vanguard of the Revolution.* Kathleen and I were on that panel. I could hear the audience cheering and clapping as the film ended.

As the stage curtain slowly began to rise, my dear sister Kathleen turned to me and said, "Did you ever think we'd live to see this day?"

We held hands. She smiled, as I said, "No!"

Just as the velvet stage curtain was fully raised, Kathleen quietly said, "I didn't either!"

There were tears in our eyes. As if on cue, there was a standing ovation, for the women and men of the Black Panther Party. The audience was beautiful: inspired, hopeful, young people of color. I will never forget that poignant moment—memorable because many women and men of the party ask this question daily. We are still here to tell the history out loud, to encourage young people to repeat our successes and to carefully recognize our failures.

Kathleen Cleaver
San Francisco Chapter, LA / Algiers International Chapter
(a tribute by Ericka Huggins)

July 28, 1968 Oakland, California: George Murray, Minister of Education for the Black Panther Party speaks at a "Free Huey" rally in DeFremery Park, which the Panthers re-named Bobby Hutton Park, in honor of their slain 17-year-old comrade. Murray was a leader of the San Francisco State student strike, which was put down by Governer Ronald Reagan. Left is Kathleen Cleaver, BPP Communications Secretary.

1968 *All Power to the People, Black Power to Black People* – Peace and Freedom Party, courtesy of Lincoln Cushing and Lisbet Tellefsen.

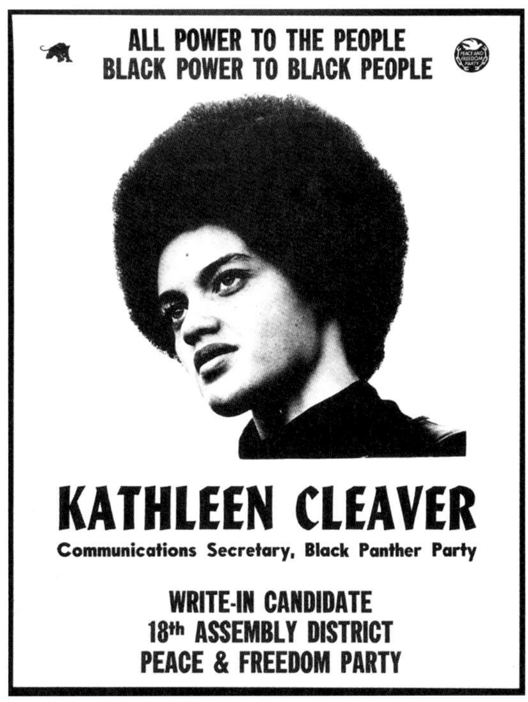

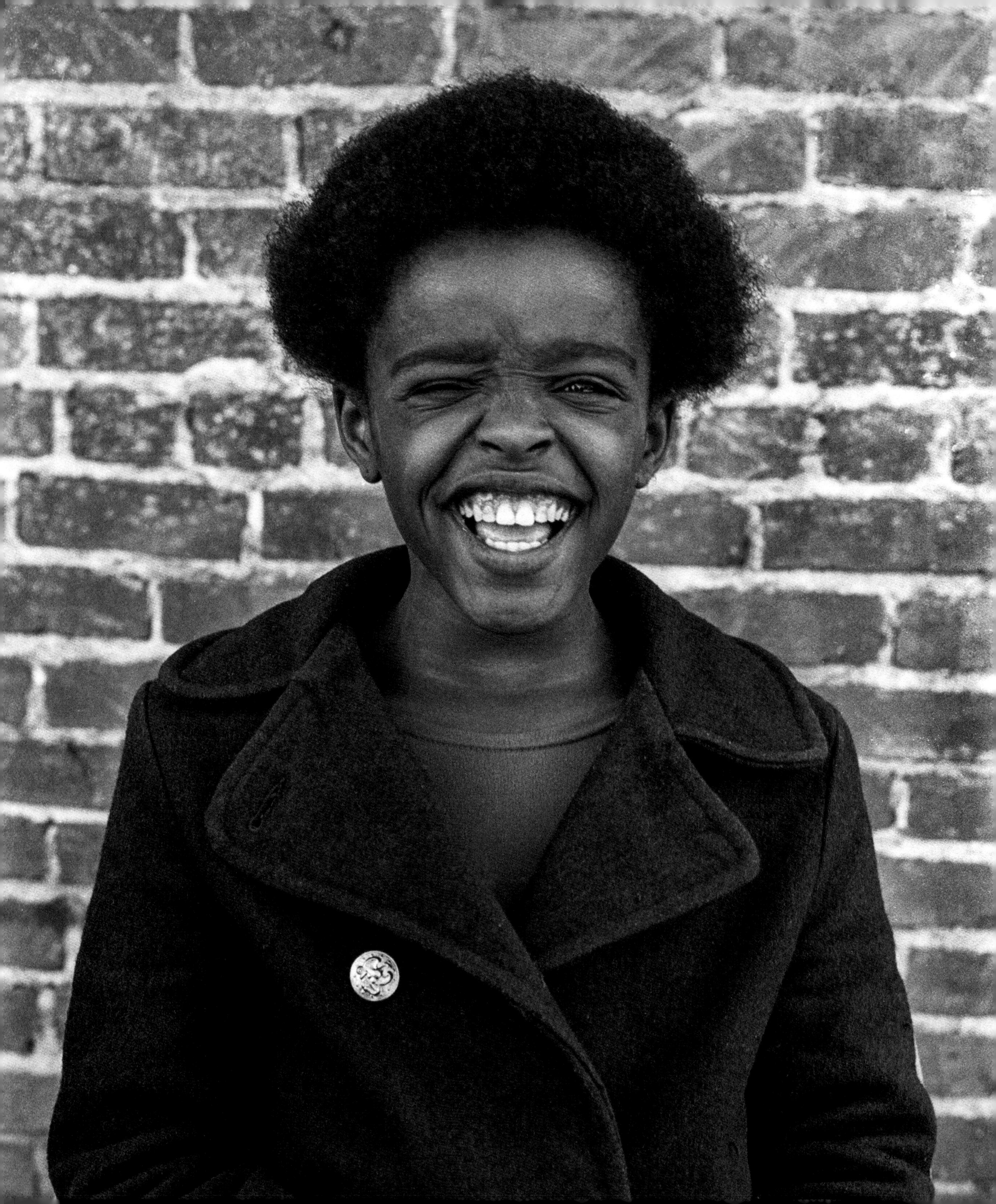

I joined the party because the men in my family, who were serving this country in the armed services, came back and were arrested and always in and out of jail. I asked my grandmother: "Why are my cousins always going to jail?"

They didn't do anything. I loved my cousins. I looked up to them. They were the older men in the family. When I read the BPP newspaper and noticed that what I saw in TV interviews with Huey and Bobby mirrored the reality of the men in my family, it made me feel, *there is a connection here. I can do something about this.*

I wanted to join the Black Panther Party. My grandmother preached that we should serve the people, and so I did.

Katherine Campbell
San Francisco Chapter, CA / Oakland Chapter, CA

I was in school studying accounting and finance. I was pushed into the finance ministry of the Jamaica chapter of the Black Panther Party.

What I think is so interesting is how the party valued the skill you brought. The party went with whatever experience you had, or what you thought you could do. I think this was the beauty of the party. You could have just a little bit of knowledge, and you were put in that position. I'll never forget that.

After the party, I went on to a career in finance. I've worked for many community nonprofit organizations for over 40 years. When people ask me, "How did you get into non-profit work?" I say, "That little bit of knowledge that I started with, in the Black Panther Party, it's still there."

I wonder if it ever crosses sisters' minds that we were the strength of the party.

Yasmeen Sutton Majid
Corona Chapter, NY / Queens Chapter, NY

1970 Oakland, California:
Patrice, daughter of David Hilliard,
at the Intercommunal Institute.

I grew up in Boyle Heights, an underserved Latin, Black, and Asian community in Los Angeles. In college, I fought for Asian Studies. For me, the WWII concentration camps was the reality that helped me understand my history, yet every day I would hear about Black mothers losing their sons on the streets, and I felt there must be more to do.

Since my focus was on education, I was invited to go to the LA Free Breakfast for School Children Program and help. That prompted me to join the BPP, and eventually I moved to Oakland.

I started to work at the Oakland Community School. It was a time of struggle, but the Party's world outlook, theories, and practice were a good fit for me. It was a natural fit because we were working together for the same goals.

Many years have passed. I'm older, and still I think the platform and programs of the BPP will guide change. There were many memorable moments, but the relationships that developed from our trust in each other were inspiring, and working at the school was joyous.

I would tell young women today to have the courage to believe in their worth and move forward even when you don't have all the answers. Seek the support and inspiration of like-minded folks to achieve your goals.

Ruth Wakabayashi-Kondo
Los Angeles Chapter, CA / Oakland Chapter, CA

I came from the Detroit Chapter to Oakland. I served for almost 10 years as the secretary for the Oakland Community School, and the administrative assistant to the director, Ericka Huggins.

What I want women and girls to know about serving the community is that our voices historically have been silenced, have been suppressed, and we keep coming through, stronger and stronger. And that's because our voices are empowering. We have very powerful voices when we speak the truth. It's our time!

Lorene Banks, Sr
Detroit Chapter, MI / Oakland Chapter, CA

March 31, 1972 Oakland, California: Black Panther member Ericka Huggins laughs with comrades after the Black Community Survival Conference. She served in the Los Angeles, New Haven, and Oakland offices of the party.

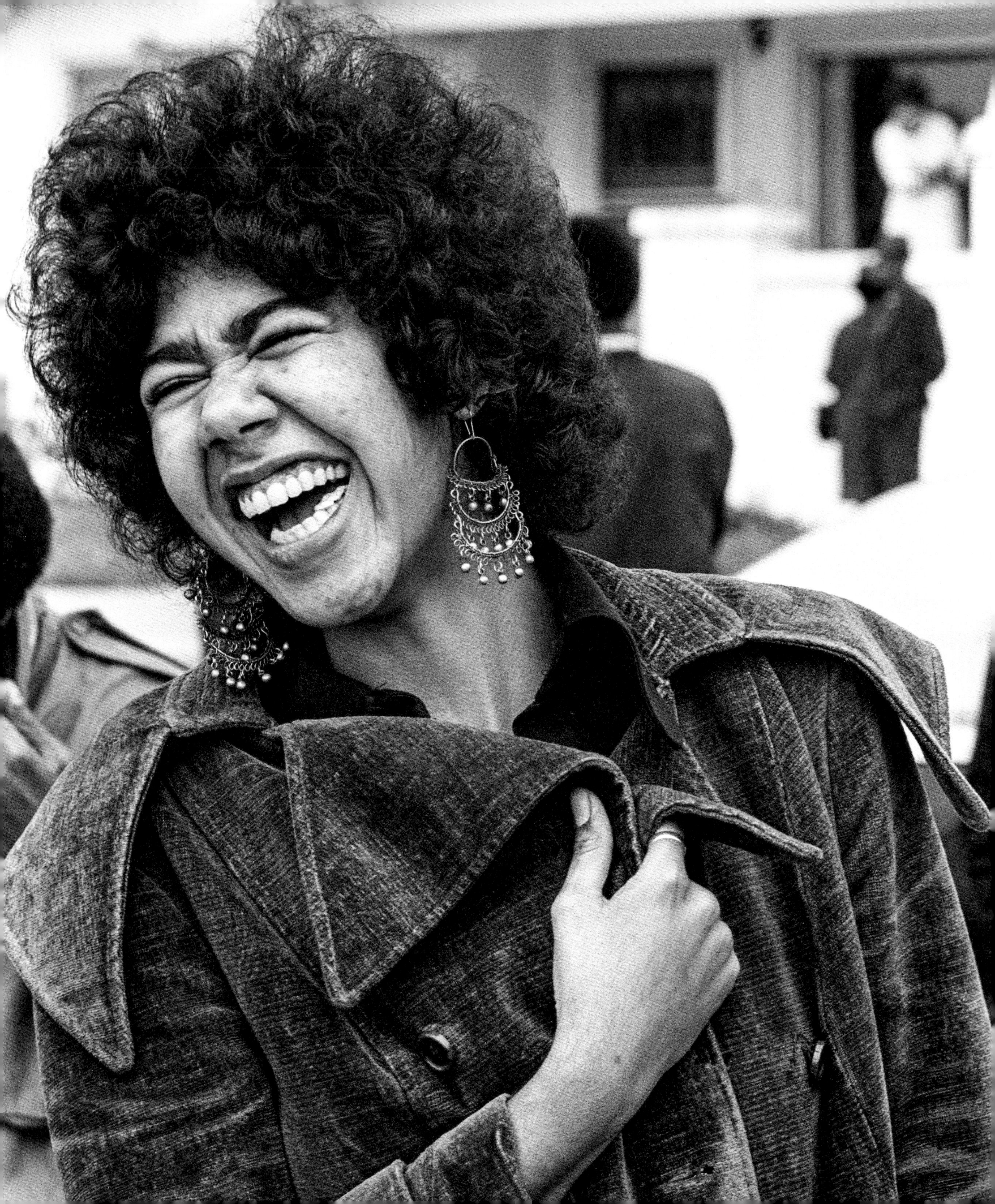

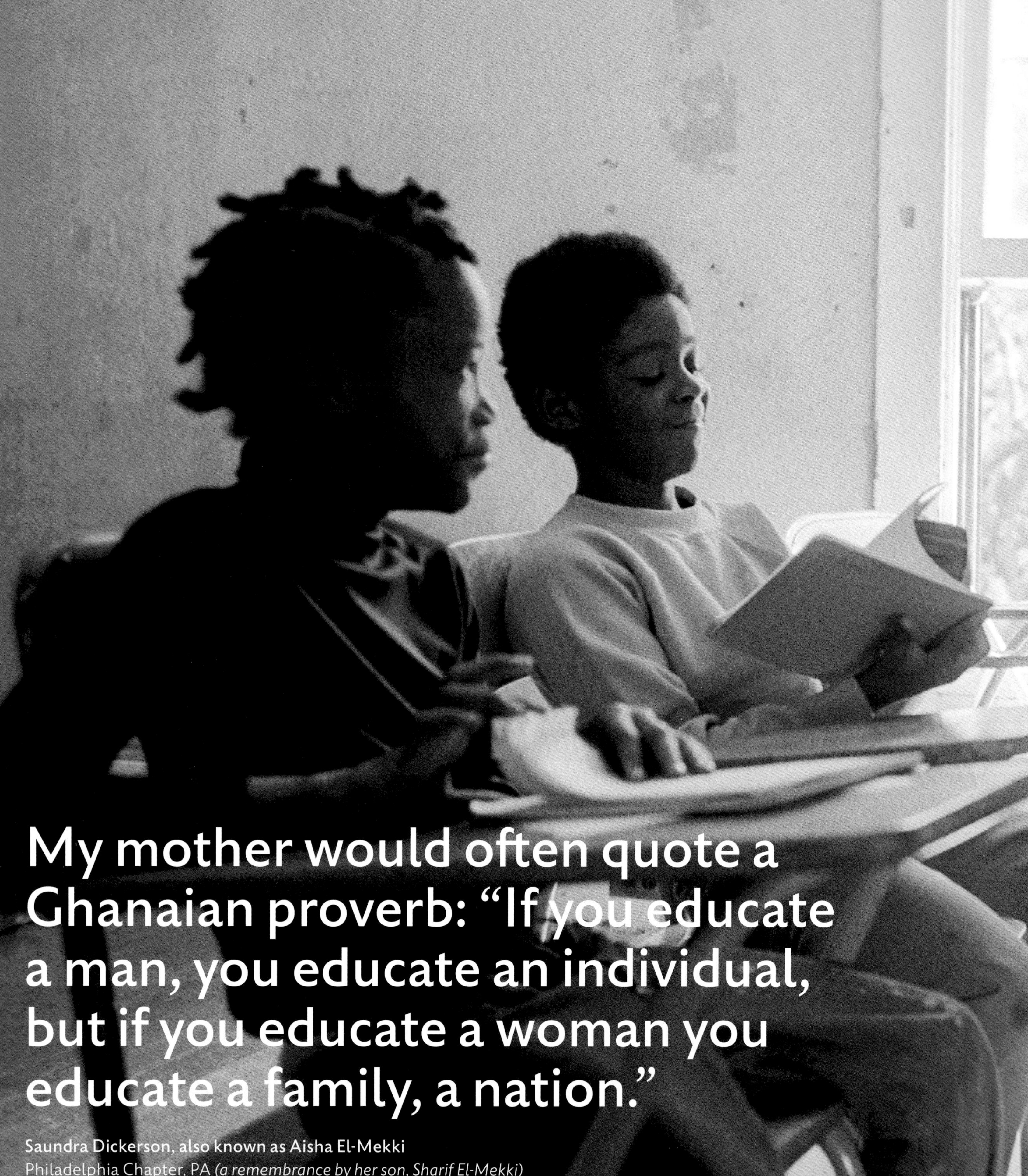

My mother would often quote a Ghanaian proverb: "If you educate a man, you educate an individual, but if you educate a woman you educate a family, a nation."

Saundra Dickerson, also known as Aisha El-Mekki
Philadelphia Chapter, PA (a remembrance by her son, Sharif El-Mekki)

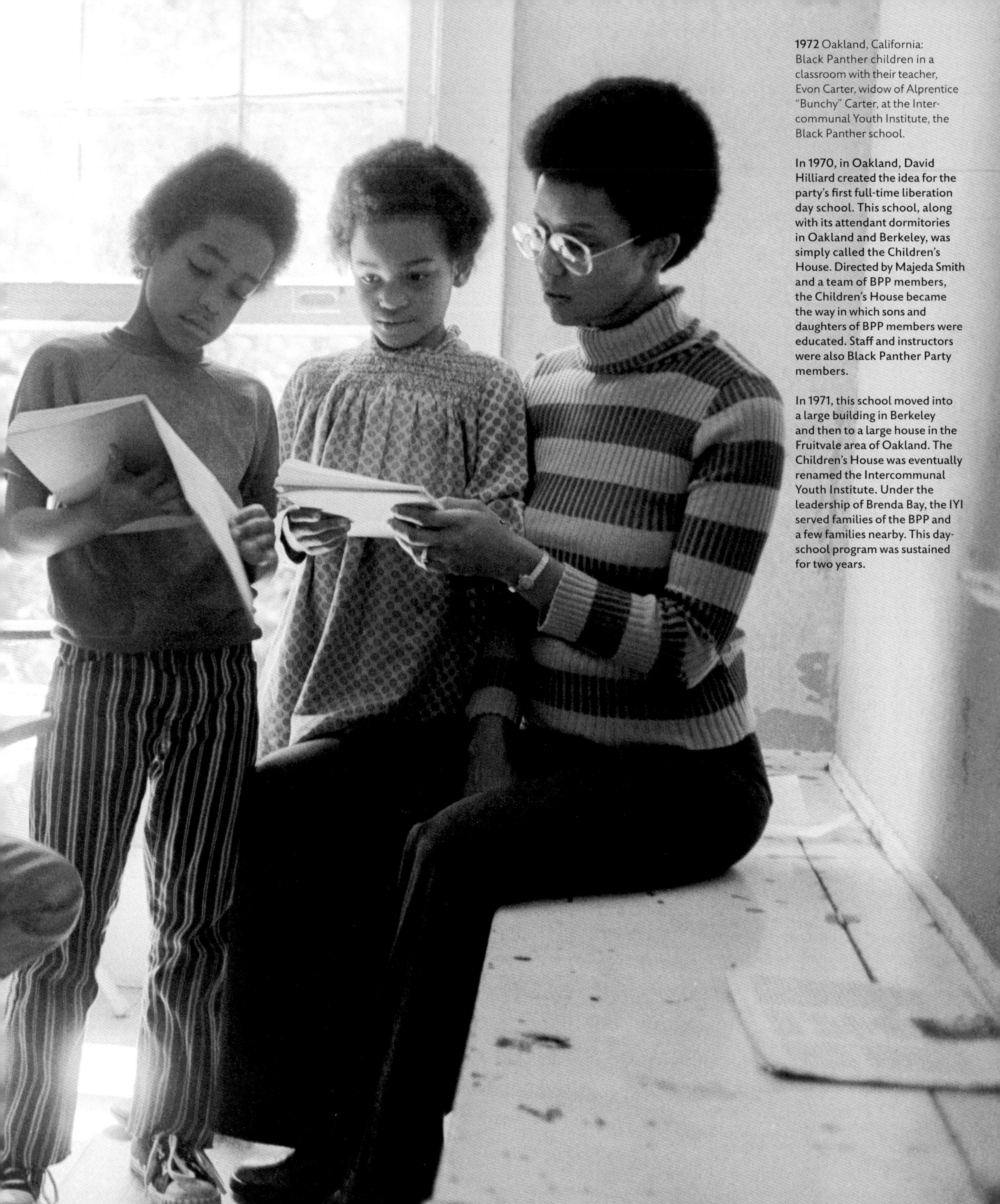

1972 Oakland, California: Black Panther children in a classroom with their teacher, Evon Carter, widow of Alprentice "Bunchy" Carter, at the Intercommunal Youth Institute, the Black Panther school.

In 1970, in Oakland, David Hilliard created the idea for the party's first full-time liberation day school. This school, along with its attendant dormitories in Oakland and Berkeley, was simply called the Children's House. Directed by Majeda Smith and a team of BPP members, the Children's House became the way in which sons and daughters of BPP members were educated. Staff and instructors were also Black Panther Party members.

In 1971, this school moved into a large building in Berkeley and then to a large house in the Fruitvale area of Oakland. The Children's House was eventually renamed the Intercommunal Youth Institute. Under the leadership of Brenda Bay, the IYI served families of the BPP and a few families nearby. This day-school program was sustained for two years.

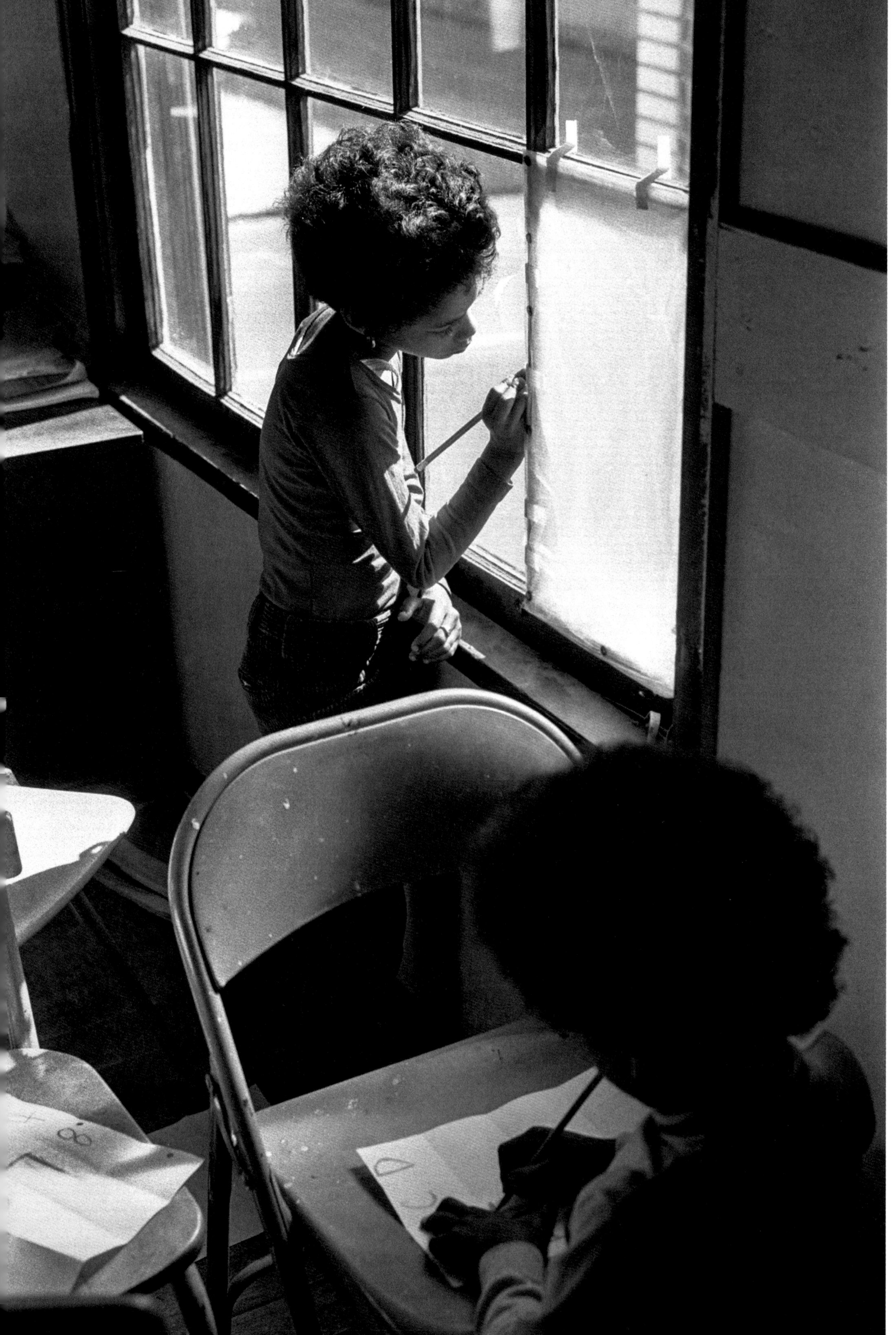

I'm the son of Kaye Washington and Amar Casey. They met as students at the University of Michigan and, at age 19, were able to join the Venceremos Brigade in one of its trips to Cuba to support the people there. Shortly after graduating from the university, my parents moved to Oakland, California, to join the Black Panther Party. My mom was drawn to the party because of her heart; she was one of the most generous people I've met.

She was a giver, a healer, a helper. I really miss her. She passed in 2019 due to cancer. She was 68.

I think one of my mother's most memorable moments in the Black Panther Party was being a teacher at the Oakland Community School, where I attended and my father taught. I was speaking to my wife [Janae Casey] and she remembered that, decades later, my mom would talk about how she enjoyed working with the children there more than being a corporate attorney.

I would like to believe that another of her more memorable moments was seeing how confident and secure I was at a young age at the school. I walked around like I owned the place, with my head held high and my chest poked out. I mean, you couldn't tell me anything; I had my mother and my father at the school! Oakland Community School was one of my favorite schools, and it made an early impression on me. The confidence that we exuded was priceless. We knew who we were as a people and we knew our history at an early age. So, job well done.

For my mother, serving the community was essential to creating a better world. She lived with the understanding that giving is also receiving. She gave of herself fully, wholeheartedly, and freely. For her, it goes without saying that the backbone of the Black Panther Party was women. I think she would want girls to know that they can be whatever they want, and also sincerely serve the community with love.

Kaye Casey (Kaye Washington Casey)
Oakland Chapter, CA *(a remembrance by her son, Camilo Casey)*

1970 Oakland, California: Sons and daughters of members of the Black Panther Party work on an art project at the Intercommunal Youth Institute.

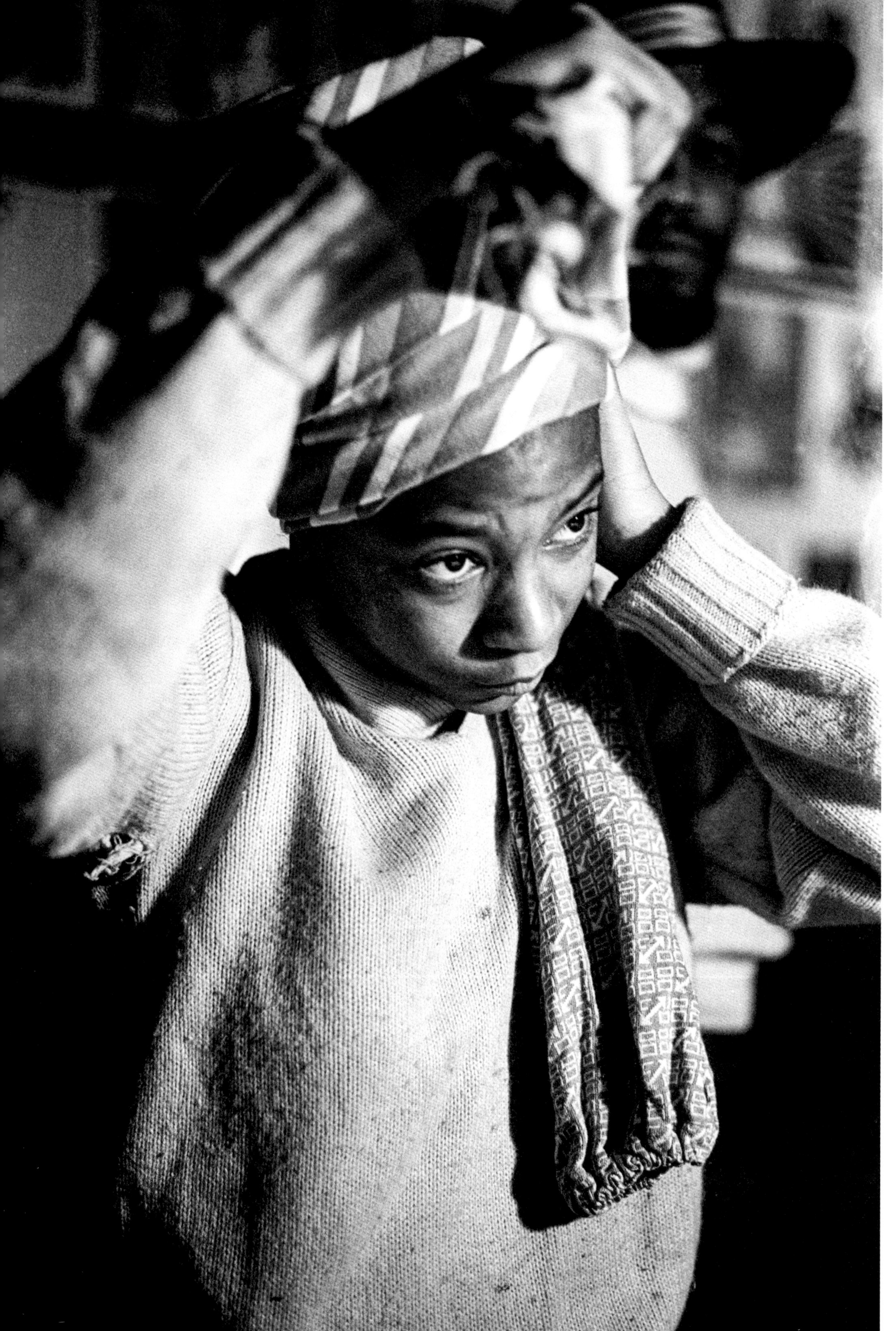

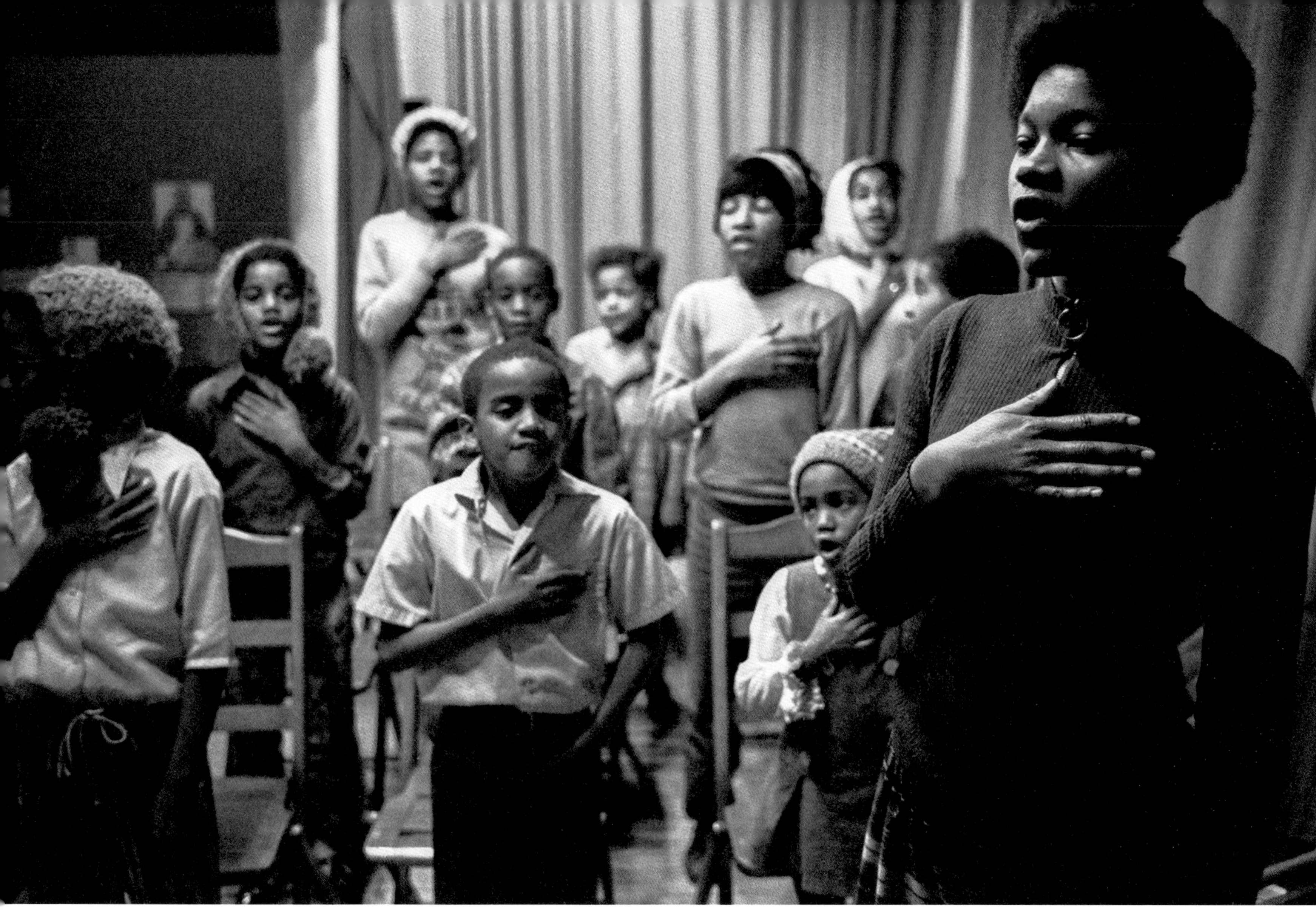

1971 New York, New York:
A woman of the Black Panther
Party wraps her hair at the
Harlem office.

1970 New Bedford,
Massachusetts: Black Panther
Liberation School.

In early 1968, shortly after John Huggins Jr. and I joined the BPP In Los Angeles, we met Elaine Brown, a talented musician, brilliant mind, and tender soul. Los Angeles was an everchanging Black political and cultural zone. The growing Black Panther Party chapter was a huge part of it. Artists and the activists worked in tandem.

Like so many of us who focused our lives on serving the people, Elaine became our friend, and soon became a leading voice in the Los Angeles Chapter of the party. As with John and me, the party gave Elaine's life purpose. Elaine became my sister in struggle. She was funny, serious, and fiercely dedicated. Many of us came to the party with jobs of all kinds; our lives in the '60s were entirely fluid, and yet we were driven.

Many years have passed since then. Though the party formally ended in 1982, like the BPP's principles and programs, Elaine Brown's drive, creativity, and love for communities of color never dissipated. Many don't know that Elaine is a composer and songwriter. Elaine's song "Assassination," which honors John Huggins Jr. and Alprentice "Bunchy" Carter, is hauntingly beautiful.

In 1976, Elaine wrote the lyrics and the melody for a song, "We Can Do Anything." This song was written for the children of Oakland Community School (OCS), a model elementary school in East Oakland, started in 1973 and sustained until 1982 by women and men of the Party. My daughter and her OCS friends remember this song as their personal anthem. One of them recently shared, "No matter how old I get, every time I sing it or hear it, I cry. I remember every word with love." The message in the song is a light in the darkness. It is a testament to the power in us all.

Elaine Brown
Los Angeles Chapter, CA *(a tribute by Ericka Huggins)*

1971 Oakland, California: Michelle, daughter of Evon Carter, stands at a blackboard at the Intercommunal Youth Institute. the school for the sons and daughters of the BPP.

September 11, 1974 *Are We Wrong?*, artwork by M. Gayle Asali Dickson.

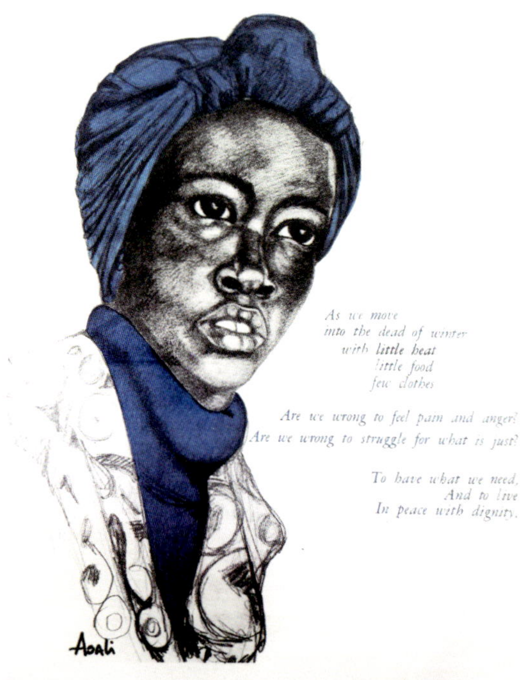

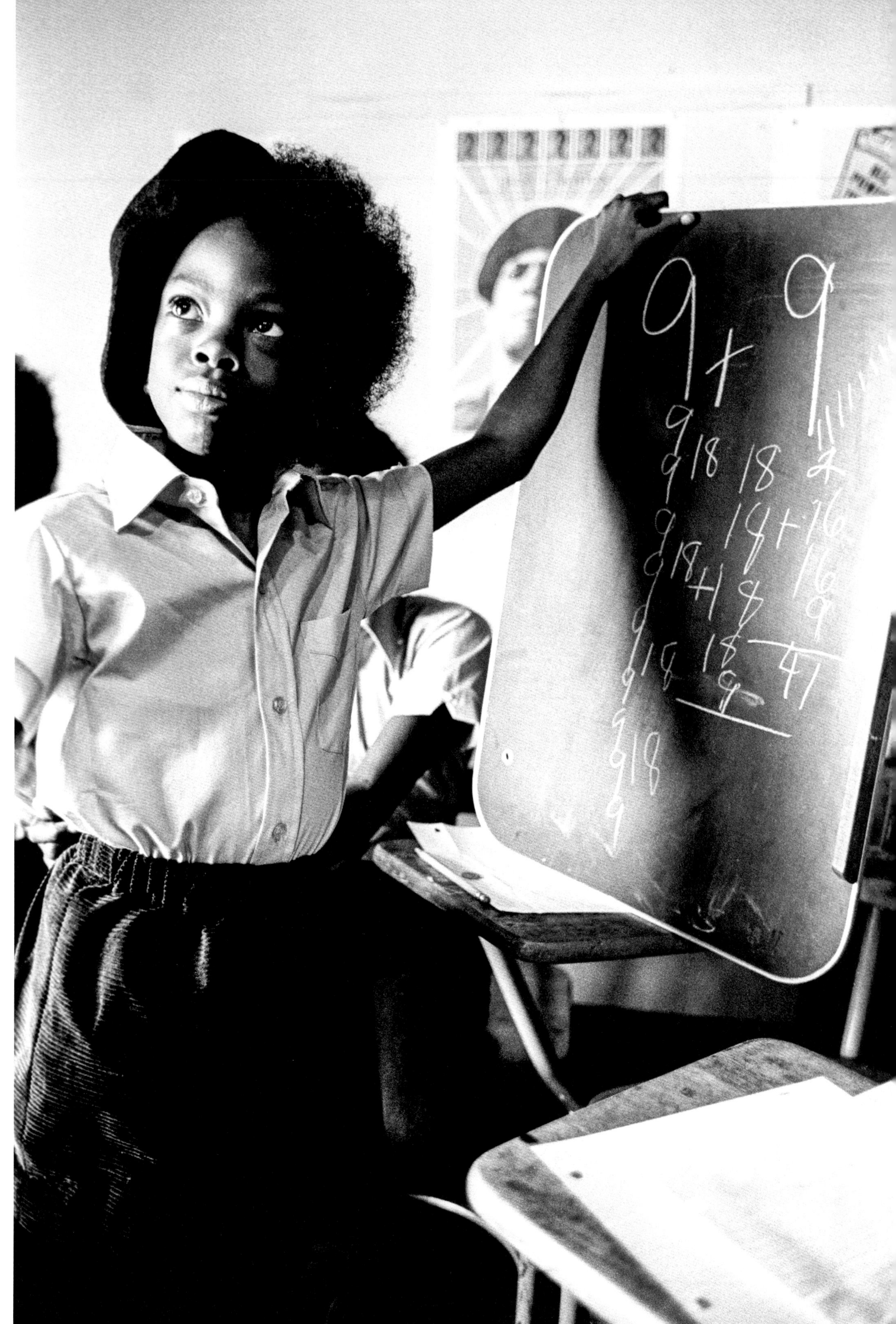
9 + 9
9 18 18
9 18 18 + 16
9 18 18 16
9 18 18 9
9 18 47
9 18
9

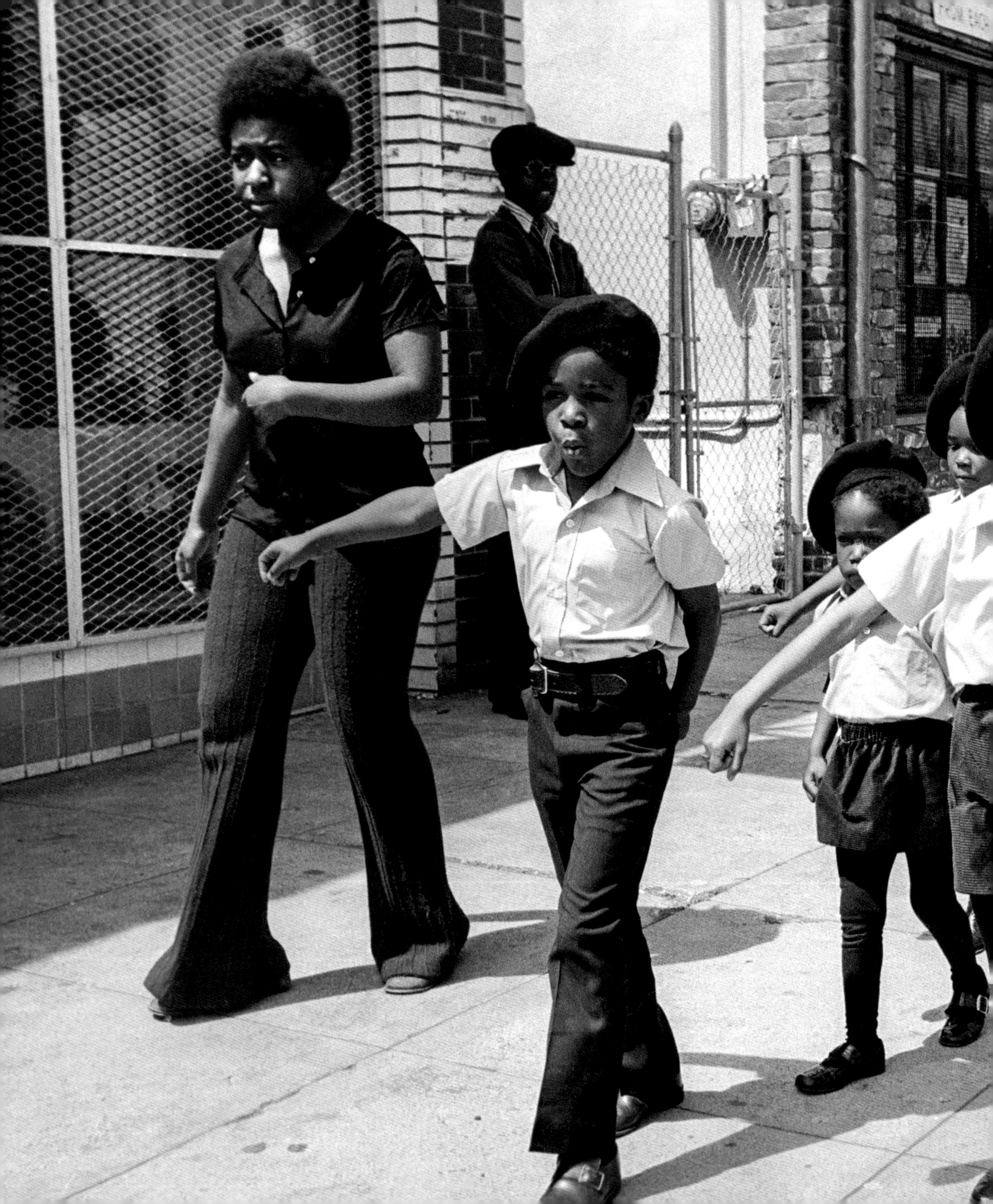

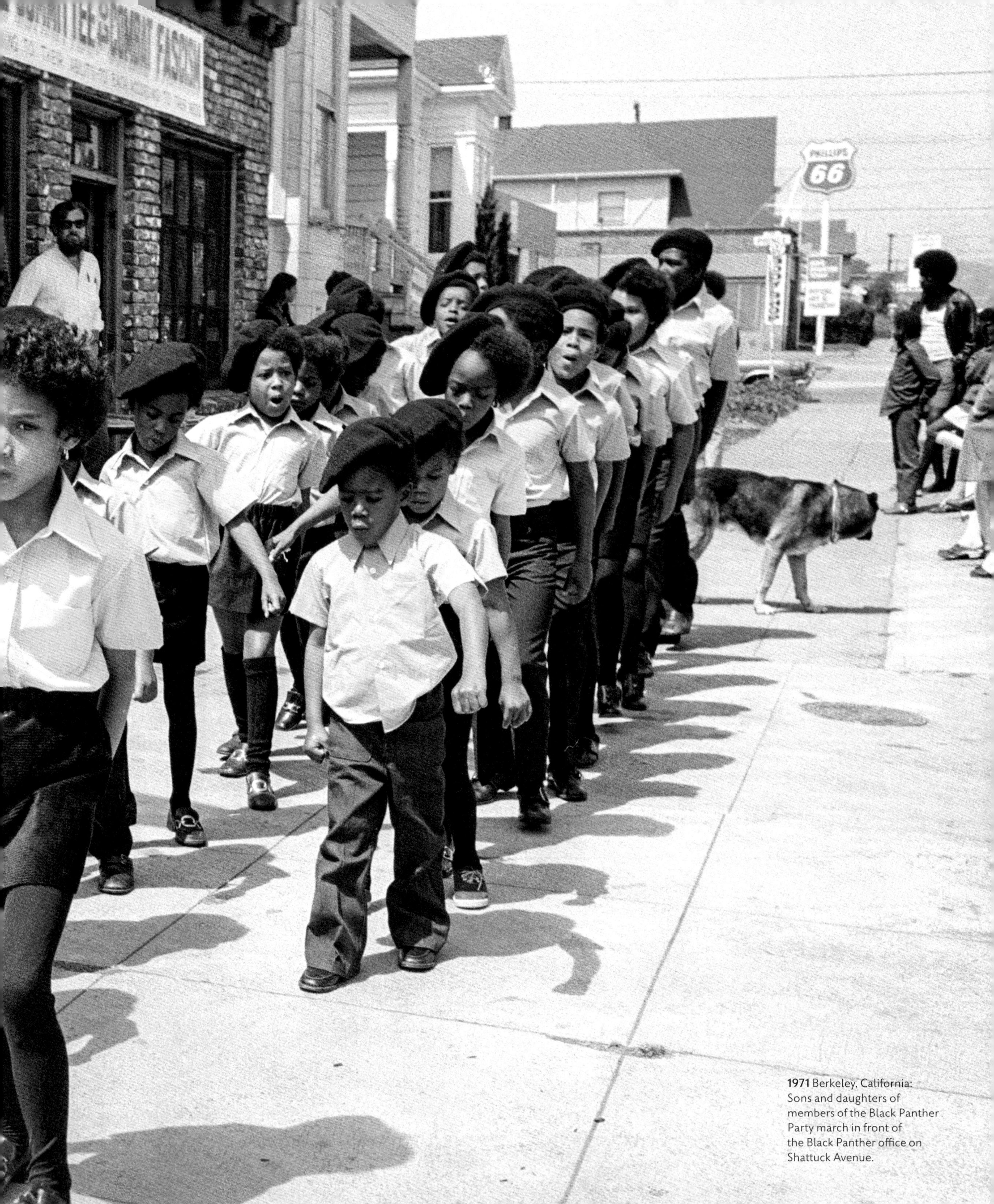

1971 Berkeley, California: Sons and daughters of members of the Black Panther Party march in front of the Black Panther office on Shattuck Avenue.

I came from New York. When we moved to San Francisco, I met a young man [Lamar Donald] who sold the Panther paper. He told me about the Breakfast Program, on Downey St., and asked if I wanted to volunteer, which I did, for a while. What drew me to the Black Panther Party was that the Party had a very clear platform. *We need food. We need shelter. We need them to stop arresting us for no reason.* Stop the killing of Black people! I mean, what could be clearer?

It appealed to me intellectually. Finally, somebody had said something that made sense. *This is what we want: food, shelter, education, and stop putting us in jail for no reason and stop killing us.*

I had been a professional proofreader, so I worked for the Party newspaper for a while. But that was later. My work with the Party began at the Oakland Community School after we moved to Oakland. Thank God, because I have two biracial children. They are Black in America, and I didn't want them to be confused about that.

I started in the kitchen, which I loved! I could make really healthy food for the kids, from scratch! Later, I taught English in the classroom and wrote the school curriculum. I did it with a lot of help, of course. Did I know American history? Well, I'm this smart-ass; I can research anything. I can go to the library and get books, and I can write decently. So, I wrote the American History section of the curriculum. I got through the whole thing and I realized there was no Black history. None. I was so embarrassed. Mortified, actually.

Amar Casey, the school's history teacher, came to help. I kept saying, "I can't believe I did this." Amar was very sanguine and calm. He said, "This is what happens, because there's nothing in the history books." We went through and rewrote it. It was never clearer to me that our people's history is left out of the official history books. It is hopeful to see that from about the 1970s to the present, many books have been written by Black people, Indigenous people, People of Color and others to counter this lack of a complete history of the U.S.

What I want people to know is that to serve their community, they must try to live a life of service. That doesn't mean that you don't have a career, family, friends, or fun. It means that you see everything—your job, your kids, your partner—as though you're there to help them. If you come from a place of service, you can serve the people of your community, body and soul.

Carol Granison
Oakland Chapter, CA

1972 Oakland, California:
Black Panther Party member
teaches at the Intercommunal
Youth Institute.

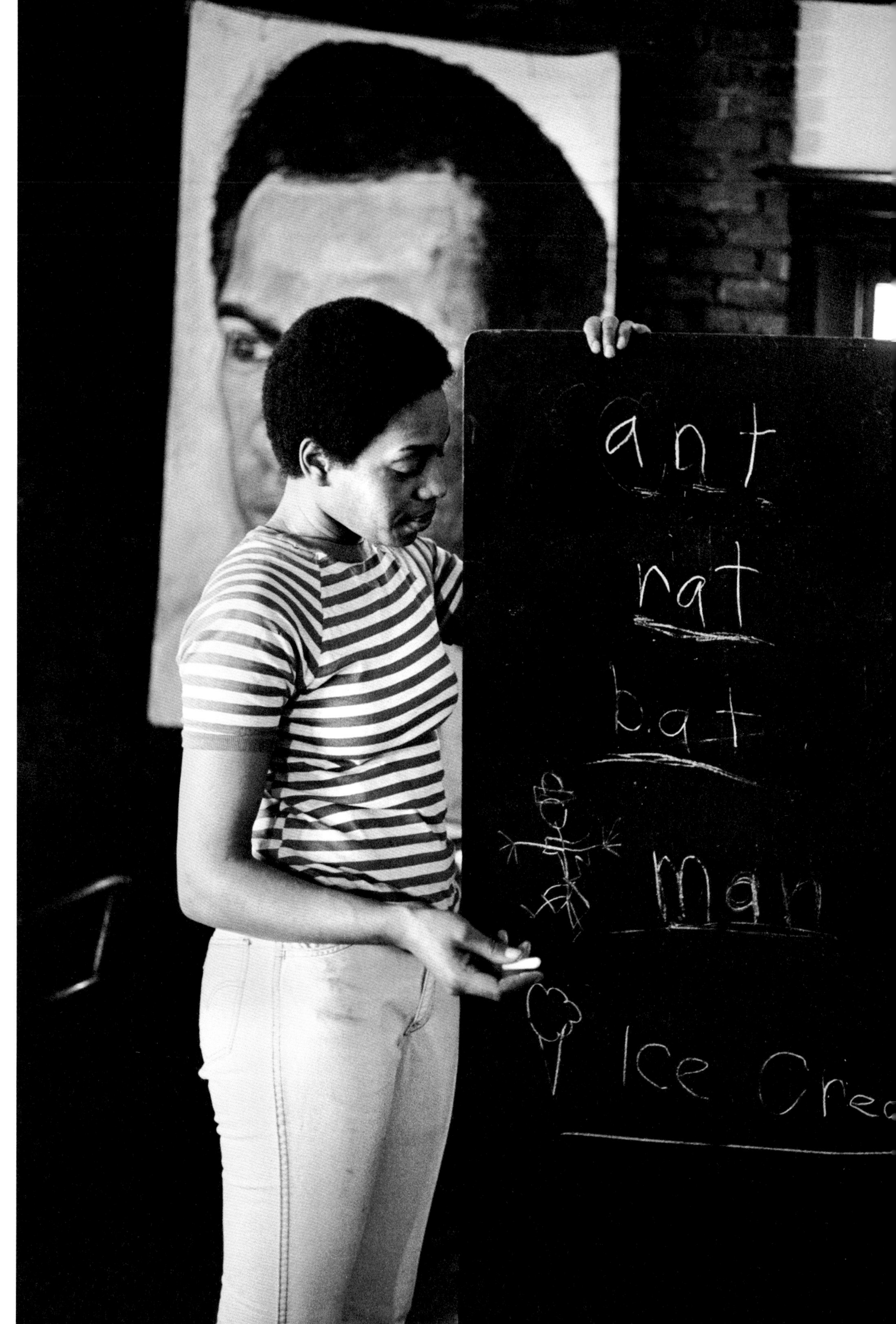
ant
rat
bat
Man
Ice Crea

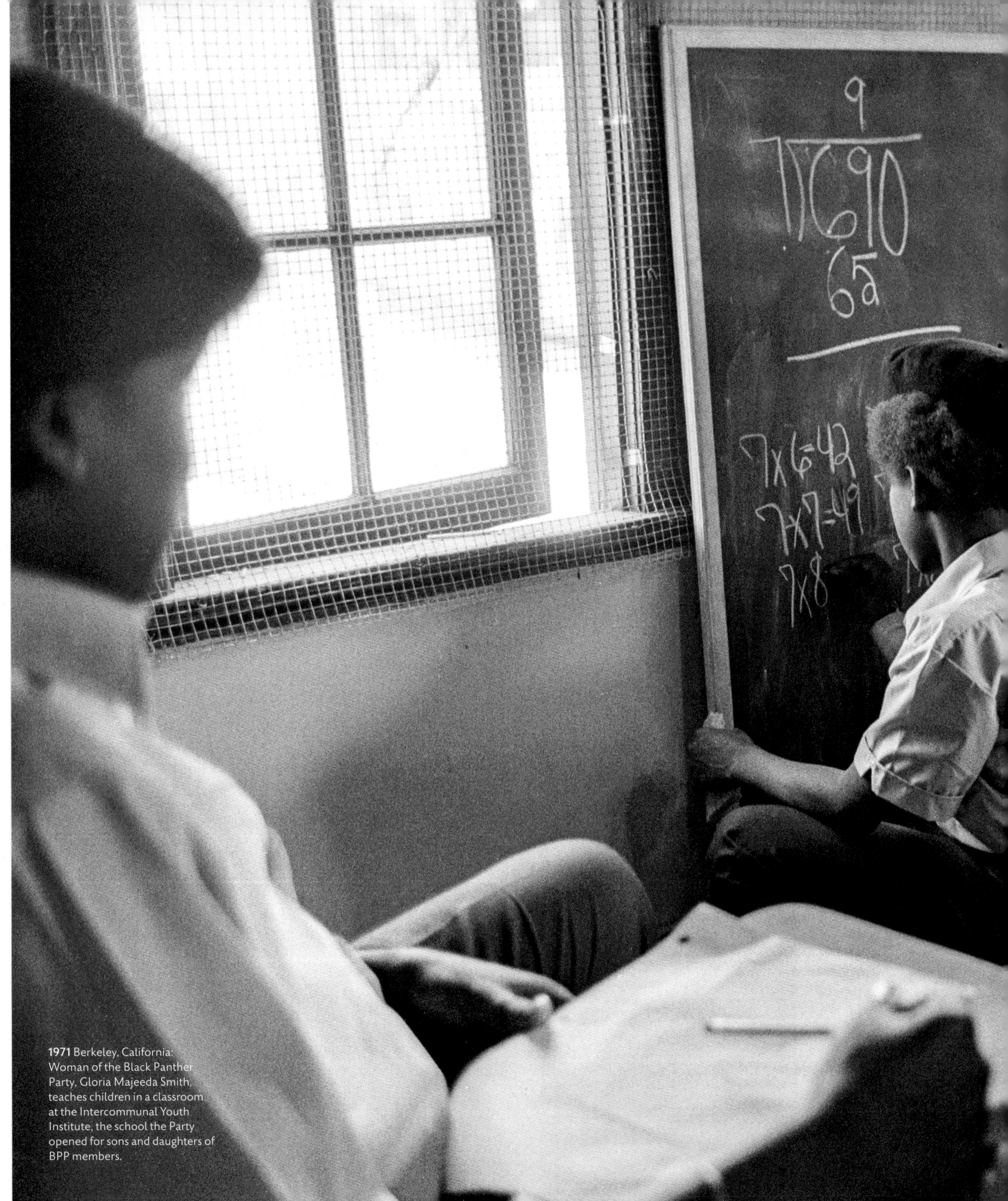

1971 Berkeley, California: Woman of the Black Panther Party, Gloria Majeeda Smith, teaches children in a classroom at the Intercommunal Youth Institute, the school the Party opened for sons and daughters of BPP members.

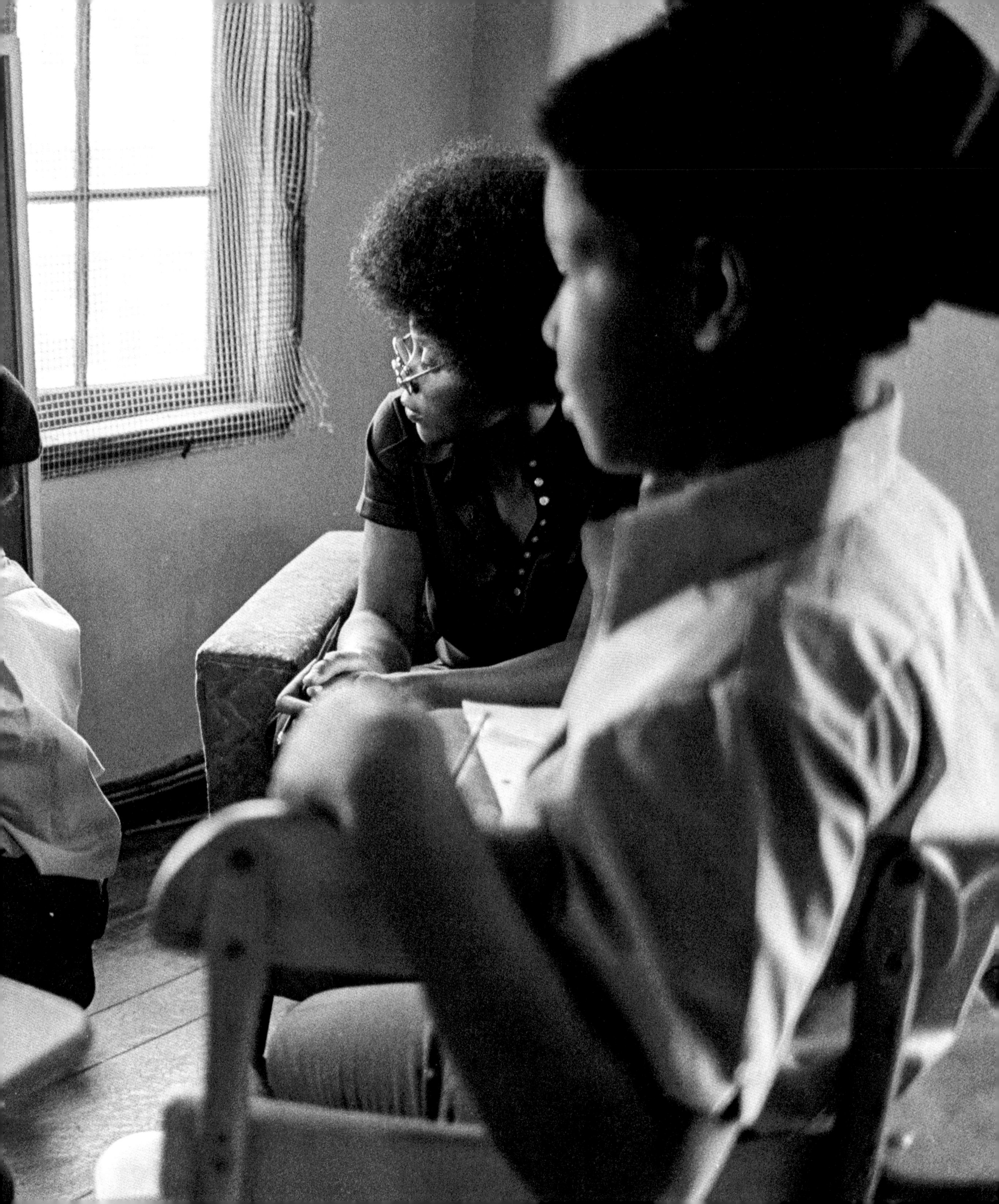

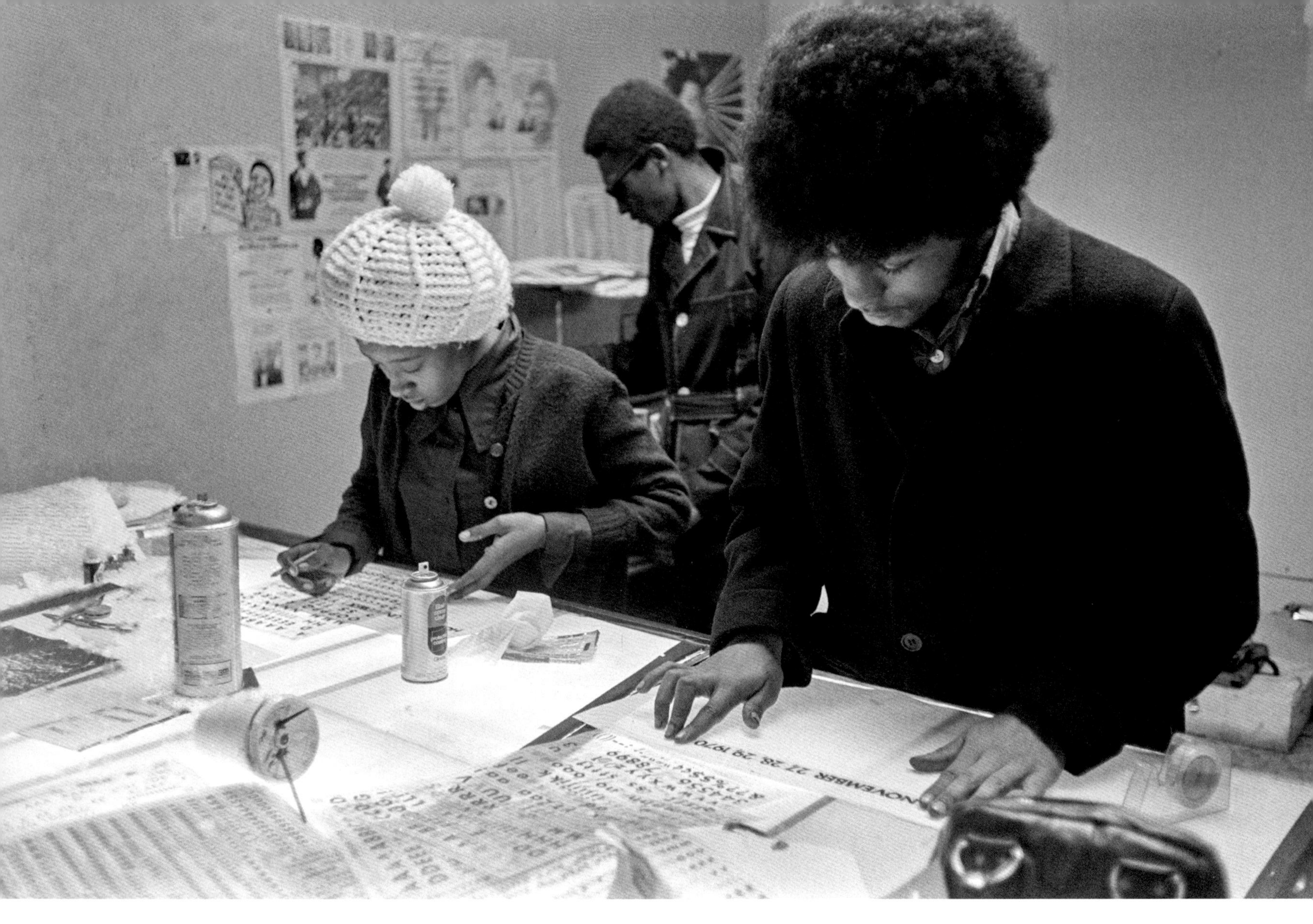

1969 Oakland, California:
Black Panther Party members
design leaflets for events.

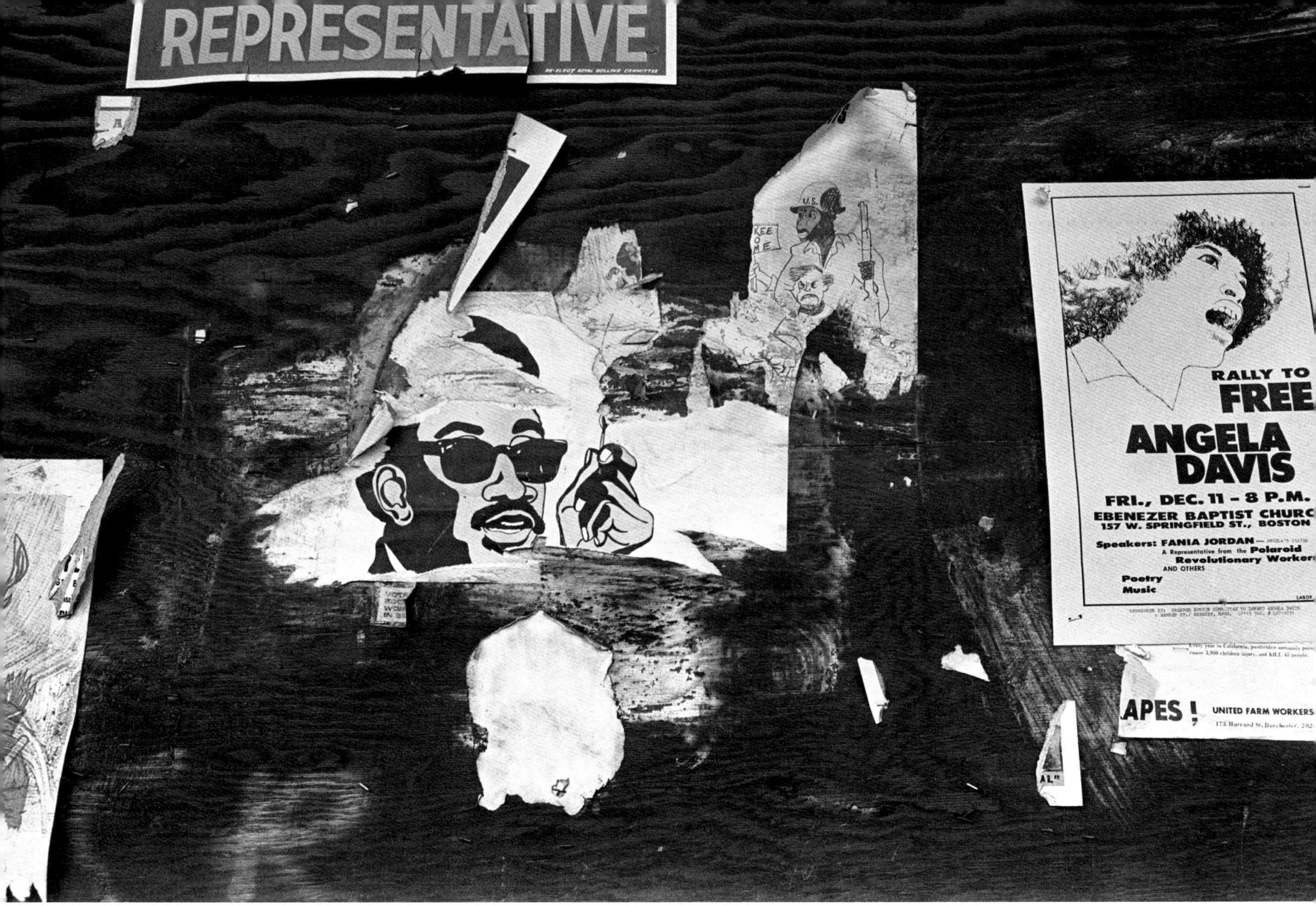

1970 Boston, Massachusetts:
Posters for Angela Davis and
H. Rap Brown.

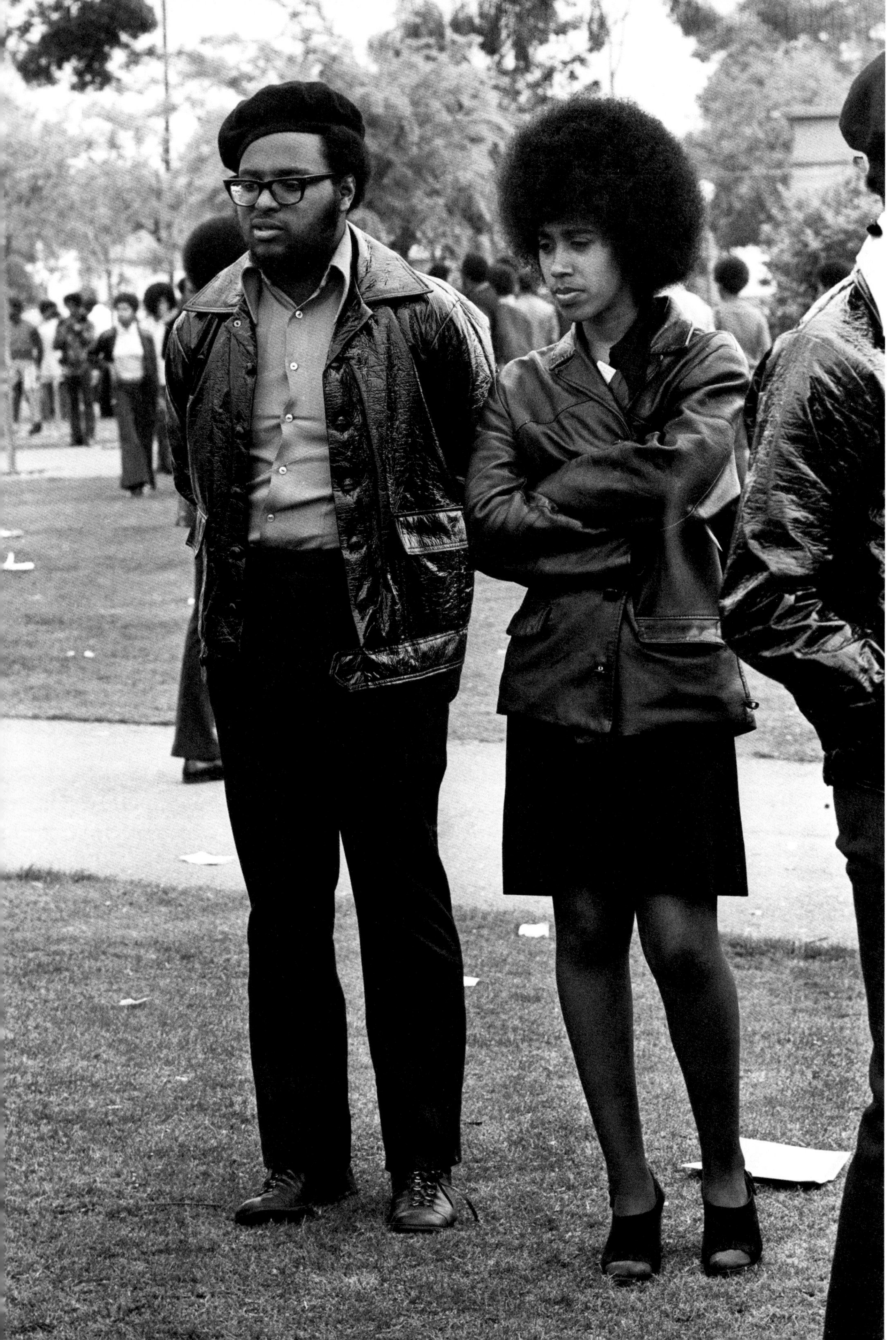

While I was on the BPP newspaper cadre—it was around 1973–1974—I began hearing about the Oakland Community School. Simultaneously, the Vote for Survival campaign was happening. Bobby Seale ran for Mayor and Elaine Brown for City Council. As the campaign gradually came to an end, I was beginning to feel a little burned out due to the pace we had kept. That feeling was especially strong after talking to a comrade who worked at the school. I requested a transfer to the Oakland Community School.

It seemed to me that members of the school cadre functioned more like a "family"—a family I wanted to be part of. The feeling of family and community was and is important to me. In the Seattle Chapter, we literally functioned as a family as we went about serving the community, body and soul.

I started out at the OCS as a preschool teacher. Later, I became the school's art teacher, after working as an assistant to Emory Douglas, and then teaching classes by myself. I began with 10 children in my class. I had no previous experience as a teacher. However, I was given a curriculum, which helped me to support the children in learning to advance to the next level. The way I "stepped up to the plate" was to use art as a tool to teach my preschool students the cognitive skills they needed to advance.

One memorable experience is of the day my class went on a field trip to Coit Tower in San Francisco. We rode in the school van; me pointing out the clouds and birds in the sky and the boats on the water and informing them that there were fish under the water. I also pointed out the SF cityscape before us.

Upon returning, and while the children were napping, I rolled out some butcher paper and made a paper mural of the field trip showing the children in the drawing, waving to the children in the classroom. When they woke up from their nap, we all sat down in front of the "mural" and *they* retold, out loud, the story of their field trip, talking about all the details from beginning to end.

Afterwards, I told them to be sure to tell their parents or a guardian about their trip. One little girl in my class did not enunciate words. She spoke in a sing-song voice, and it was very difficult to understand her words. However, when her mother came to pick her up, the child ran and grabbed her mother and excitedly said, "Come here, come here!" That little girl, speaking very clearly so that her mother and I could understand every word, told us about the field trip she and her classmates took that day, from the beginning to the end.

At OCS, we were allowed to use the skill that was our gift to help teach the children how to think, not what to think.

M. Gayle Asali Dickson
Seattle Chapter, WA / Oakland Chapter, CA

March 31, 1972 Oakland, California: M. Gayle Asali Dickson stands with Anthony Ware at the Party's Black Community Survival Conference. Anthony and Asali were originally from the Seattle Chapter.

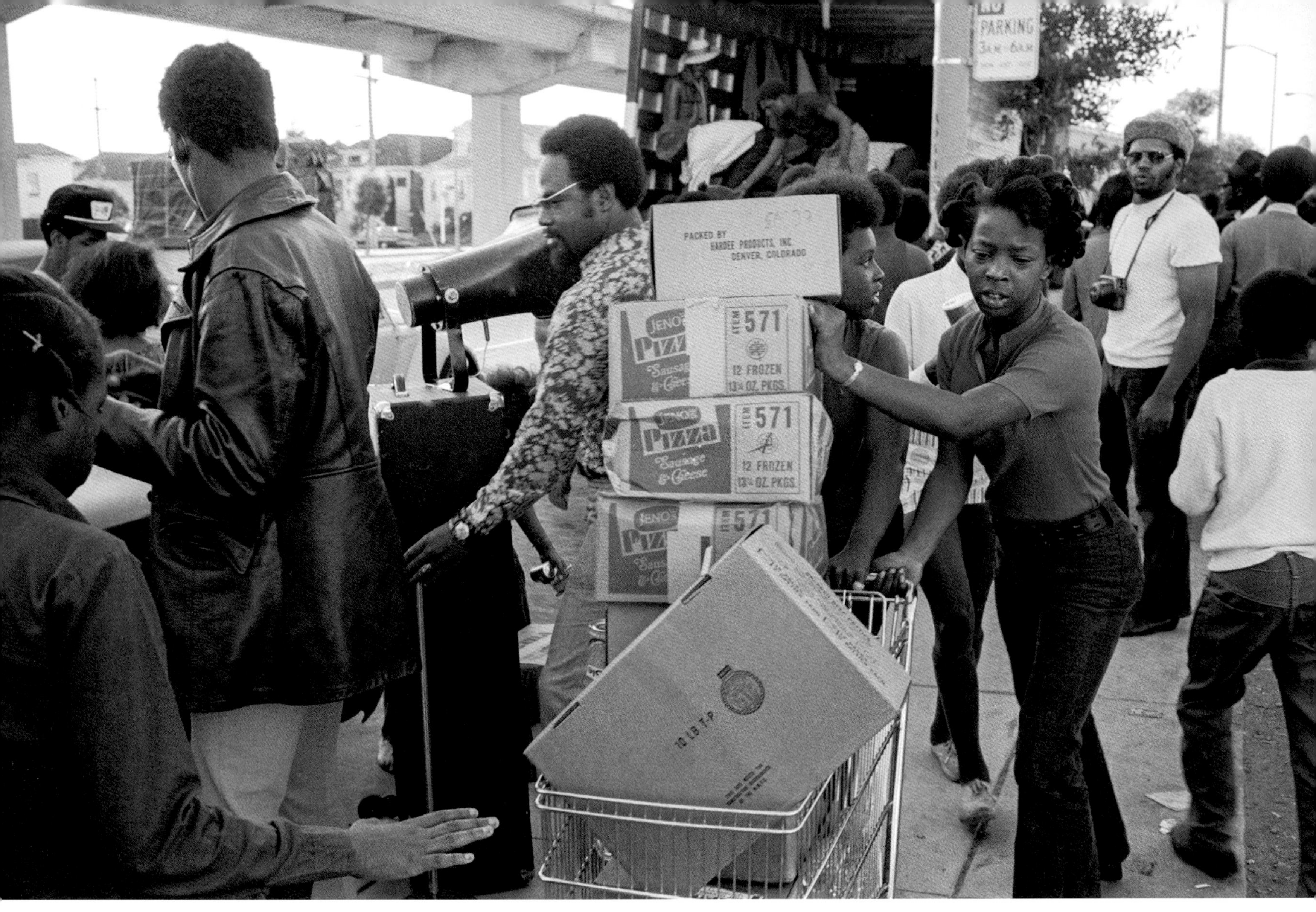

August, 1971 Oakland, California: Black Panther food give away in the community. Left of boxes is Panther artist and central committee member Emory Douglas.

1970 Boston, Massachusetts: Woman of the Black Panther Party, member Annette Simmons.

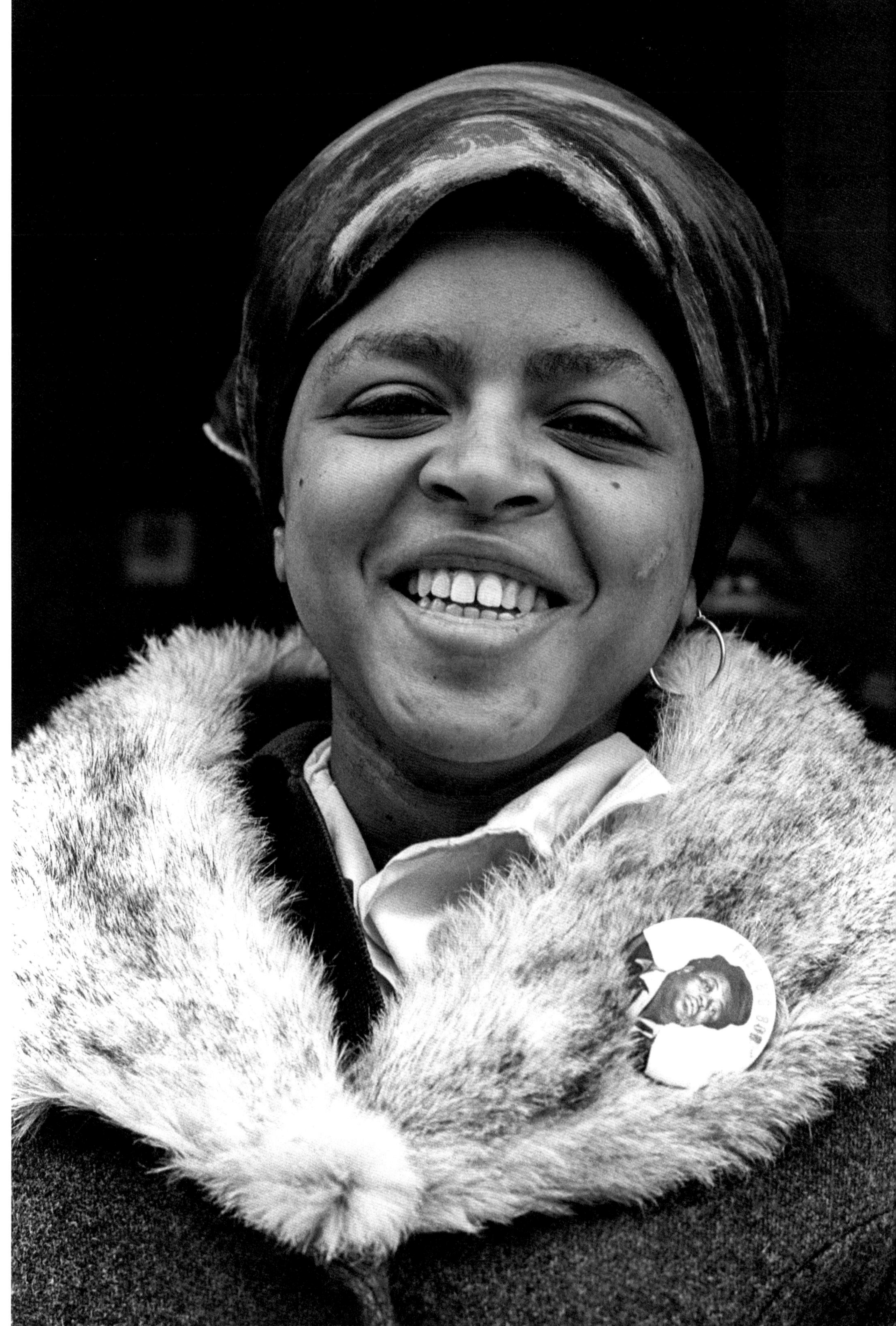

I was raised in North Berkeley. I was almost 18 when I joined the party. I felt that camaraderie: working side by side and leaning on each other for long hours. We got it done!

I worked on the party newspaper, learning how to typeset. Such tireless dedication: working at the George Jackson People's Free Clinic in Berkeley, learning how to take blood samples, and distributing WIC vouchers (for the federal Women, Infant, and Children nutrition program) to the community. It all filled that empty void in my life, that need to find a family. As a youth on the verge of being homeless, living in a foster home, I found a safe place at the Oakland Community Learning Center as a part of the Son of Man Temple singers. This was a place where I found a sense of home and family.

When I departed, it took me a while to get it together because something was missing. In the party, we all shared the same vision and goal. My most important experience with the BPP, which I still apply today, was the use of food as a tool to organize community. Now, almost 15 years later, each week I help to ensure that people can actually eat a real cooked meal. I am the visionary of the Self Help Hunger Program; its roots are the seed of the BPP Free Food Program.

I started cooking more and more. We use a vacant lot; public land for public good. We have four community events a year, and we share fruits and vegetables every day of the week through the Melvin Dickson Memorial Produce Bin. *All Produce to the People.* Melvin was the main cook at the Oakland Community School, and after the party, he started a Youth Literacy Program that lived until he passed on. It's all still going, and the stewardship is growing.

Frances Moore (affectionately known as "Aunti Frances")
Oakland Chapter, CA

1971 New York, New York: Woman of the Black Panther Party sells the Black Panther newspaper in the 8th Avenue bus terminal.

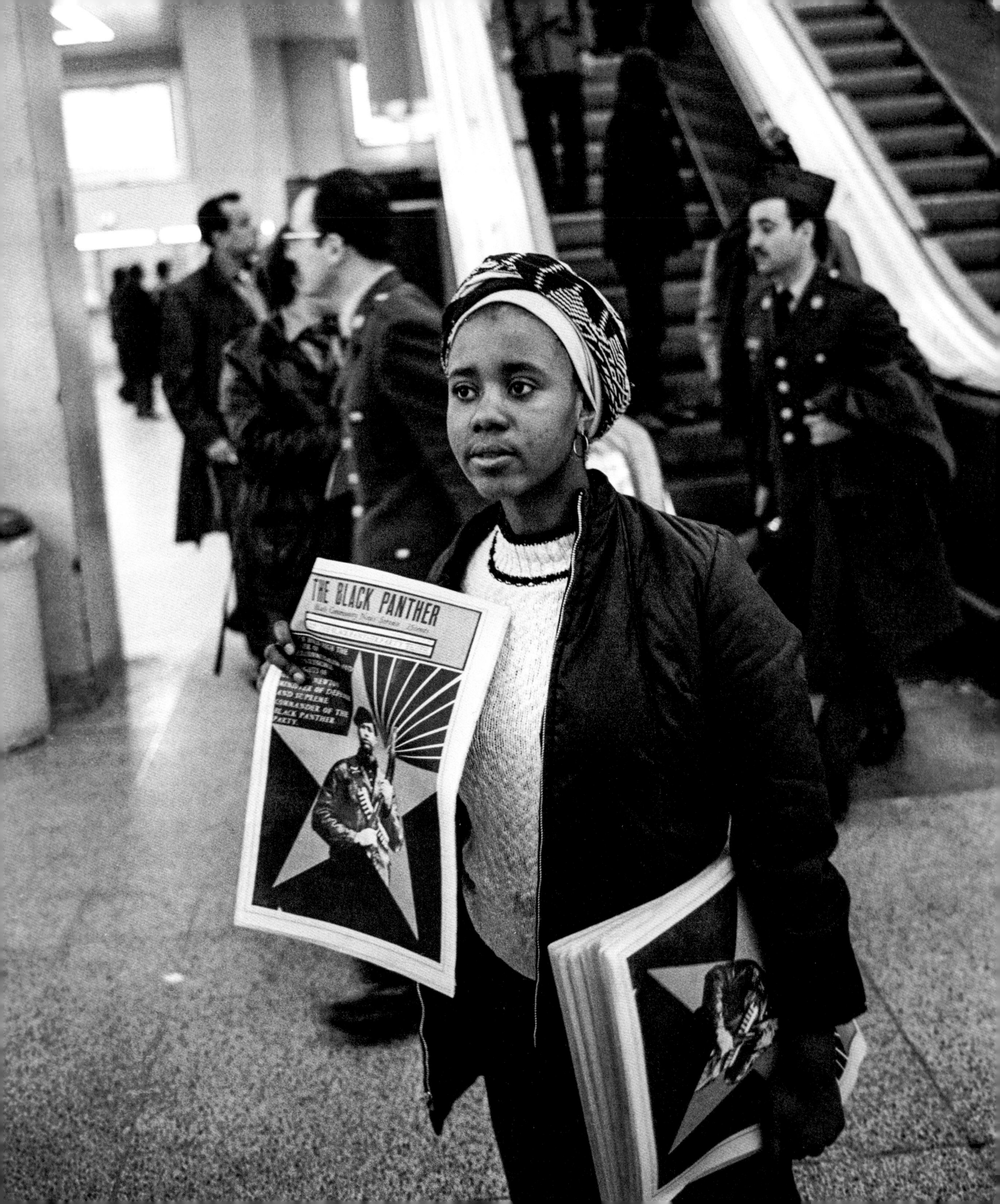

THE BLACK PANTHER
Black Community News Service
MINISTER OF DEFENSE AND SUPREME COMMANDER OF THE BLACK PANTHER PARTY

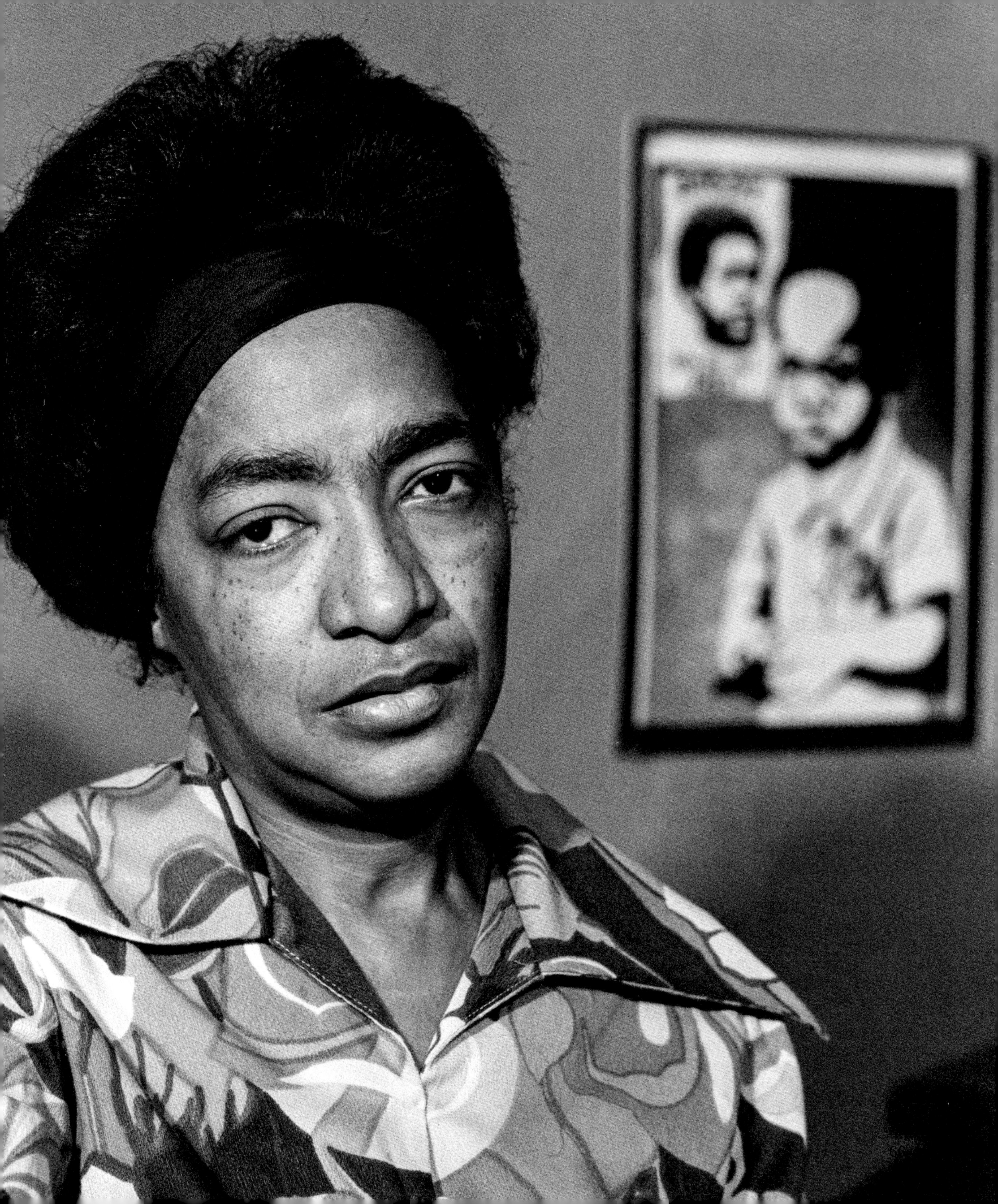

A huge, life-changing moment was, of course, the two-to-three-day period when Martin Luther King and little Bobby Hutton, the first member of the Party, were killed. Both men were assassinated.

I was with my boyfriend (later husband) Buzz, a member of the Party. We'd gone out to eat and we came back to my little apartment in Berkeley, and it looked like someone had broken in through the front window of the apartment. Inside were Bobby Seale, Joanne Mitchell, Alex, and Elsa—the white couple from KPFA radio station. They explained to us that we were all on the run from the police.

All I could see was my dirty laundry and my underwear, spilled all over the living room floor. And Bobby said, "We've got to go."

For the rest of that night, Evelyn Proctor and Janice Garrett Forte, Bobby Seale, Joanne, Buzz and me were eluding the police. We were literally running through backyards in Oakland and Berkeley. We finally made it to a safe apartment. Bobby told us that Huey said that Oakland was not to go down in flames. Oakland was not going to have a riot after these horrendous events!

Judy Juanita Hart
San Francisco Chapter, CA / Oakland Chapter, CA

1971 Oakland, California: Woman inside Black Panther National Headquarters. 1048 Peralta Street, West Oakland.

1968 Poster protesting the murder of "Lil' Bobby" Hutton by the Oakland police force on April 6.

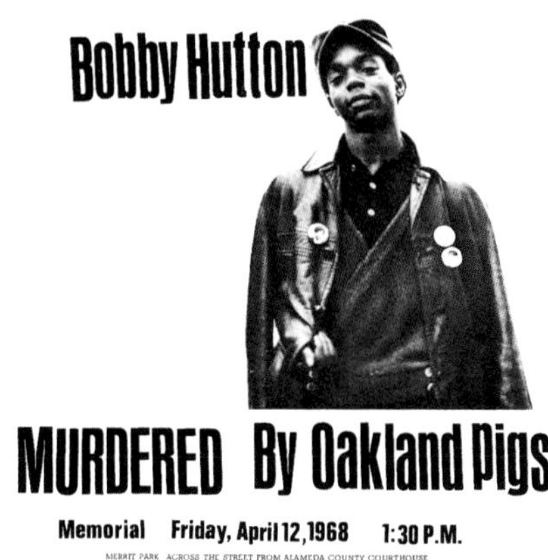

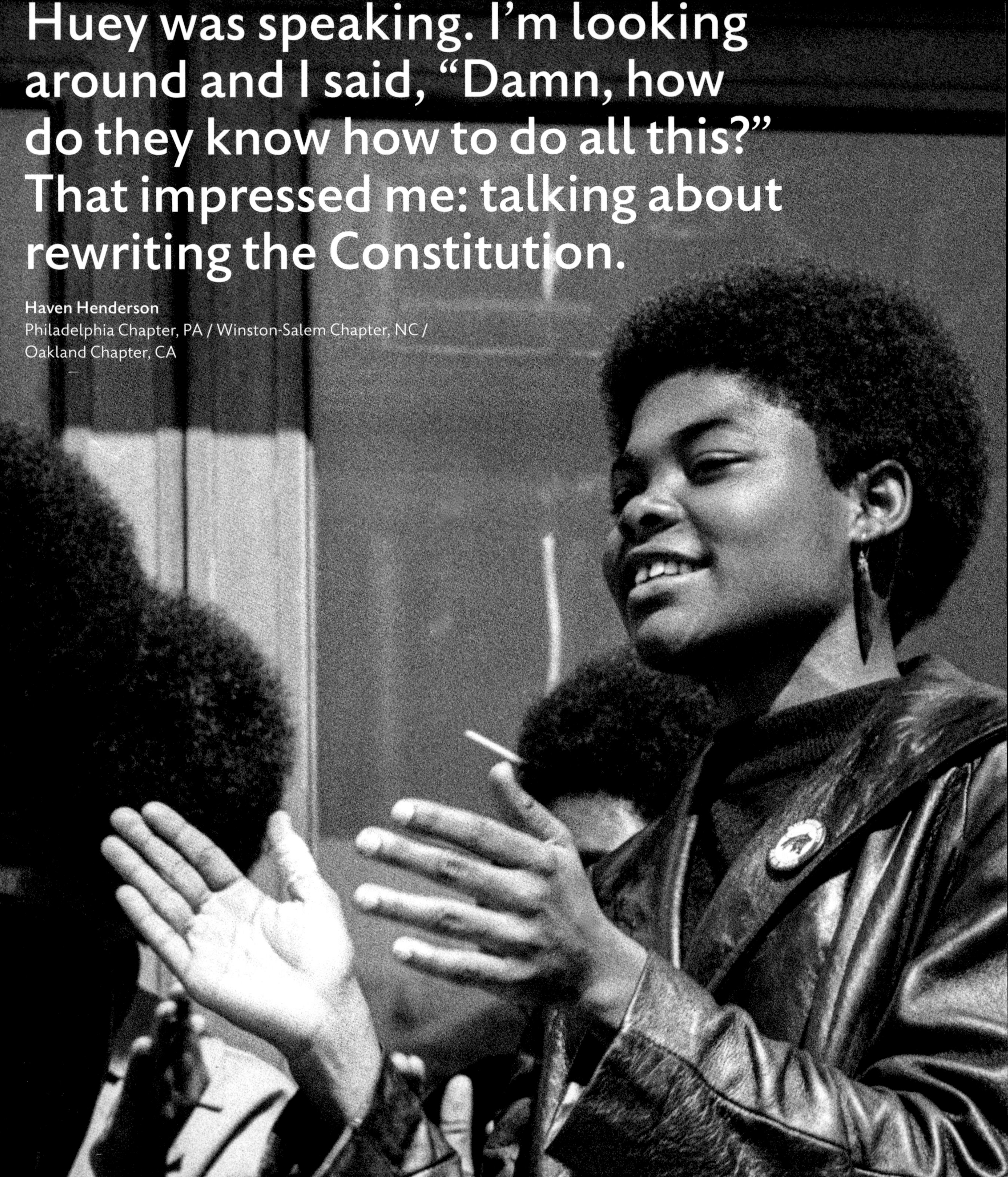

Huey was speaking. I'm looking around and I said, "Damn, how do they know how to do all this?" That impressed me: talking about rewriting the Constitution.

Haven Henderson
Philadelphia Chapter, PA / Winston-Salem Chapter, NC / Oakland Chapter, CA

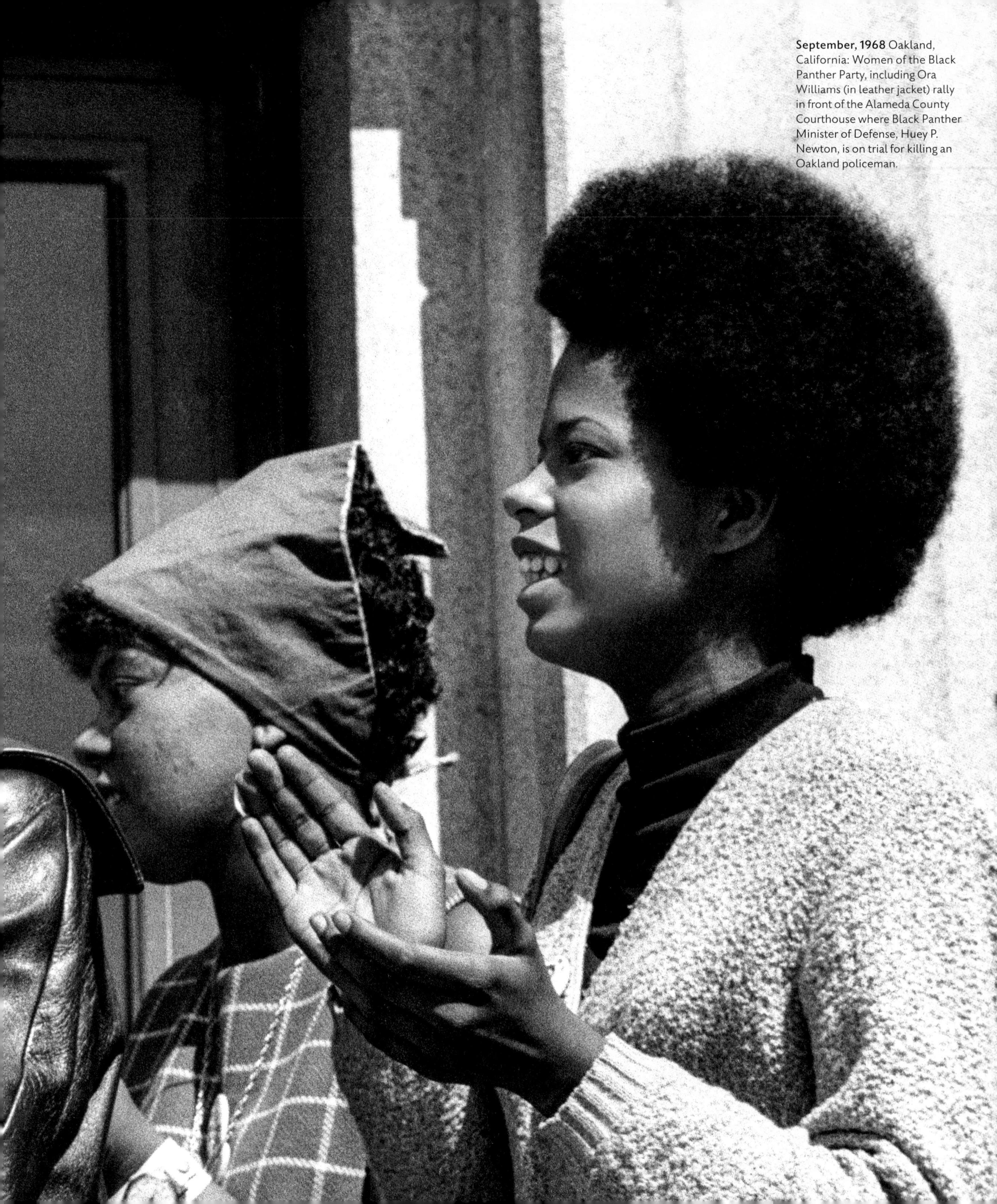

September, 1968 Oakland, California: Women of the Black Panther Party, including Ora Williams (in leather jacket) rally in front of the Alameda County Courthouse where Black Panther Minister of Defense, Huey P. Newton, is on trial for killing an Oakland policeman.

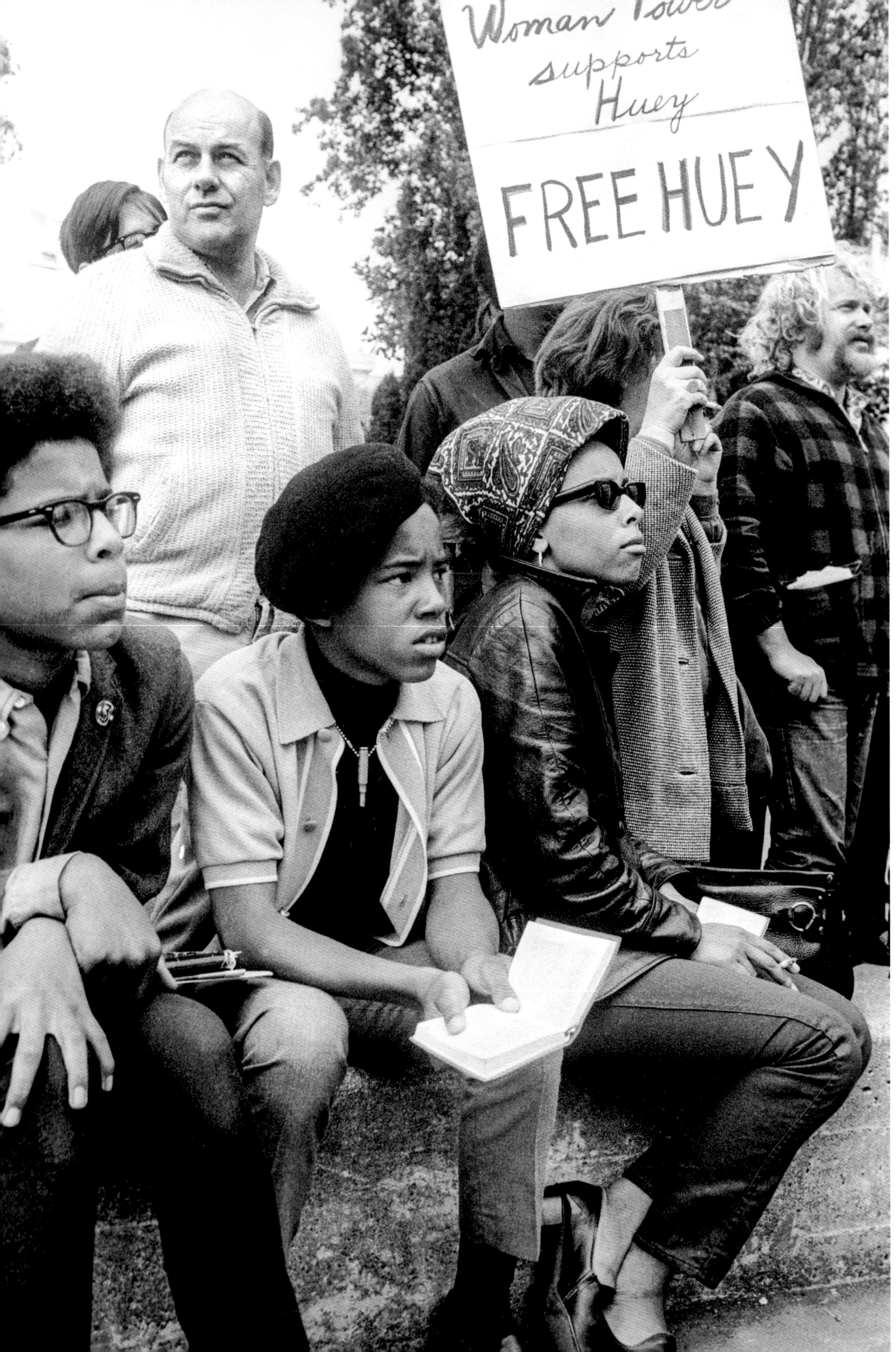

Woman Power
supports
Huey
FREE HUEY

I joined the BPP when I was 20 years old. I was mainly in the Oakland Chapter, but I think I began in San Francisco. I lived in a part of town where the Free Breakfast for School Children Program ran. I was interested in cooking breakfast for children. We got up at 3:00am; it was a real mission, but it was beautiful. We gave those children a full breakfast every day. Cooking that breakfast was the most memorable part, because everybody got up so early and everybody worked together.

After the breakfast program, I worked with the Huey P. Newton Defense Fund at Merritt College in Oakland. I worked directly with Huey's brother, Melvin Newton. I traveled all over the U.S. raising money. I went to New York, Los Angeles, Detroit—all over the country—and I saw very strong movements organizing in those places. It was amazing.

In the Party I met Ducho Dennis, the father of my children. He was a photographer. He was my political education teacher. My other memory was speaking to 10,000 women about police brutality and speaking against fascism at the United Front Against Fascism. It was a very politically involved time.

Women and girls of all ages, I want you to know that serving the people is the best thing that you can ever do.

Carol Henry
San Francisco and Oakland Chapters, CA
(remembrance by Senay Alkebu-Lan, grandson, and Refa One, son of Carol Henry and Ducho Dennis)

October 28 1967 Oakland, California: Police officer John Frey was shot to death in an altercation with Huey P. Newton during a traffic stop. In the stop, Newton and backup officer Herbert Heanes also suffered gunshot wounds. Newton was convicted of voluntary manslaughter at trial, but the conviction was later overturned. At the time, Newton claimed that he had been falsely accused, leading to the "Free Huey" campaign.

This incident gained the party even wider recognition by the radical American left. Newton was released after three years, when his conviction was reversed on appeal. As Newton awaited trial, the Black Panther Party's "Free Huey" campaign developed alliances with numerous individuals, students, and anti-war activists, "advancing an anti-imperialist political ideology that linked the oppression of antiwar protestors to the oppression of blacks and Vietnamese." The "Free Huey" campaign attracted black power organizations, New Left groups, and other activist groups.

The Black Panther Party collaborated with the Peace and Freedom Party, which sought to promote a strong antiwar and antiracist politics in opposition to the establishment Democratic Party. The Black Panther Party provided needed legitimacy to the Peace and Freedom Party's racial politics and in return received invaluable support for the "Free Huey" campaign.

1968 Berkeley, California: L–R: Jeffrey Scales, unidentified person, Barbara Cox, Stu Albert at a "Free Huey" rally in Provo Park. The official name of the park was Constitution Park, but it became Provo Park to Berkeley residents, in honor of the Dutch Provos. In 1983 it was re-named Martin Luther King Jr. Civic Center Park.

I have to acknowledge a particular brother—my late husband Donald Cox, or DC. When Emory Douglas introduced me to DC, that really brought me a new way of looking at life. DC introduced me to travel. I spent one night in Algiers, and then went to North Korea, then to Germany. When I came back to the U.S. there were a lot of changes. That feeling of loss when the Party split and people went every-which-way was hard.

I settled in Philly. I looked for something I could belong to, but I never found anything like the Black Panther Party. No matter what faults we had, the work we did and the way we did it, has helped me all these years. I suspect it will hold me until I leave here, you know.

My mother defined for me what real love is. Love is what tied me to the party; it exemplified how I understood love. And that is: you have to love people to serve them. I was so loved. So blessed on this earth because of my sisters, all of us, who came into the Party. It's lacking today, when I look out on this landscape in America.

I'd like to say to the young people of tomorrow, especially women: if you're from a strong family of women—aunties, cousins, mothers—listen to their stories. I would also say, if you have a good father or a good uncle, listen to his story also. I'm my father's daughter and my sister is my mother's daughter —she can cook. I can't cook. What I can do is make you smile. I can make you laugh. I can listen to your story, and we can exchange ideas.

Young people, come back into the fold. Love yourselves, love your history, love our culture, and the history of being in Babylon, America. The world is not in a cell phone. You can get out there and experience it. No matter at what age, if you meet somebody that makes you think about how to survive this world, listen to them. Please listen to us. That's it.

Barbara Easley-Cox
Philadelphia Chapter, PA / International Chapters

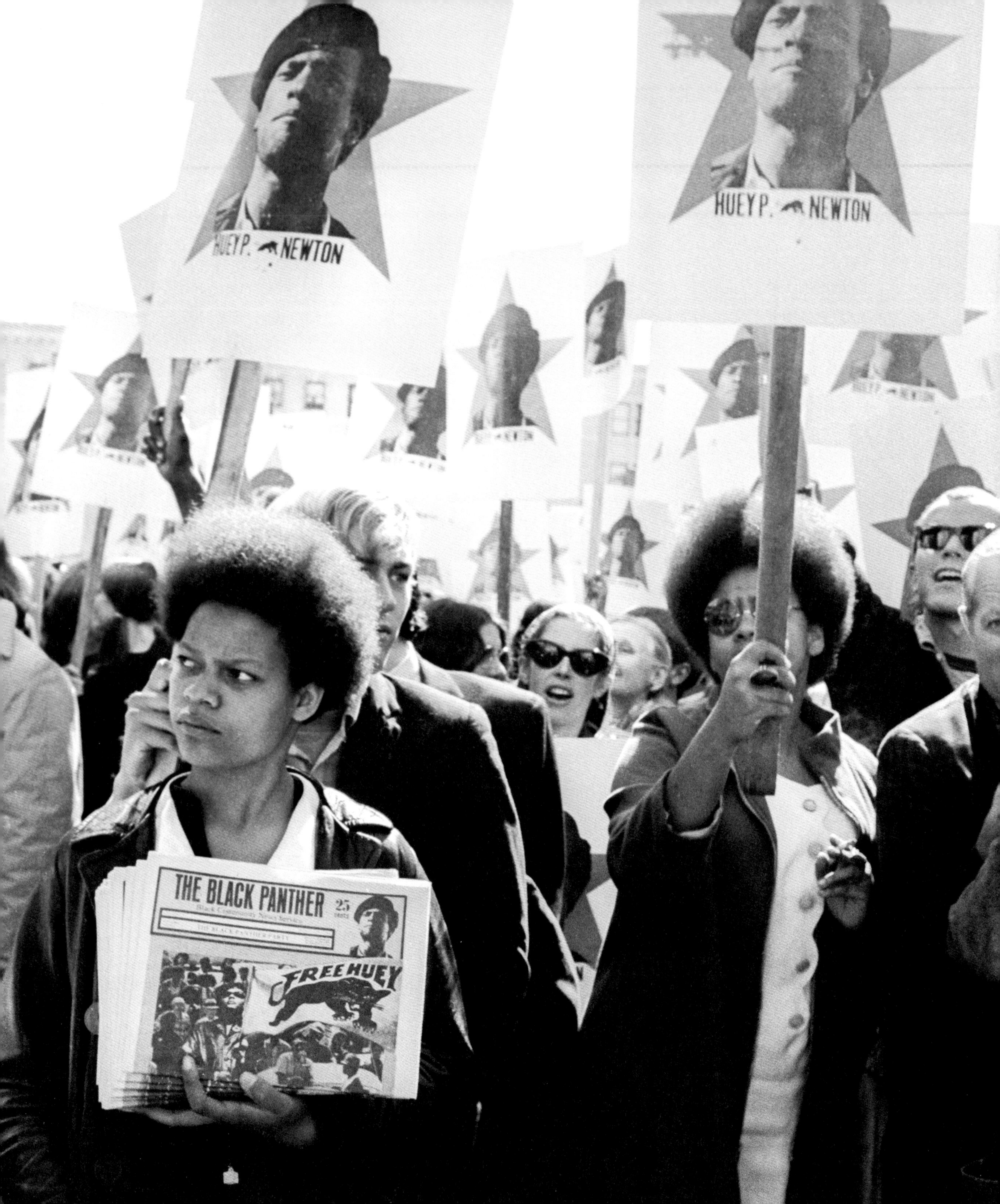

HUEY P. NEWTON
HUEY P. NEWTON
THE BLACK PANTHER
25 CENTS
FREE HUEY

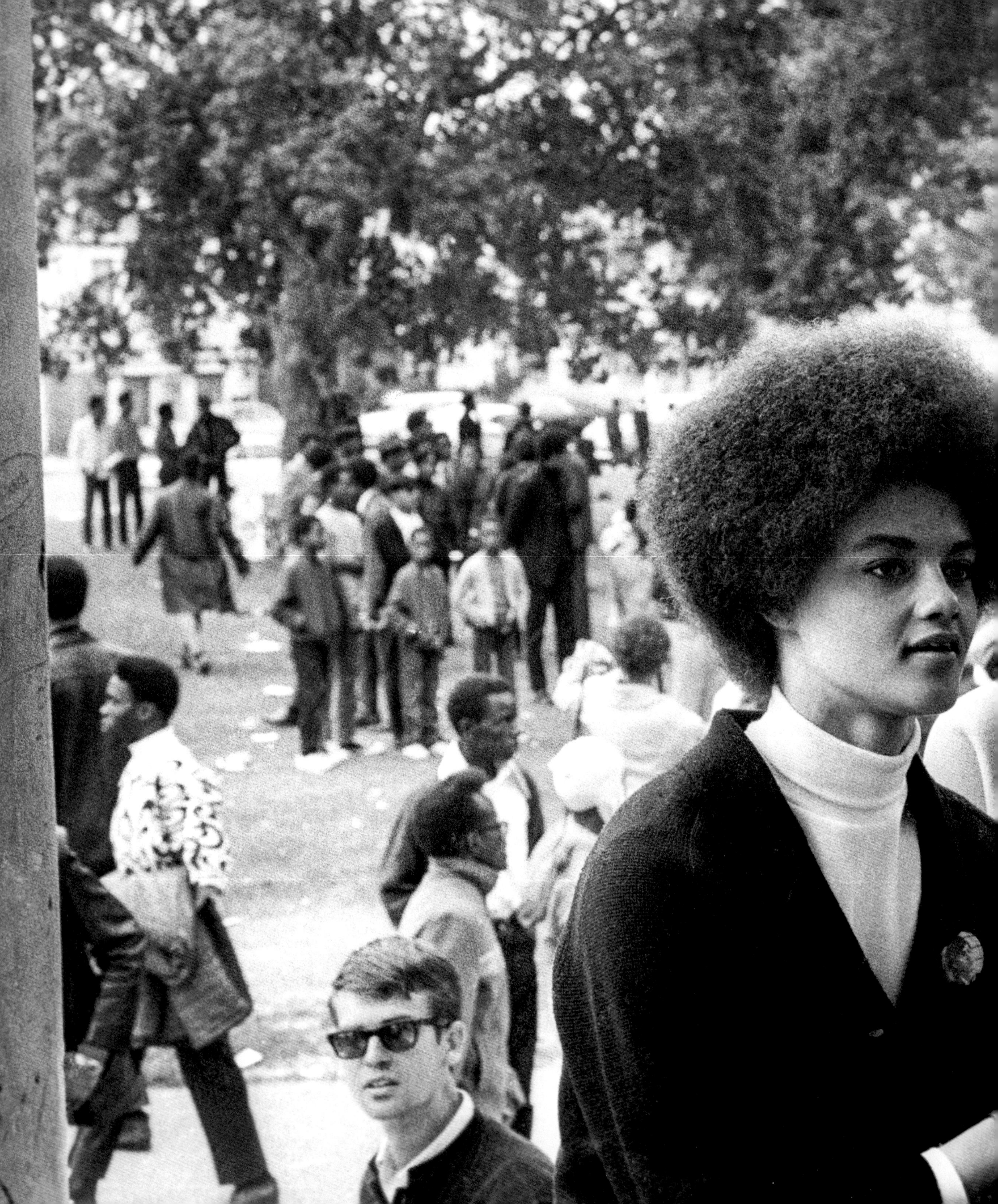

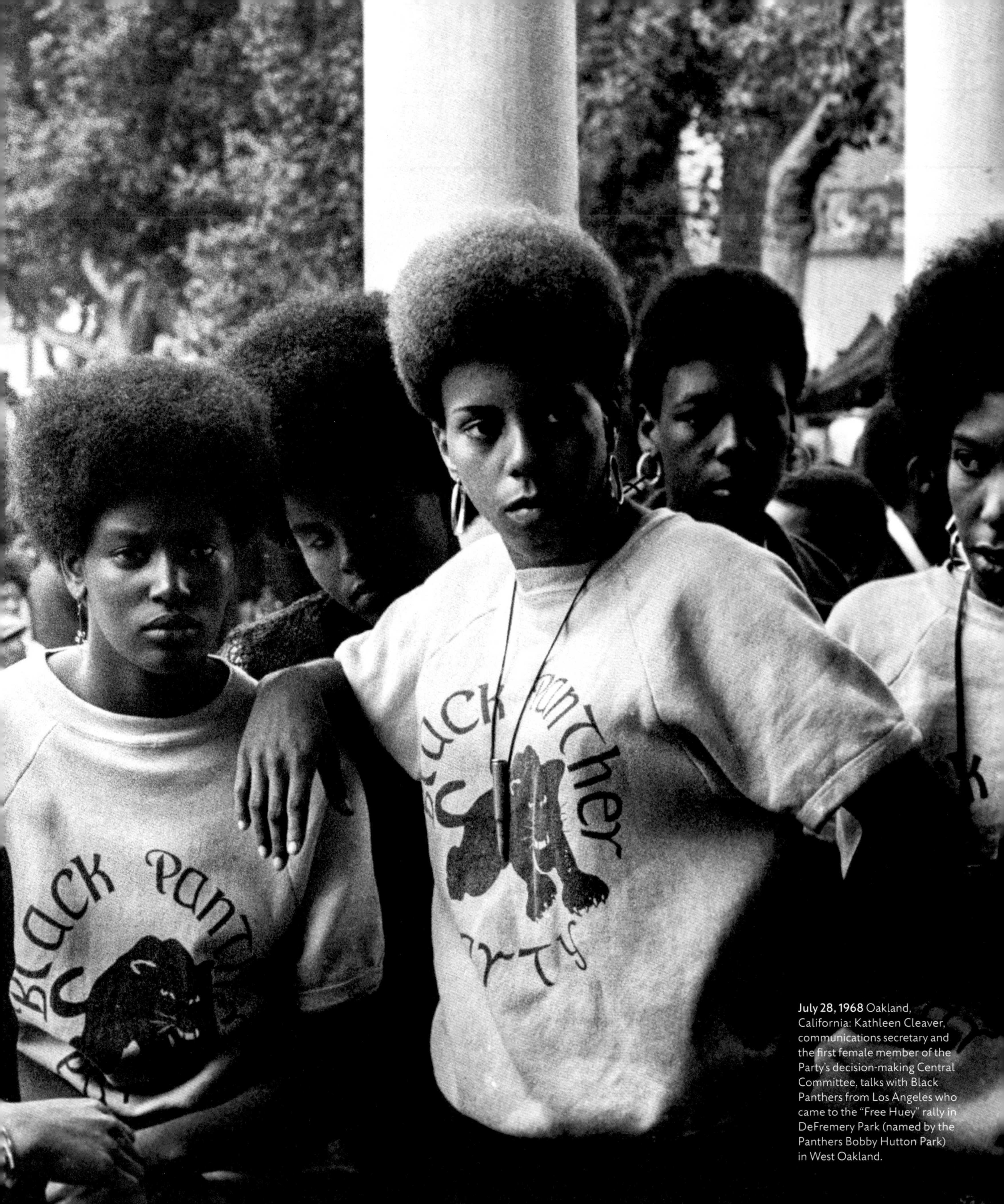

July 28, 1968 Oakland, California: Kathleen Cleaver, communications secretary and the first female member of the Party's decision-making Central Committee, talks with Black Panthers from Los Angeles who came to the "Free Huey" rally in DeFremery Park (named by the Panthers Bobby Hutton Park) in West Oakland.

Kia ora. I was born in Auckland. My father is Maorī and Tongan; my mother is Tongan and Fijian. I'm the daughter of a 28th Maorī Battalion veteran. This colored my sense of justice.

When my father returned without a job, he sent me, my mother, and my four siblings to Kaitāia, where his Maorī people lived. Later, we returned to Auckland and I joined the Panthers in 1971. Others stayed in Auckland, and I set up the Polynesian Panther branch on the South Island in Dunedin. I was upset about the daily injustices. Down at this end of the world on South Island, people like myself were fairly obvious—dark-skinned, with a big afro.

The most memorable work for me is the legal aid program. A legal aid booklet was written. I didn't let that book out of my hands. With it I could talk to people, and as a result, people would find me and ask for help. I'd go down to the police station. I'm female, so they thought I was the least threat. They let me into cells to talk to the men and work out what they were up for. I would contact a lawyer friend who did legal work pro-bono. I was also able to work at the women's prison and visit the Pacific and Maorī women. As the years passed, I was grateful for the Quakers, the student Christian movement, and the community workers. They were what we call Pakeha, white people who supported us.

Now, I have two beautiful little granddaughters and they have fair skin with light brown blonde hair. They are mixed race–Maorī, Pasifika, and European. What I want to say to them is this: "Know who you are. Be respectful of your culture and traditions. Have a goal, a plan. Seek support from a strong role model and do things with confidence." This is all I want to say to my mokopunas.

Mere Meanata Montgomery
Auckland, Aotearoa

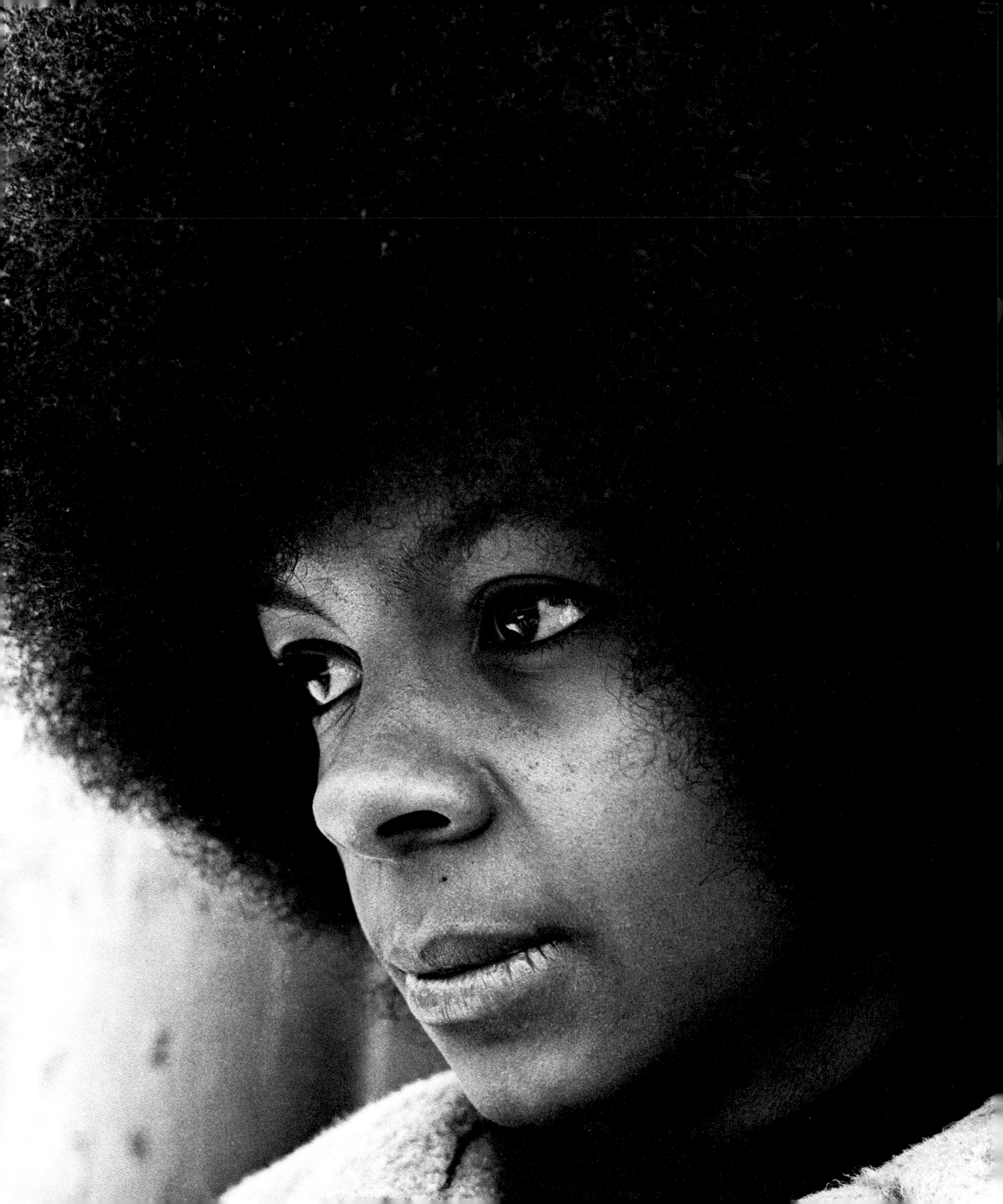

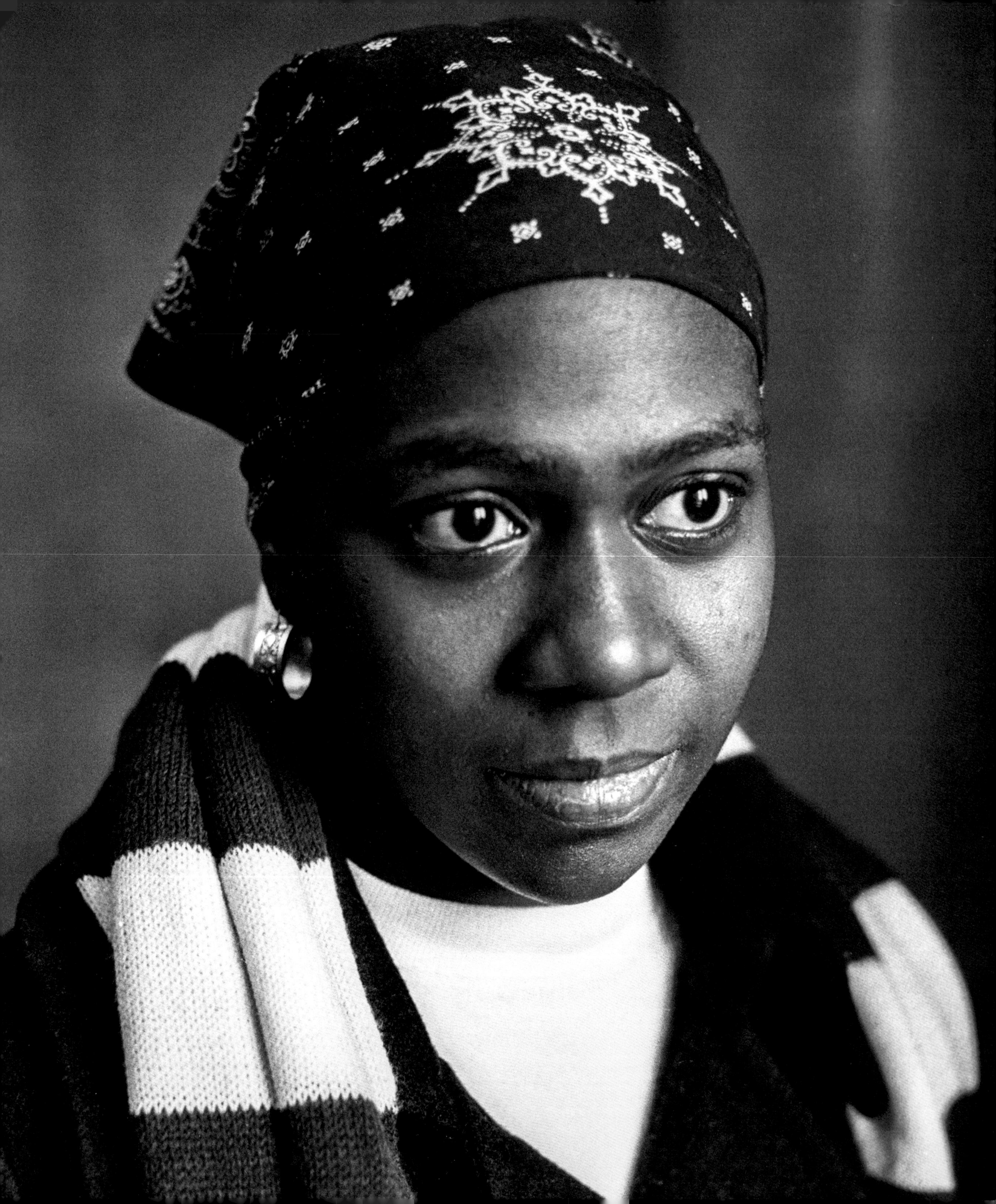

I was originally in the Philadelphia Chapter of the Black Panther Party. I was later transferred to New Haven to help in the rebuilding of the chapter after a series of arrests and the imprisonment of the leadership. Despite the common harassment and 24-hour police surveillance of our office, there were some important and memorable moments.

On Sundays, a cadre of us would drive down from New Haven to the Harlem branch of the Party, where we had political education classes. I looked forward to those weekends because Afeni would be there teaching the classes, and afterwards sharing sisterly moments with all of the women.

Oh, I loved Afeni Shakur. She affirmed everything that I believed in, and she supported what all of the women were doing in New Haven to rebuild the organization, while creating new programs. She was so real—what a sense of humor she had! I admired her intelligence and her bravery. I respected her ability to dispatch tasks to the men who also looked up to her. She had that no-nonsense ability to be direct and to lead, in a way that was not intimidating but firm. She didn't take shit from the inside or the outside, regardless of who you were. That's what I loved about her.

Afeni Shakur
Defendant in the Panther 21 trial and a leader in the Harlem
Branch of the New York BPP
(*a remembrance by Rosemari Mealy*)

1970 New York, New York: Afeni Shakur inside the Black Panther Party's Harlem office. Ms. Shakur (born Alice Faye Williams January 10, 1947 – May 2, 2016) was an American music businesswoman, political activist and member of the Black Panther Party. She was the mother of the late rapper Tupac Shakur.

July 15, 1972 *We The People Demand A Change … Reparations! Reparations! Reparations!*, artwork by M. Gayle Asali Dickson.

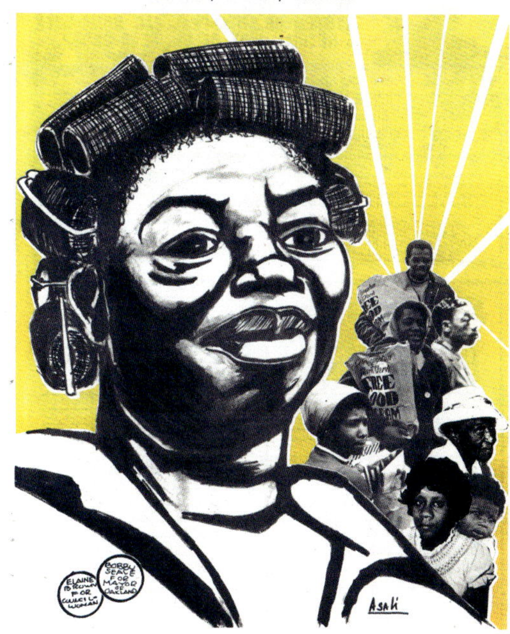

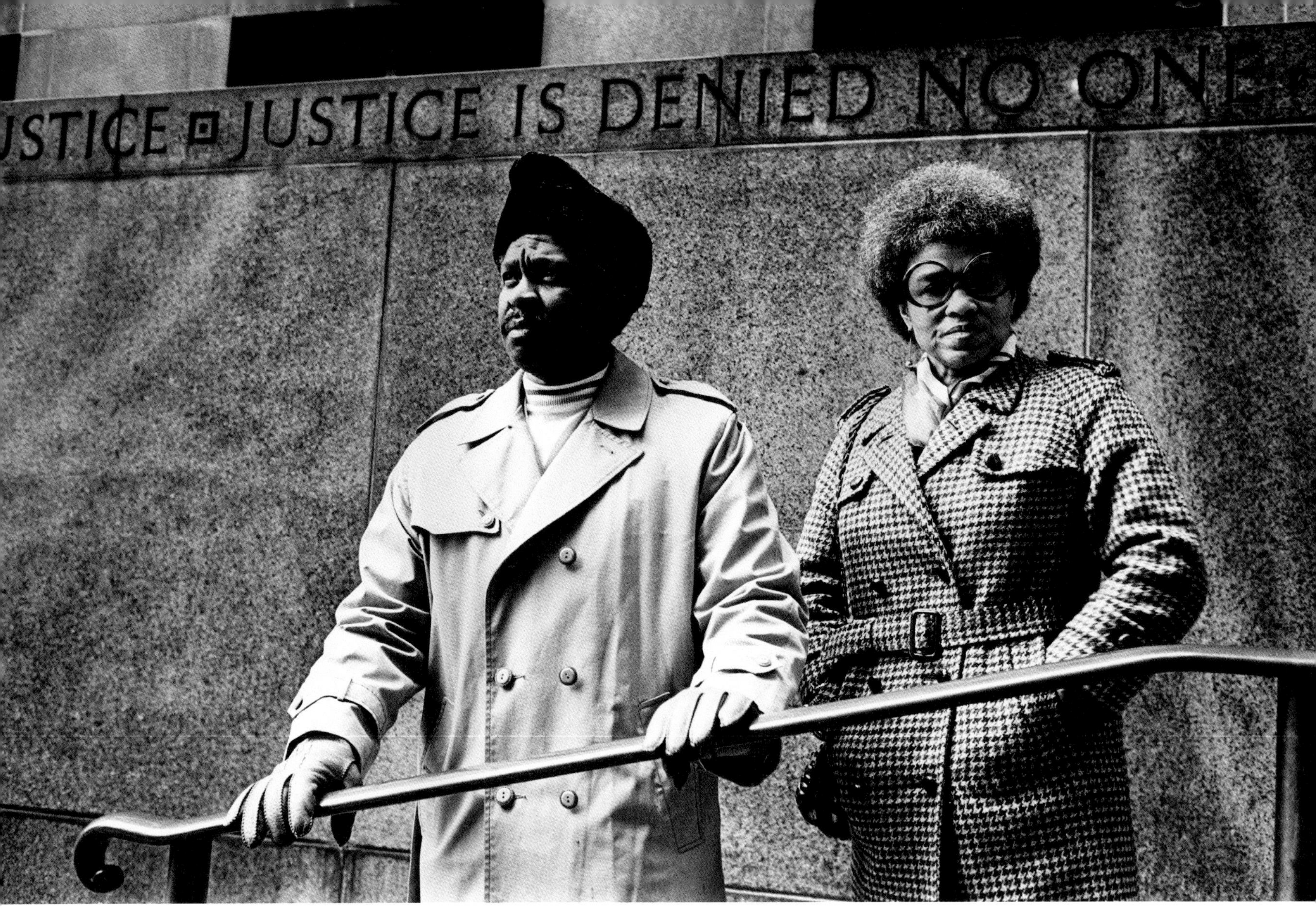

1970 New York, New York: Outside Manhattan courthouse during New York 21 trial. Left: El-Hajj Salahdeen Shakur "Aba" father of Zayd Malik Shakur and Lumumba Abdul Shakur. El-Hajj Salahdeen (Dec 13, 1919 – May 21, 1993) was an international merchant and owned several businesses, African Hip Boutique, Afro Artifacts, Hagar's House, Inc, and Timbuktu Inc.

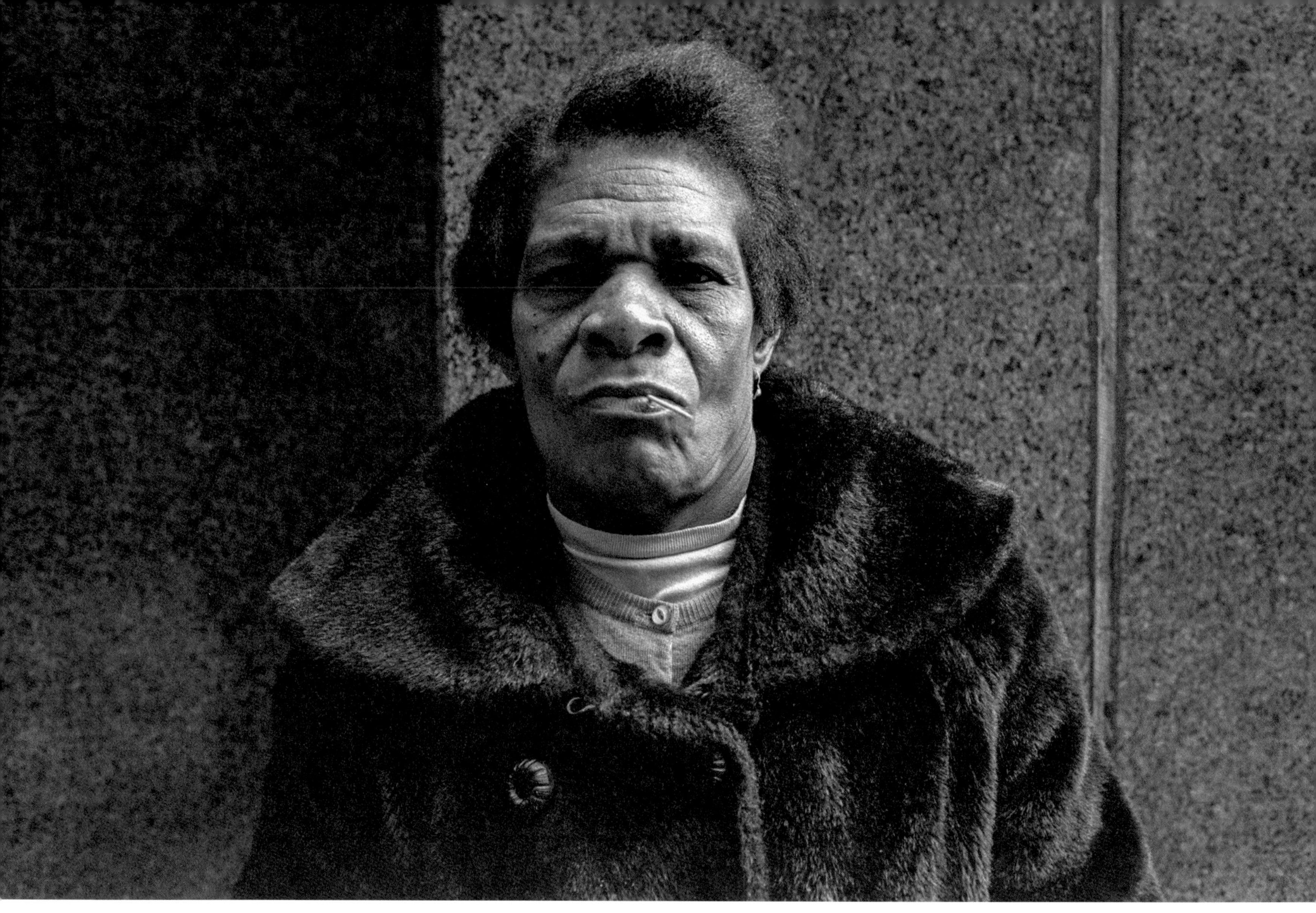

1970 New York, New York:
The Panther 21 is a group of 21
Black Panther members who
were charged with conspiracy to
kill several police officers and
to destroy a number of buildings,
including four police stations,
five department stores, and the
Bronx Botanical Gardens. The
trial eventually collapsed and
the 21 members were acquitted.
The eight-month trial was the
longest and most expensive in
New York State history.

1970 New York, New York: Afeni
Shakur's mother at rally for
the Black Panther New York 21,
standing outside a Manhattan
courthouse during the trial.

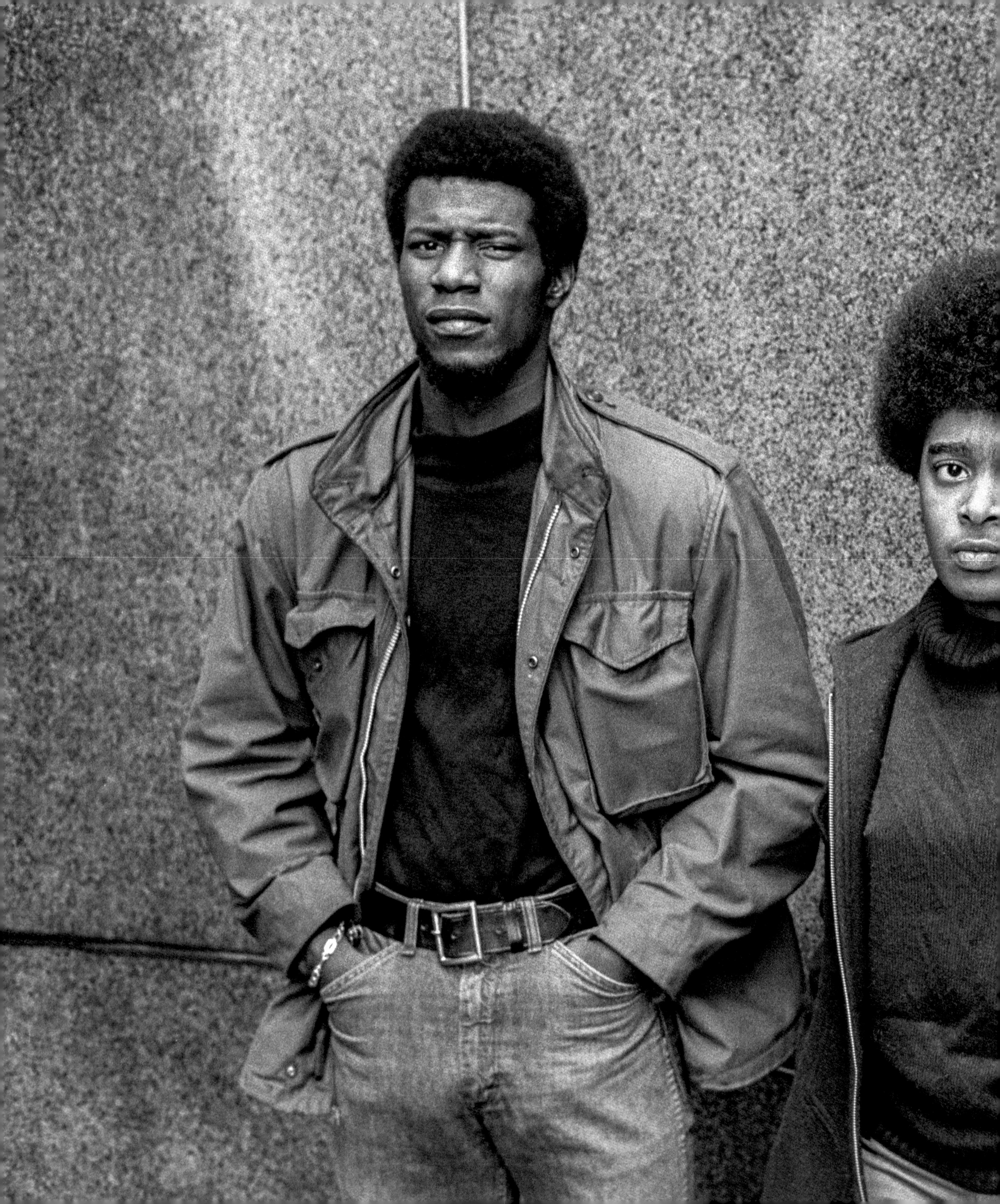

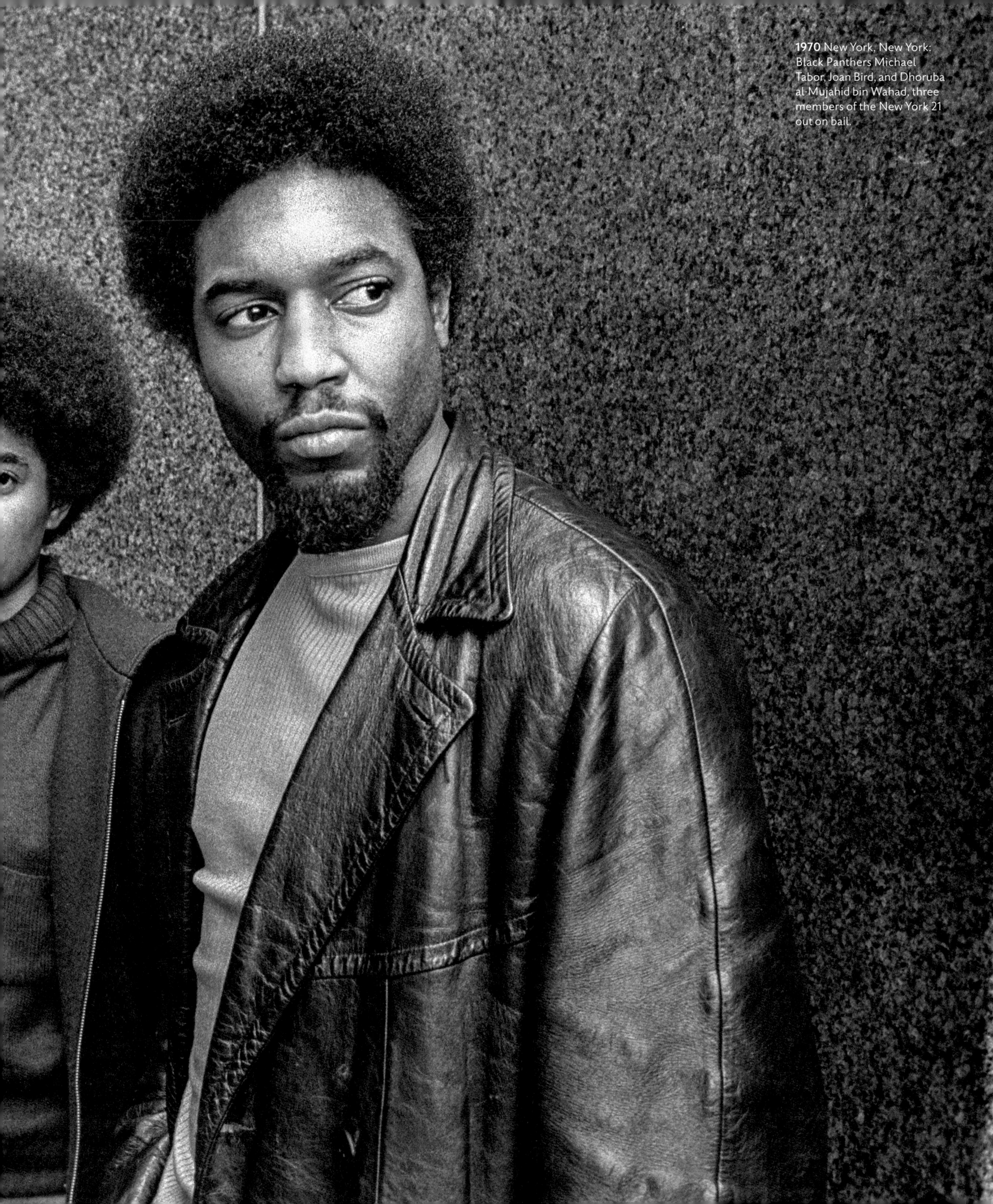

1970 New York, New York:
Black Panthers Michael
Tabor, Joan Bird, and Dhoruba
al-Mujahid bin Wahad, three
members of the New York 21
out on bail.

As a Winston-Salem State University student, I became the secretary of the Student Government Association (SGA). The president of SGA was a member of the Black Panther Party, the Winston-Salem Chapter. He was recruiting people from campus to work with some of the Community Survival Programs. So, I became involved with the Black Panther Party's Free Ambulance Program at age 20. I made a real commitment to that and trained as an EMT.

When I was in college for the EMT certificate, a woman in the community died because the ambulance service came to pick her up and she did not have money. They told her she would be okay. They left her there and she died. That was unheard of for me, that someone should be refused a ride to the hospital. That was what started the whole push for funding a People's Free Ambulance Program. I dedicated quite a bit of my life to that. My parents did not send me to college for that. At one point I dropped out of college to devote myself full-time to the Party.

I remember the Joan Little trial so vividly. I will never forget that sister and what we did to help secure her freedom and her safety in 1975. She defended herself from sexual assault by a prison guard, and was charged for that. We organized her defense and brought national attention to her case. That stands out in my mind.

My parents had such high hopes for me when I went away to school. They did not envision me dropping out of school to join the Panther Party. However, the first time my mother joined me on a march was for Joan Little. I get emotional about that, even to this day, because my mother understood. When I went to Winston-Salem state and started working with the Party, it was like family. It was a community. It was a camaraderie that I had never experienced before.

The Party understood that due to the plight of Black America, we as a people need to address it. That was what I always felt. And the Party addressed the need.

Vivian McMillan
Winston-Salem Chapter, NC

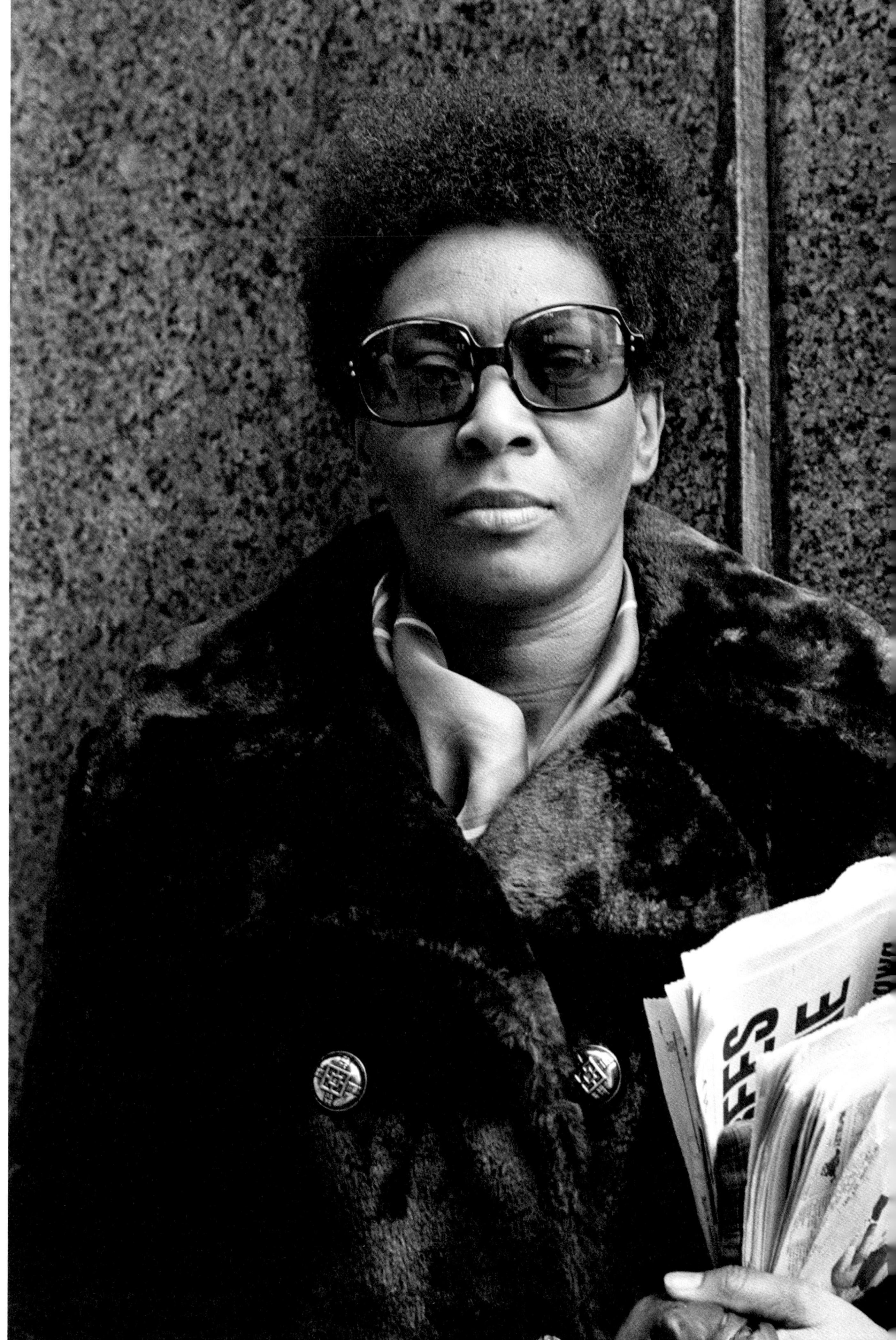

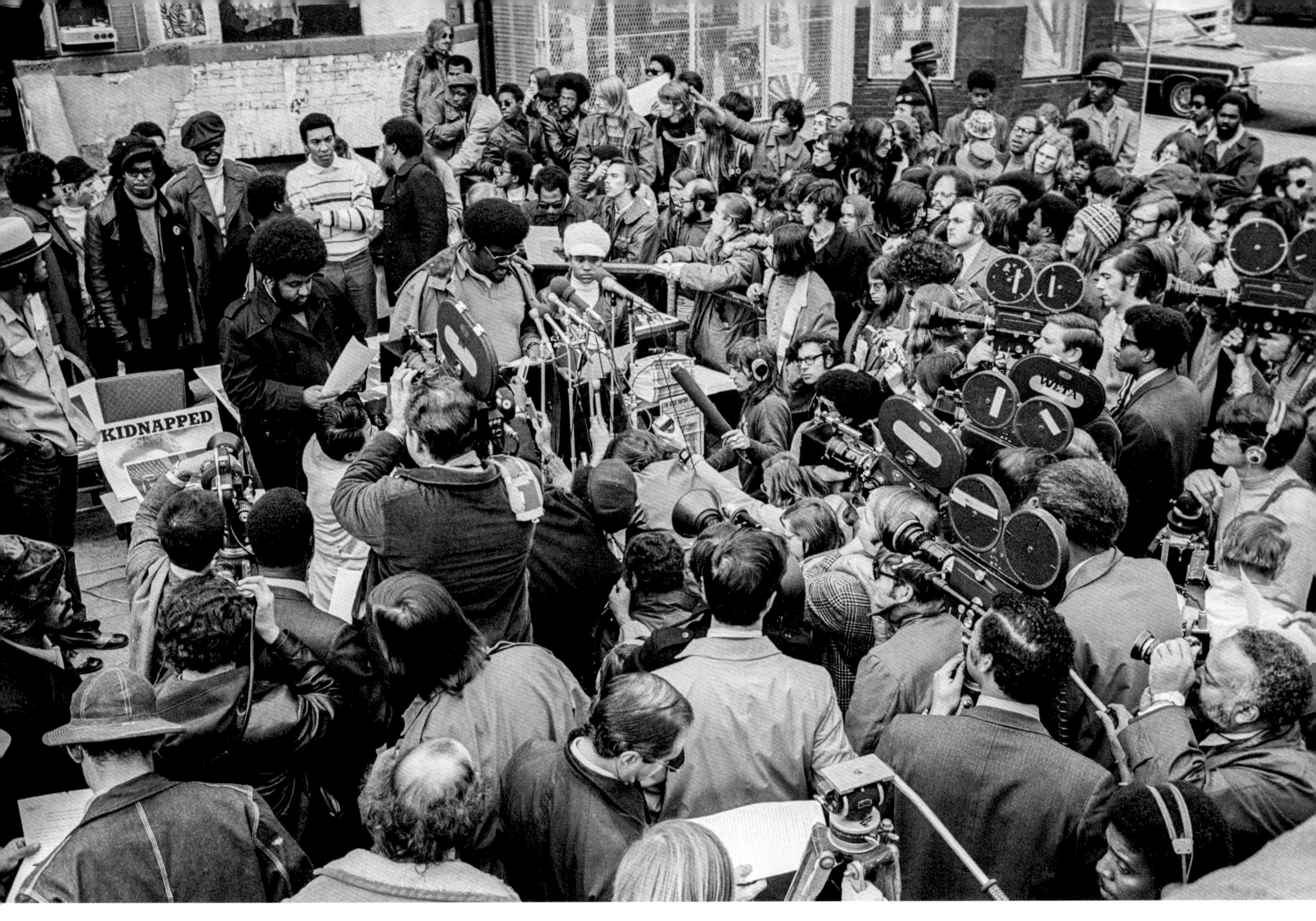

1971 Washington, DC:
Big Man was one of the four original Panthers. He was deputy minister of defense and national/international spokesperson. He went to Merritt College with Huey.

1971 Washington, DC:
Elbert Howard, known as Big Man, and an unidentified woman of the Black Panther Party hold a press conference about the Constitutional Convention in front of the Panther office. The convention was held in Philadelphia.

I was in high school when I learned about the Black Panther Party. I was 18. Coming from parents who were very engaged in the civil rights movement and politics, despite struggling to keep food on our table, I learned a little more, I'd say, than the average high schooler. I passed a newspaper stand while walking to school one day and saw that image of the Black Panthers on the steps of the State Capitol with guns to protest against the Mulford Act in Sacramento. I knew then: *soon as I graduate high school, I'm going up north.*

I loved working at Central Distribution for the party paper. The thought of being able to educate communities worldwide about the struggle was empowering to me. This was one of my first experiences as a woman in the Party. We had a showdown about that. When I first started, the men would go to the warehouse at the end of the day to throw the boxes, load the trucks, do the airport runs. Meanwhile, us women were typing up labels for subscriptions or rolling posters and packaging goods to go out. At some point we would get that work done, and we knew there was more we could do.

One day, a couple of us went next door, where the men were loading the truck. There was a moment when the men looked at us, like, *what are you doing here?* To make a long story short, it worked out that if you're able to lift and throw a 30-to-40-pound box, get in line. Segregated work changed after that. From then on, women and men were on that side of the warehouse working together. That opened a lot of conversation. Work shouldn't have to do with your gender. It has to do with your skill and what you can contribute. I think we were beginning to have these conversations in many Party offices across the country.

Another highlight for me was working in the George Jackson Free Medical Clinic. I was really impressed with the way that we were able to get a lot of medical professionals, doctors, and nurses to volunteer their time for free, and the high level of skill that we accomplished so we could serve the community. We learned how to give tests, read slides, do all kinds of medical procedures. I think the George Jackson Free Medical Clinic, in terms of the Survival Programs, is the one that still lives with me now. I now work in the field of health and human services. I felt like the clinic was real tangible: I could see both comrades and community members actually accessing a resource that they otherwise would not have had.

Women—stay physically strong, stay mentally strong. Not everyone is meant to be on the front lines. It doesn't mean you can't be revolutionary. Everyone has a place. Get to know yourself. Find your gift, your talents. Keep your revolutionary spirit. We have to be diverse and open enough to let people bring what they do to the table and apply it in a revolutionary setting. There is so much work to do in a revolution behind the scenes.

Madalynn Carol Rucker
Oakland and San Francisco Chapters, CA

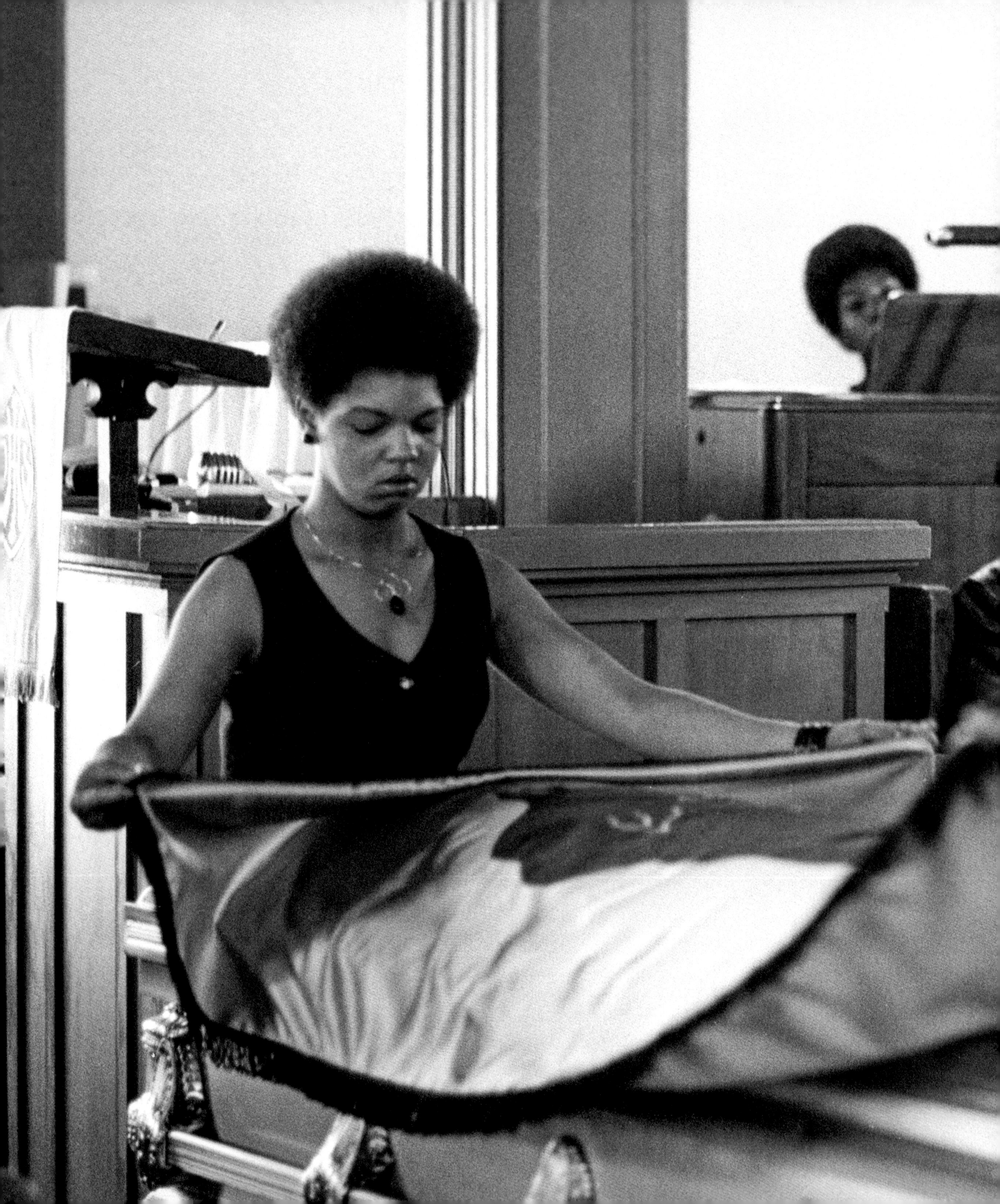

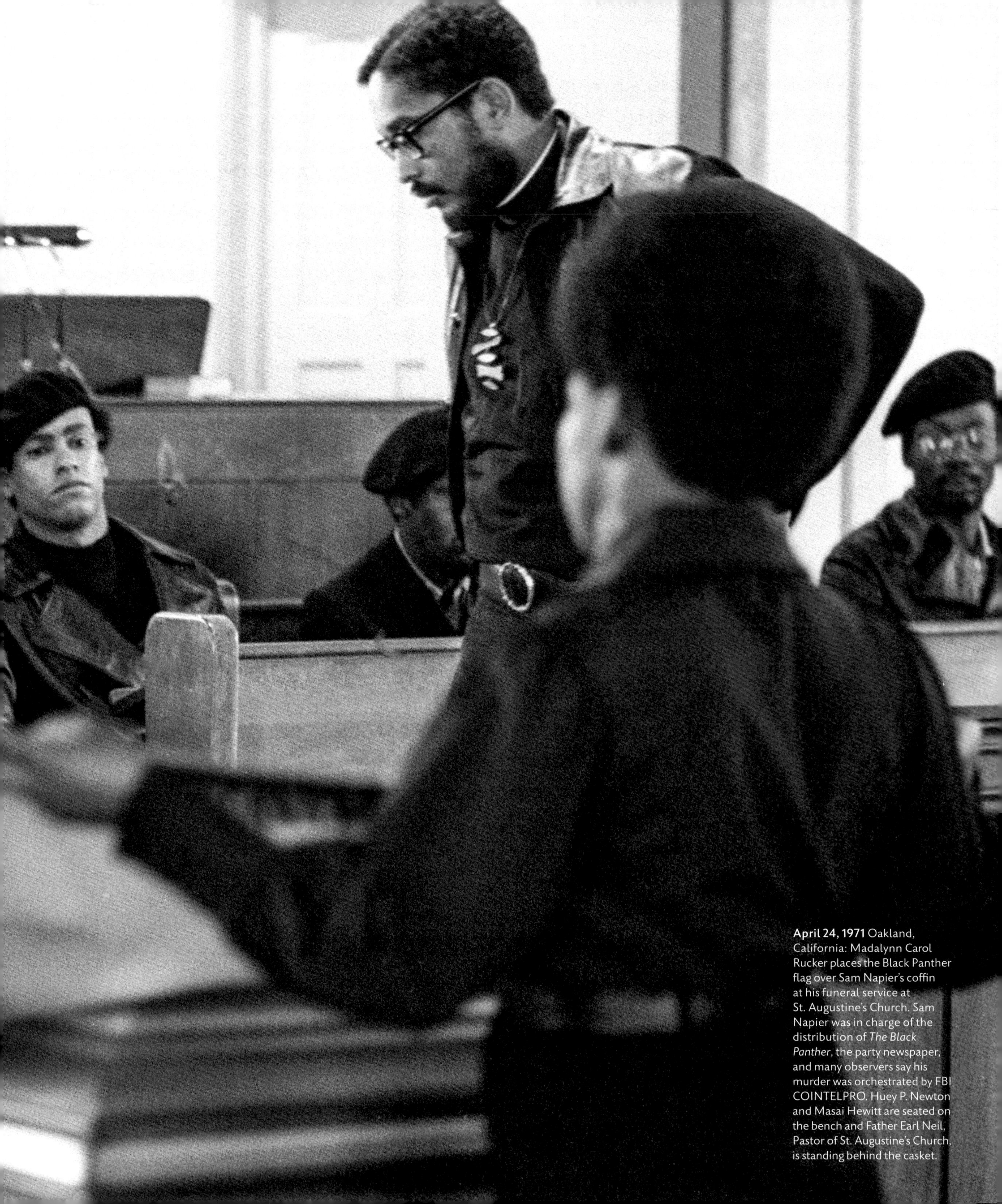

April 24, 1971 Oakland, California: Madalynn Carol Rucker places the Black Panther flag over Sam Napier's coffin at his funeral service at St. Augustine's Church. Sam Napier was in charge of the distribution of *The Black Panther*, the party newspaper, and many observers say his murder was orchestrated by FBI COINTELPRO. Huey P. Newton and Masai Hewitt are seated on the bench and Father Earl Neil, Pastor of St. Augustine's Church, is standing behind the casket.

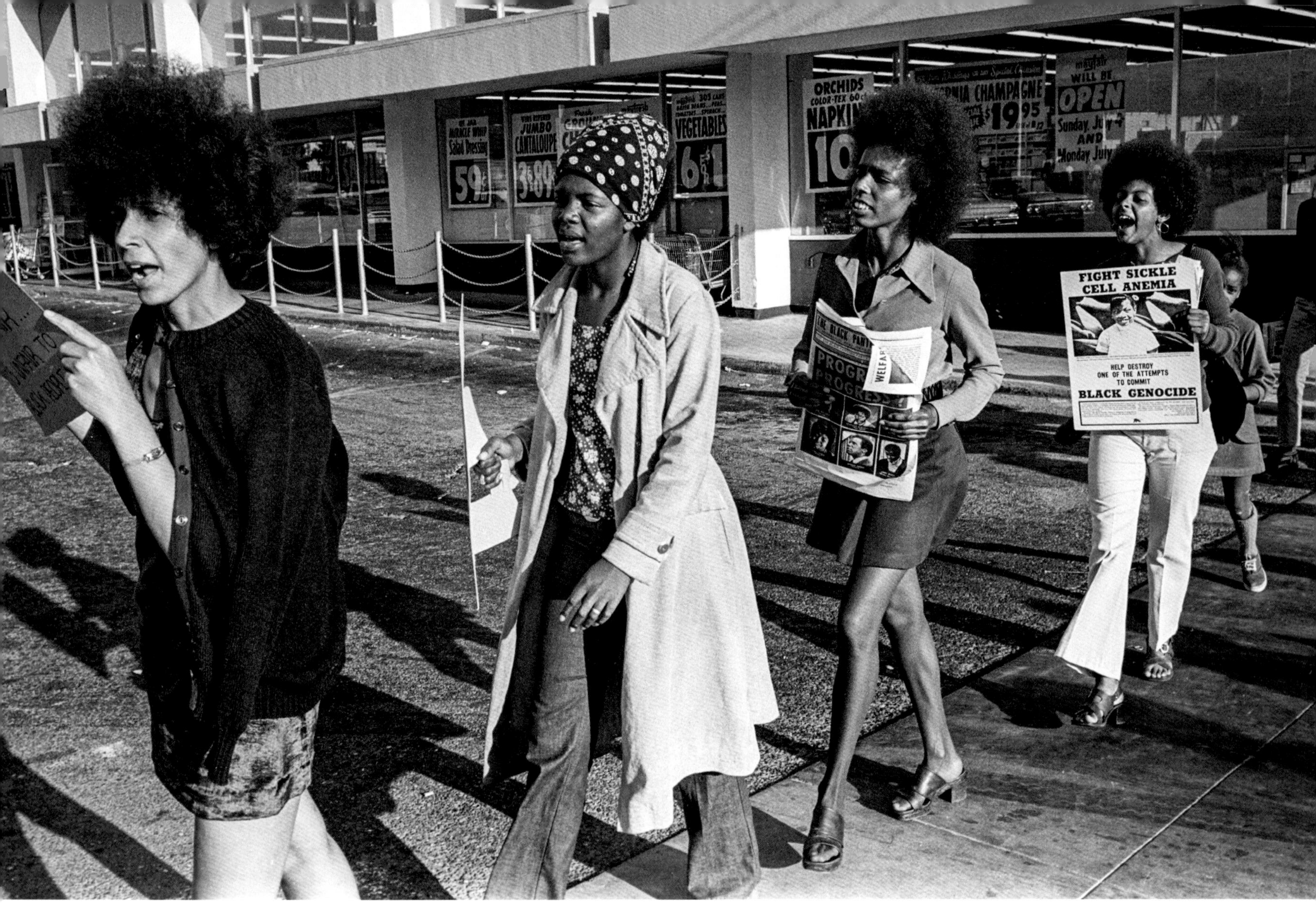

1971 Oakland, California:
Left to right: Dorothy Phillips,
unidentified woman, Gloria
Abernethy, and Tamara Lacey
boycott Mayfair supermarket.

1970 New York, New York: a
woman of the Black Panther
Party at the New York 21
demonstration downtown.

90

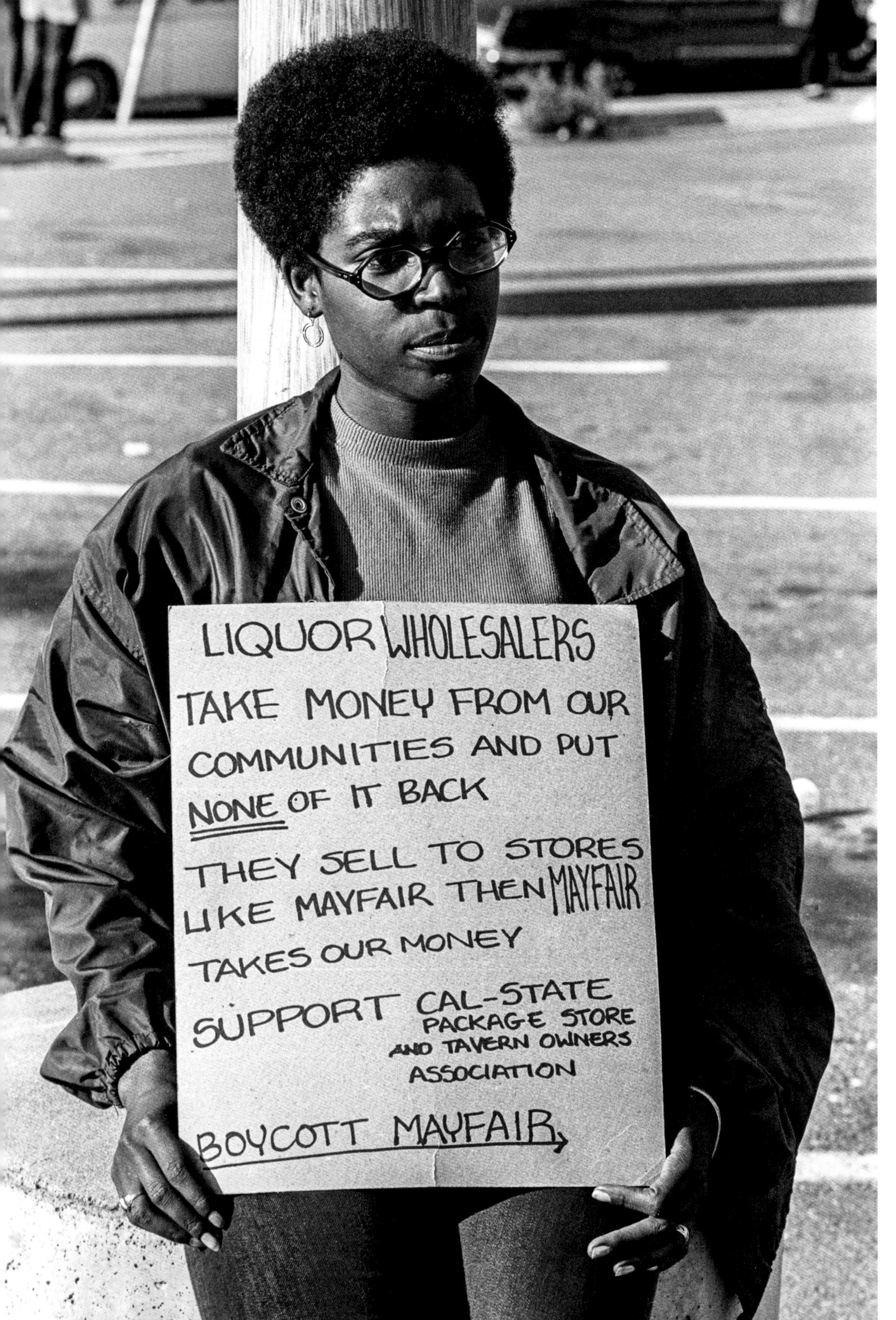

LIQUOR WHOLESALERS
TAKE MONEY FROM OUR
COMMUNITIES AND PUT
NONE OF IT BACK
THEY SELL TO STORES
LIKE MAYFAIR THEN MAYFAIR
TAKES OUR MONEY
SUPPORT CAL-STATE
PACKAGE STORE
AND TAVERN OWNERS
ASSOCIATION
BOYCOTT MAYFAIR

My name is Hazel Mae Mack. I was born in Bishopville, South Carolina. My earliest memory in life was sitting at the end of a cotton row, while my daddy and mama picked that row.

Daddy moved us to Winston-Salem, North Carolina, when I was around 17 years old. When I was 17, I met a brother who told me about the Black Panther Party. I started going to political education classes. I learned what it meant to be willing to give your all to a greater good.

In the Winston-Salem Chapter, the most popular Survival Program was the Free Ambulance Program. We started it because, as we evolved out of segregation in the city, they closed the Black hospital. When they closed the hospital, people couldn't get to the hospital way out on the other side of town. People literally died. The Party recognized what was wrong and addressed that wrong. We were willing to put our shoulders to the wheel to show our people that we can do things ourselves, without the system.

That ambulance program became a galvanizing tool, giving people hope. Party members went to school and trained as emergency medical technicians [EMTs]. Nelson Malloy, one of the leaders of the Winston-Salem Chapter, Mary McDonald, and Vivian McMillan are some of the members who became EMTs.

I learned to truly love the people I serve. Love must emanate from an understanding and knowledge of people's challenges, and the struggles we have faced due to relentless systemic oppression since being brought to these shores. It's out of that love that we do what we do.

When I was getting ready to retire, I knew I wasn't ready to sit down. I bought a house right in the middle of the Black community, next to where the first Black Panther Party office opened. I was drawn to this raggedy little house. I renovated it and started Other Suns. The name comes from one of Richard Wright's books that I read years ago. He talks about leaving the South in hopes of blooming and growing *in other suns,* so I named the house 'Other Suns'. The idea was to create a space in the community that nobody controls—not the city, nobody else. *We* control it.

I have a space where people can come every day and just *be*. A refuge. It keeps me connected to people. It keeps me alive. That's what I will do as long as I can do it. I can't do a lot of the things I used to do, but I can sit on my porch, in my rocker, while I serve the people a cup of coffee and talk to the strong women who come in. I can listen to their joys and ills, what they're dealing with, and give direction, if they want. I can talk to the homeless folks who come by—I can do all of that.

Hazel M. Mack
Winston-Salem Chapter, NC

1971 Oakland, California: CALPAC, the Black liquor distributors association, complained that Safeway and Mayfair would not purchase from them. They suggested that if the Panthers supported them, they would donate to the Party's survival programs. Mayfair settled. According to the Panthers, CALPAC reneged on the deal by offering to make a one-time donation. Huey countered that they had agreed to on-going support of the survival programs.

1971 Oakland, California: Boycott of Mayfair supermarket, which closed the store in four days.

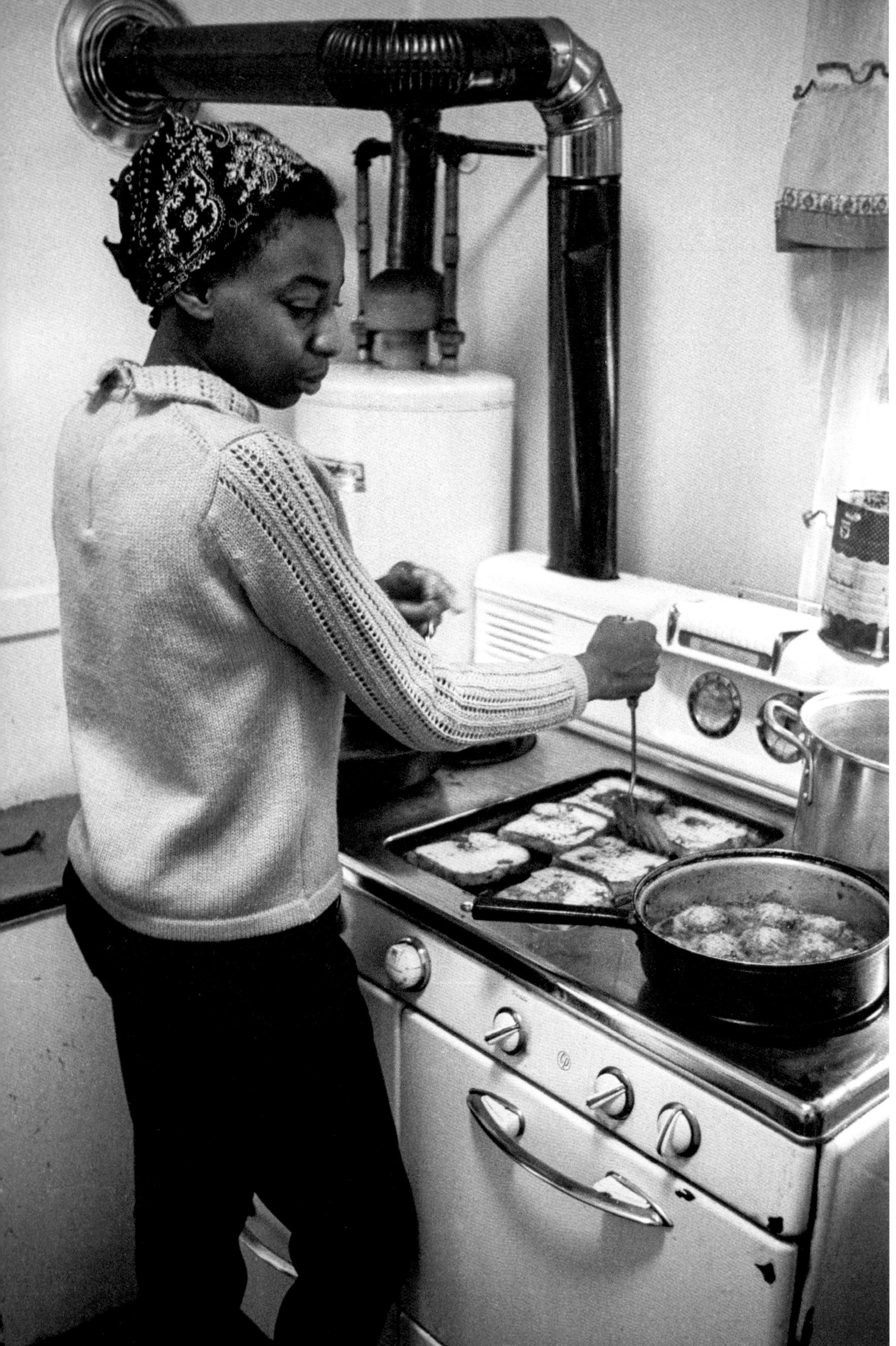

A lot of people say, "Why don't you change your name? Just be Akua Njeri." I say, "I owe my name, Deborah Johnson, to my mama, who carried me for nine months."

I was raised in Chicago, and I joined the Party when I was 18. I first heard Chairman Fred Hampton speak on a television show. Chairman Fred spoke about the Free Breakfast for School Children Program. The Black Panther Party didn't do a study to know as everyone else did, that children couldn't learn on an empty stomach. Before any free breakfast or lunch was implemented by schools, the BPP set up BFC across the country.

After I heard Chairman Fred speak, I introduced myself to him. He said, "Sister, you need to come down to the Political Education Classes." So, the next day, after school and work, I started going back: going to the office, studying, going to the Breakfast Program, selling papers. And the more I did, the more there was to do, and the more I felt different. I felt like I was doing something that was really important, really needed. Chairman Fred would say "I'm high off the People!" The work of serving the people body and soul inspired and energized the Party and the People to make Power to the People the reality.

One of the BFC sites was near Englewood High School, where Spurgeon Jake Winters was a student. Jake was assassinated by Chicago pigs on November 13, 1969. The students from that school would go to that BFC before going to class, "High off the People," doing work needed. We talked to the children at BFC about what was happening in the community, where they learned "We Serve & Protect," the logo emblazoned on pig cars, translated in the white communities to Officer Friendly getting cats out of trees. In the Black and colonized community it meant pigs disappearing our people off the streets, not knowing if they would return.

I learned from Chairman Fred Hampton Jr. that "What's good for the family may not be good for the community; what's good for the community is good for the family." Power to the People! It's not about me being a superhero freeing the world. No one has lived this thing called FREEDOM; we know that people should not be oppressed, or denied self-determination.

As a member of the BPP, I served on the Finance Cadre under the leadership of Lt. Barbara Sankey. Today I am honored to be a member of the Advisory Board of the BPP Cubs—the ideological children of the BPP.

Akua Njeri, forever known as Deborah Johnson
Illinois Chapter

1969 San Francisco, California: A woman of the Black Panther Party cooks food. Children eat a nutrious meal at the Black Panther Free Breakfast for School Children Program at the Ridge Point Methodist Church.

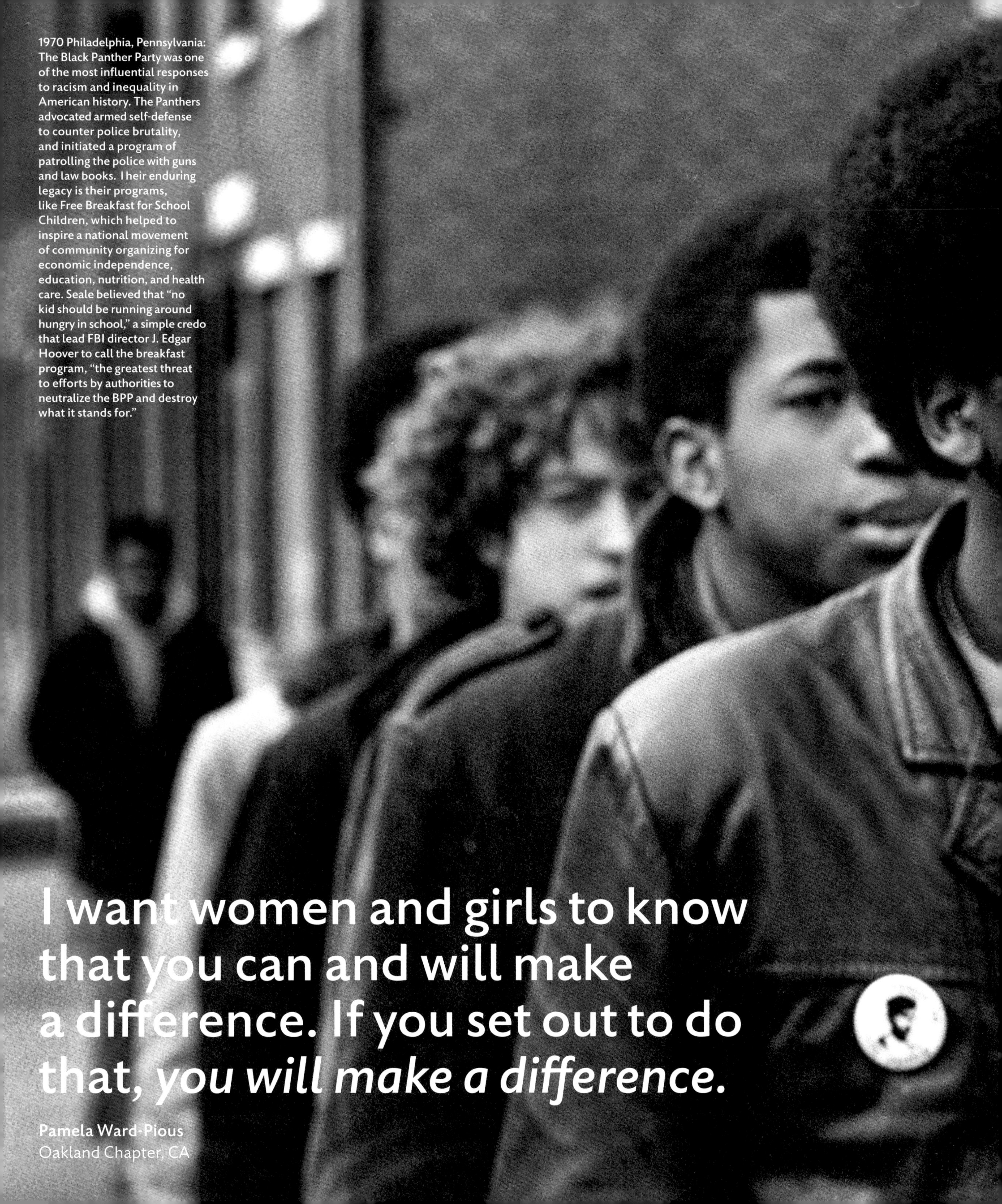

I want women and girls to know that you can and will make a difference. If you set out to do that, *you will make a difference.*

Pamela Ward-Pious
Oakland Chapter, CA

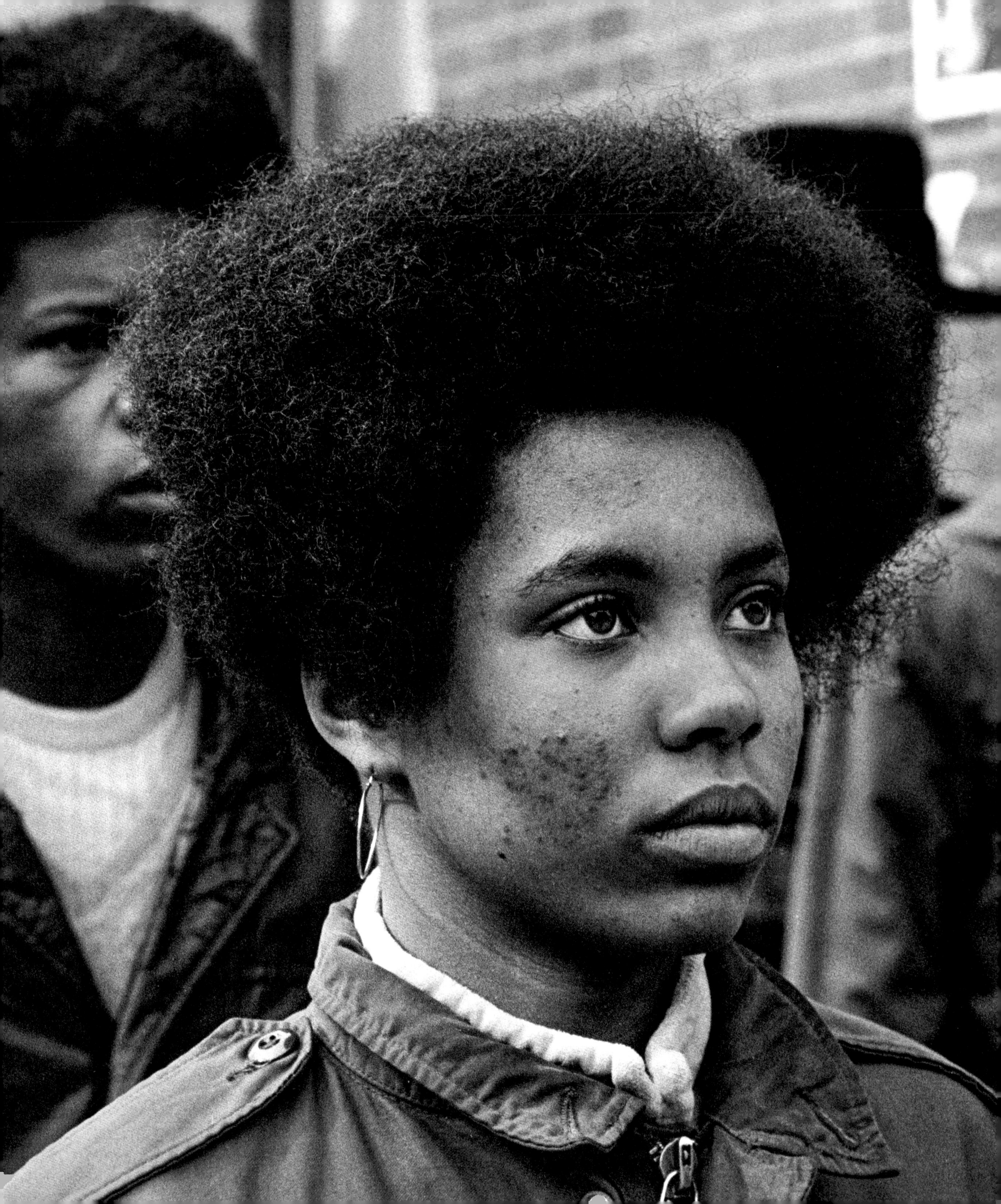

One thing that stands out is the day that Martin Luther King was killed. They called all the students into the auditorium, and we noticed that the few white children at our school were leaving, but we didn't know that Martin Luther King had died. After the white children went home with their parents, they let us out. We were met by riot police with two-by-fours. They marched us back to the Haight and Filmore. If anybody stepped off the sidewalk, they got hit with a two-by-four.

I knew that day that I would be working for change in some capacity. I was only 13, but I knew that something was going to be different for me. I went to a high school in Oakland called the Oakland Street Academy. I already knew about the civil rights movement, because we lived down the street from Medgar Evers when I was a child, growing up in Mississippi. At the Street Academy, they taught me about revolutionary movements. This moved me quite a bit.

Years later, I joined the BPP. I was 21. We worked 20 hours a day, and my focus was always on the Oakland Community School, from 1975–1982. I learned by doing. I had a high school diploma, and the work I did helped me to get my AA degree, my BA degree, my Master's degree, and my doctorate. Everything that I did there helped me to sustain myself, later on in life.

There are two memorable moments for me, during the time I was a health officer at the school. I helped one child who had seizures, and he'd be in a panic after each one. He and I started drawing pictures to show what it was like when, as he said, "the lights go out." Drawing pictures and talking, he became so comfortable in himself that he wasn't afraid. He could even tell someone just before he was going to have a seizure.

Then there was a little girl who we thought had hearing loss. I took her to the Children's Hospital in Oakland for an exam. I knew this child was not inter-acting with the other children. She seemed to float around the room as if things were going on around her, and not with her. At the hospital, I found out that her ears overproduced wax. She said to me after the day they cleaned her ears, "I can hear, I can hear now!" It brings tears to my eyes just thinking about it. Once she could hear—oh boy, she was Miss It of that classroom. She was running things.

These experiences made me aware that I can make a difference in this world. I have spent the rest of my life trying to make that difference. I want women and girls to know that you can and will make a difference. If you set out to do that, *you will make a difference.*

Pamela Ward-Pious
Oakland Chapter, CA

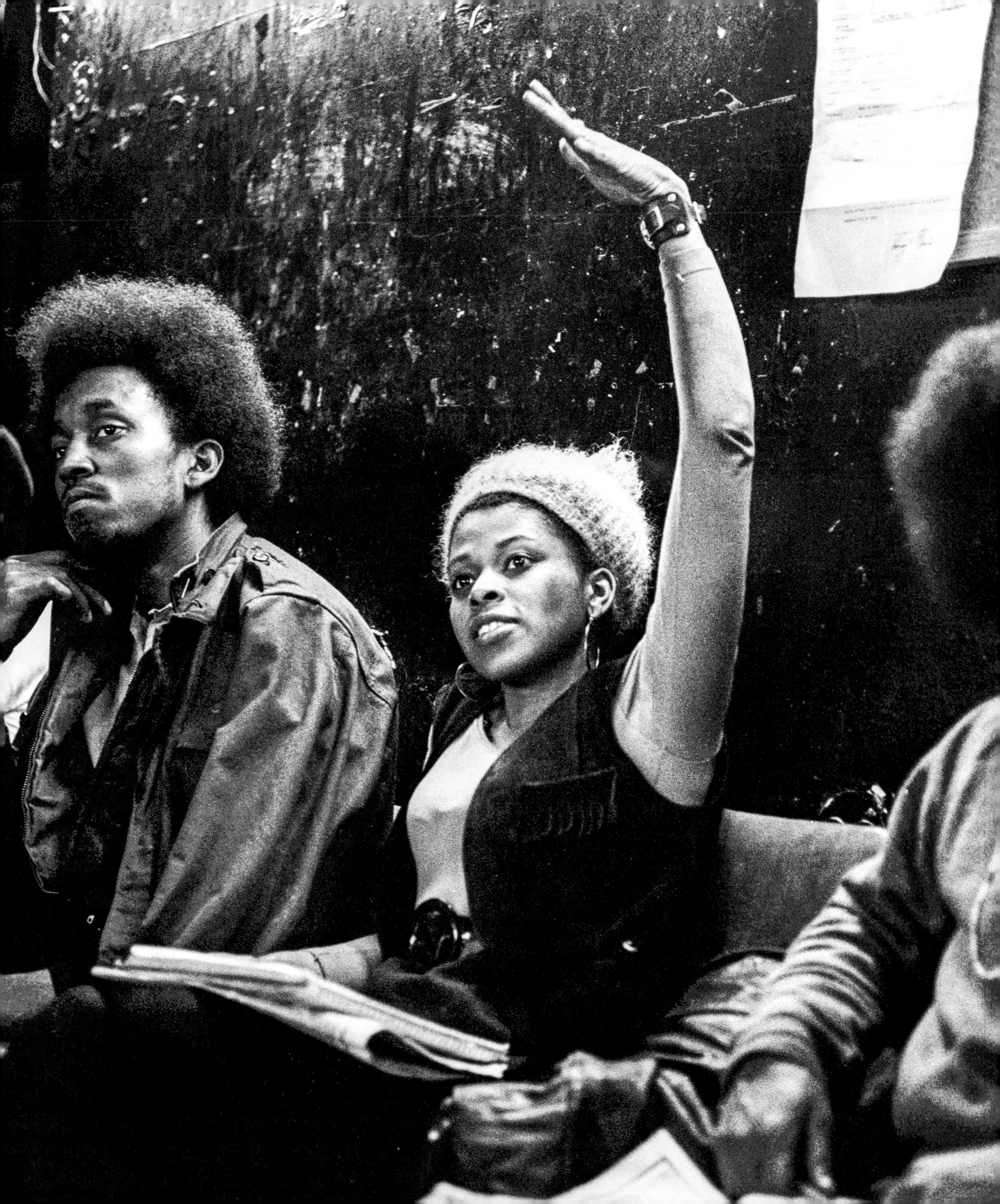

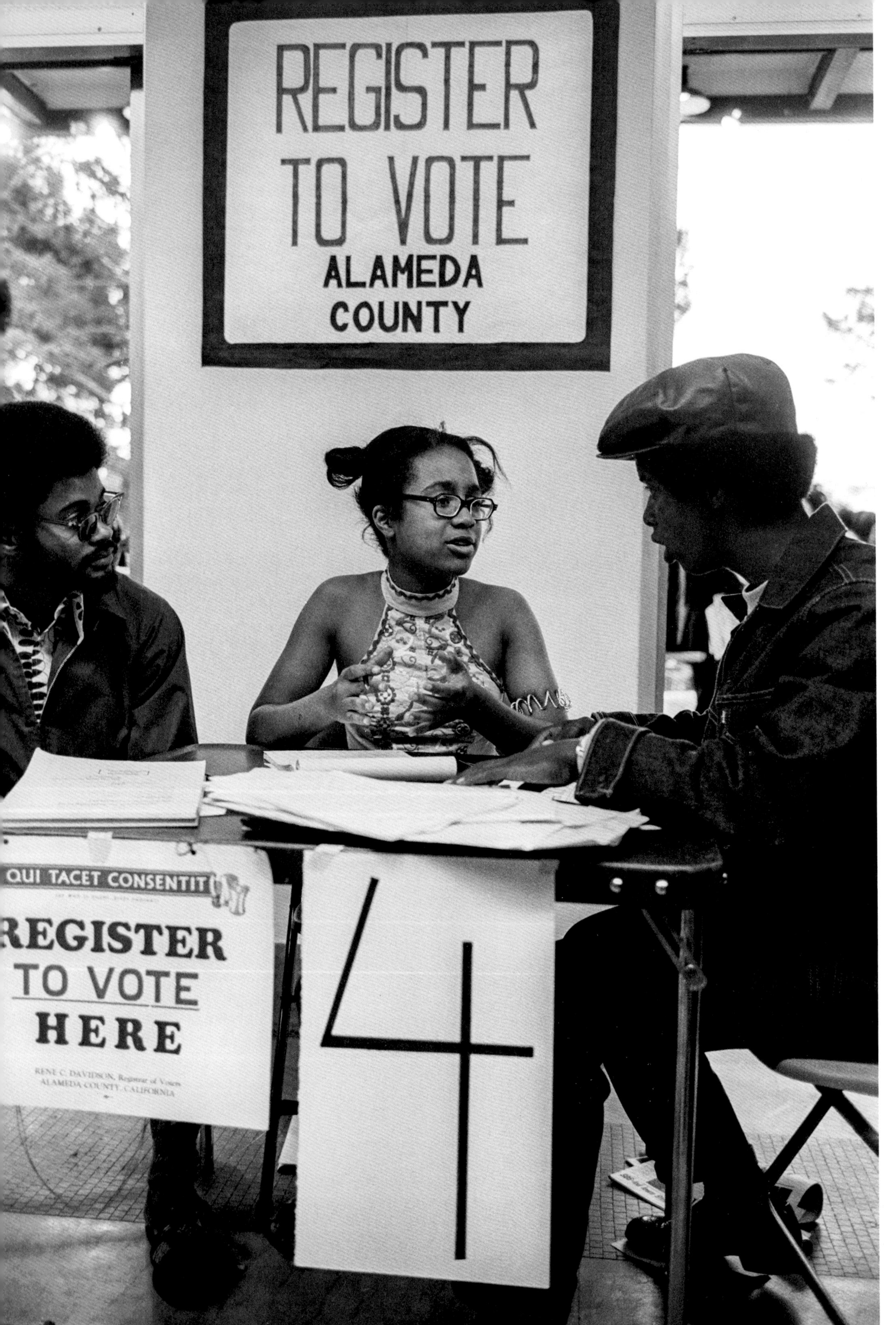

REGISTER
TO VOTE
ALAMEDA
COUNTY
QUI TACET CONSENTIT
REGISTER
TO VOTE
HERE
RENE C. DAVIDSON, Registrar of Voters
ALAMEDA COUNTY, CALIFORNIA
4

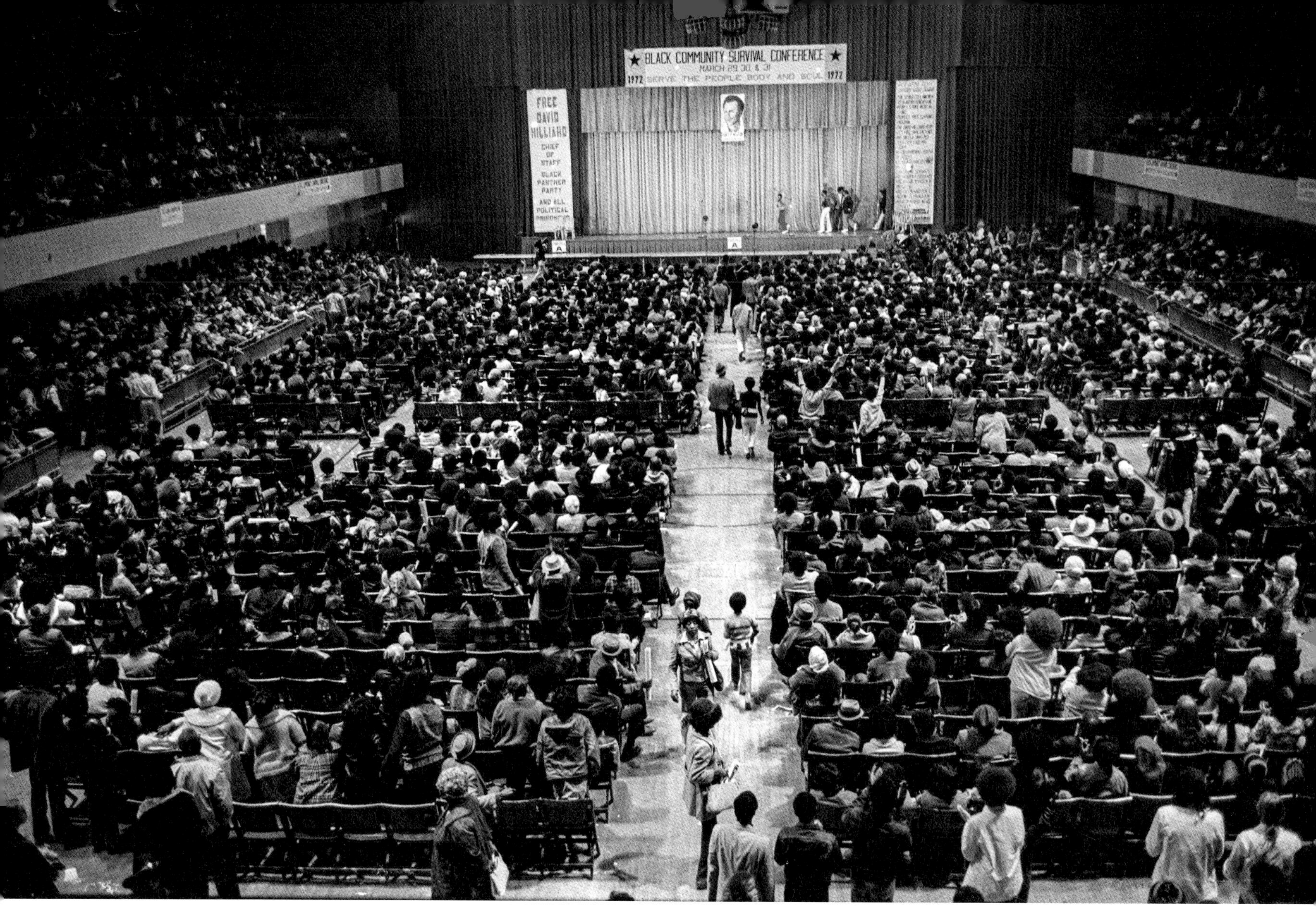

March 30, 1972 Oakland, California: Black Panther Party members register people to vote at the Black Community Survival Conference at the Oakland Colliseum.

March 30, 1972 Oakland, California: Black Community Survival Conference at the Oakland Colliseum.

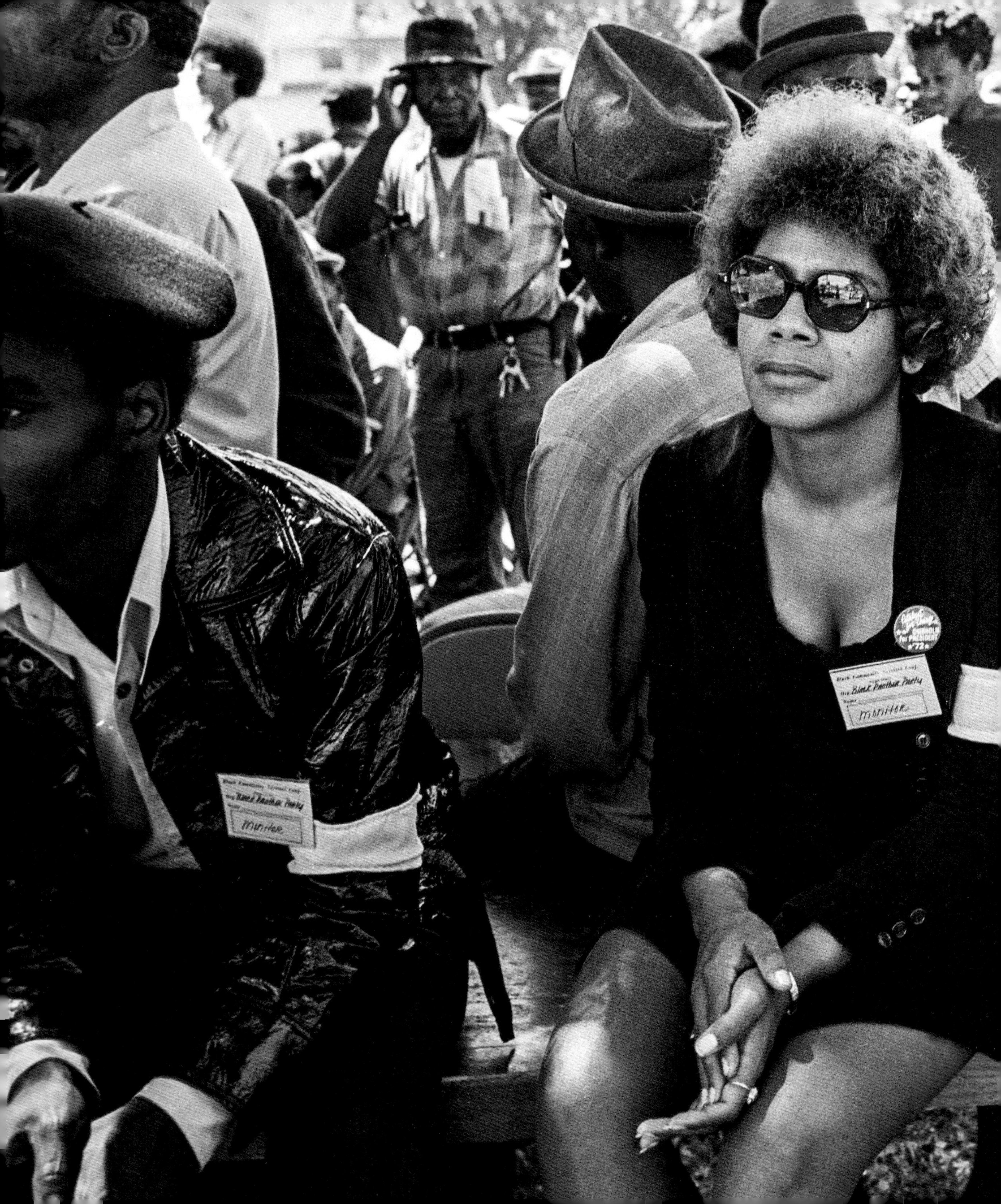

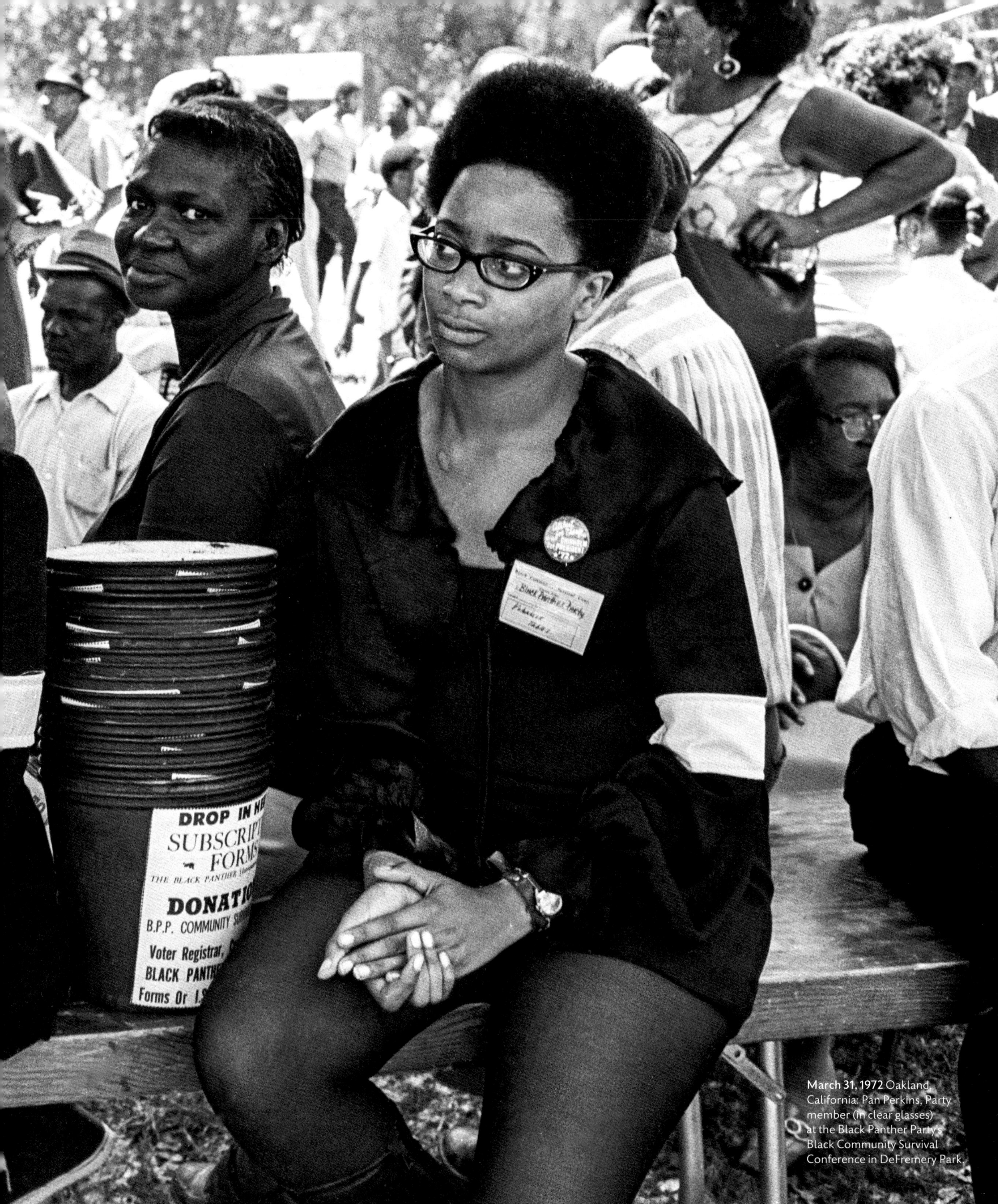

March 31, 1972 Oakland, California: Pan Perkins, Party member (in clear glasses) at the Black Panther Party's Black Community Survival Conference in DeFremery Park.

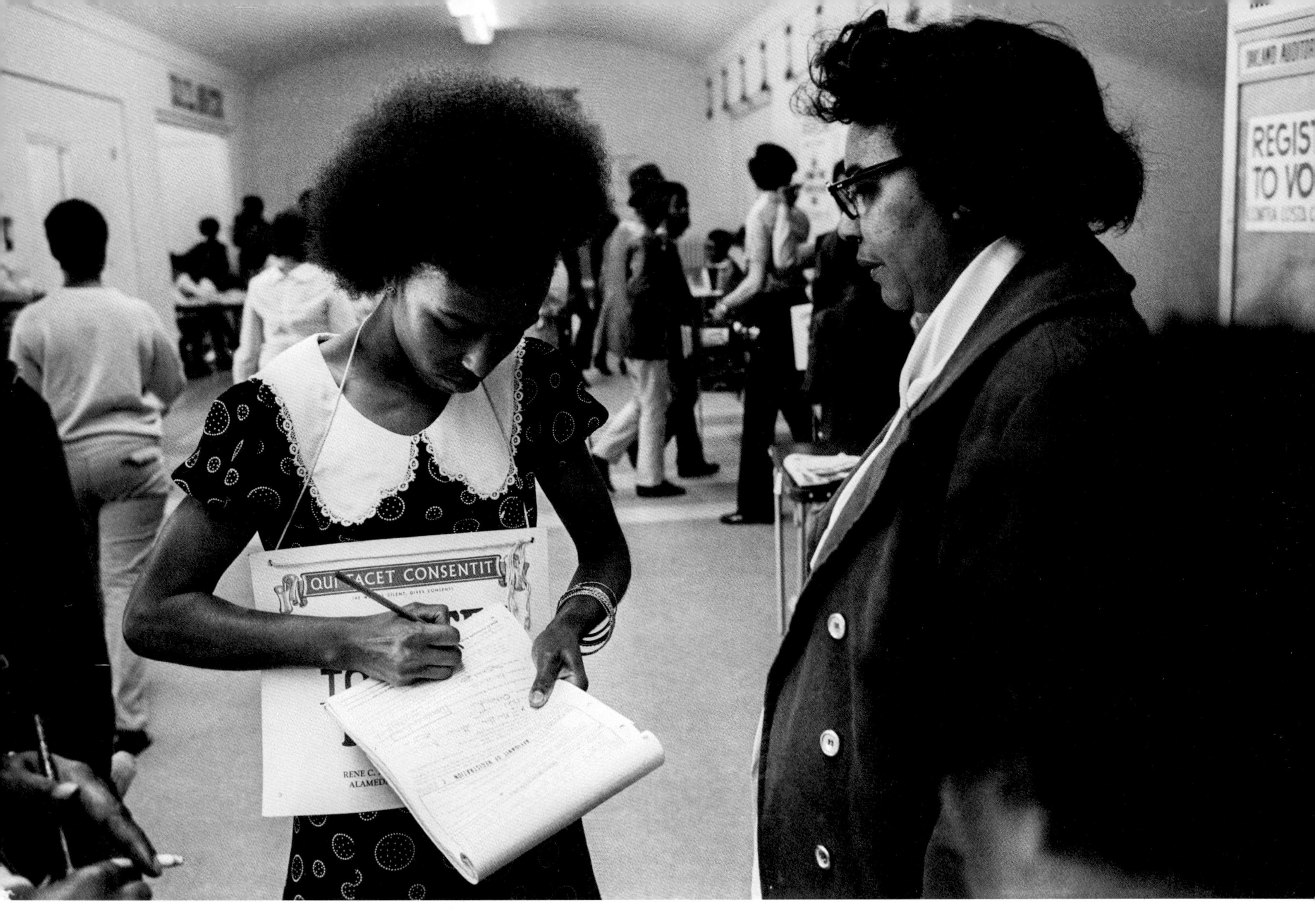

1972 Oakland, California:
Gloria Abernethy registers
people to vote during
Bobby Seale's campaign for
Mayor of Oakland.

When Martin Luther King, Jr. was killed in April 1968, I was a senior at Sacramento High. A palpable wave went through the Black students that day and many of us committed to the Party right then. The murder of Li'l Bobby Hutton, age 16, by the OPD (Oakland Police Department) solidified that commitment. I tried to keep up my work with the Party when I went to college, selling papers, going to meetings when I could. I remember being torn between the two. The Panthers won out, much to my parents' chagrin.

I had been familiar with the party since Chairman Bobby Seale led the 1966 march to the California State Capitol in Sacramento. My father and I watched the news on TV that evening and remembered how scared Governor Ronald Reagan looked when he hurriedly left a group of school children he was meeting with in Capitol Park. We both laughed.

I met Bobby Seale, Sam Napier, Emory Douglas, and John Seale in 1967. They had come to Sacramento State for a speaking engagement. After a raid and shoot-out in 1969, the Sacramento BPP Chapter was decimated. The few who were left were reassigned to the Richmond branch in the fall of 1969. We served free breakfast to school children every morning. Each Free Breakfast for School Children Program was carried out with military precision and the food was served with love and care—always on time, even when we were stopped by the infamous Richmond PD. After, we sold papers throughout Richmond. Everyday a different neighborhood: Parchester Village, Downtown, North Richmond… That was like the Wild West, with its wooden sidewalks. Some old Black people sat on their porches with guns in their laps. I remember visiting an old lady who told me, "Don't come back unless you bring us some guns."

I was later reassigned to the Oakland BPP Community Center and occasionally worked at Central Headquarters, which was down the street. We also worked weekly at *The Black Panther* newspaper distribution office in San Francisco to send out hundreds of thousands of newspapers nationally, internationally; this included free mailed copies to prisoners and those in military service. At the West Oakland Community Center, we were a hub of neighborhood activity with lots of daily visitors—local, national, international—and lots of children. People in the community, neighbors, comrades, and our children: we were all a big family. Despite all we were going through, I felt loved and safe. Walking through the Projects on my way to the laundromat (we had a free clothing program), I could hear people yell out from their windows and doors, "Hey, panther girl, hey, panther girl!" I couldn't see them but they were watching out for us.

Besides selling papers, I worked in the Ministry of Culture, producing *The Black Panther* Newspaper (which consisted of doing lay-out and headlines), and creating flyers, signs, etc. Whatever was needed. I also worked at our free health clinic in Berkeley and at the infant and toddler care center. We had lots of beautiful babies, including my daughter, Rori.

Gloria Abernethy
Sacramento, Richmond, Oakland, and Berkeley Chapters, CA /
the BPP Central HQ in West Oakland and East Oakland

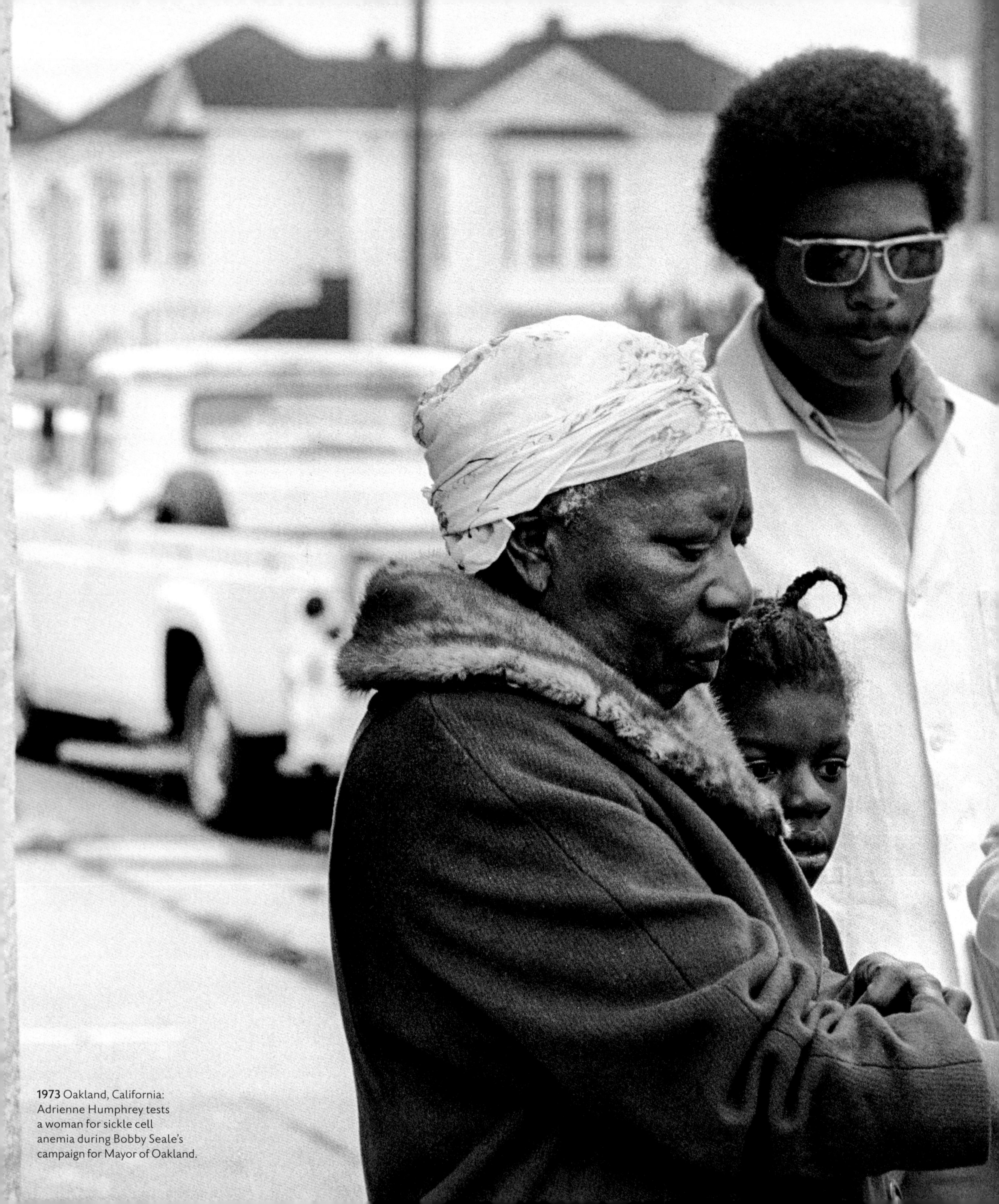

1973 Oakland, California: Adrienne Humphrey tests a woman for sickle cell anemia during Bobby Seale's campaign for Mayor of Oakland.

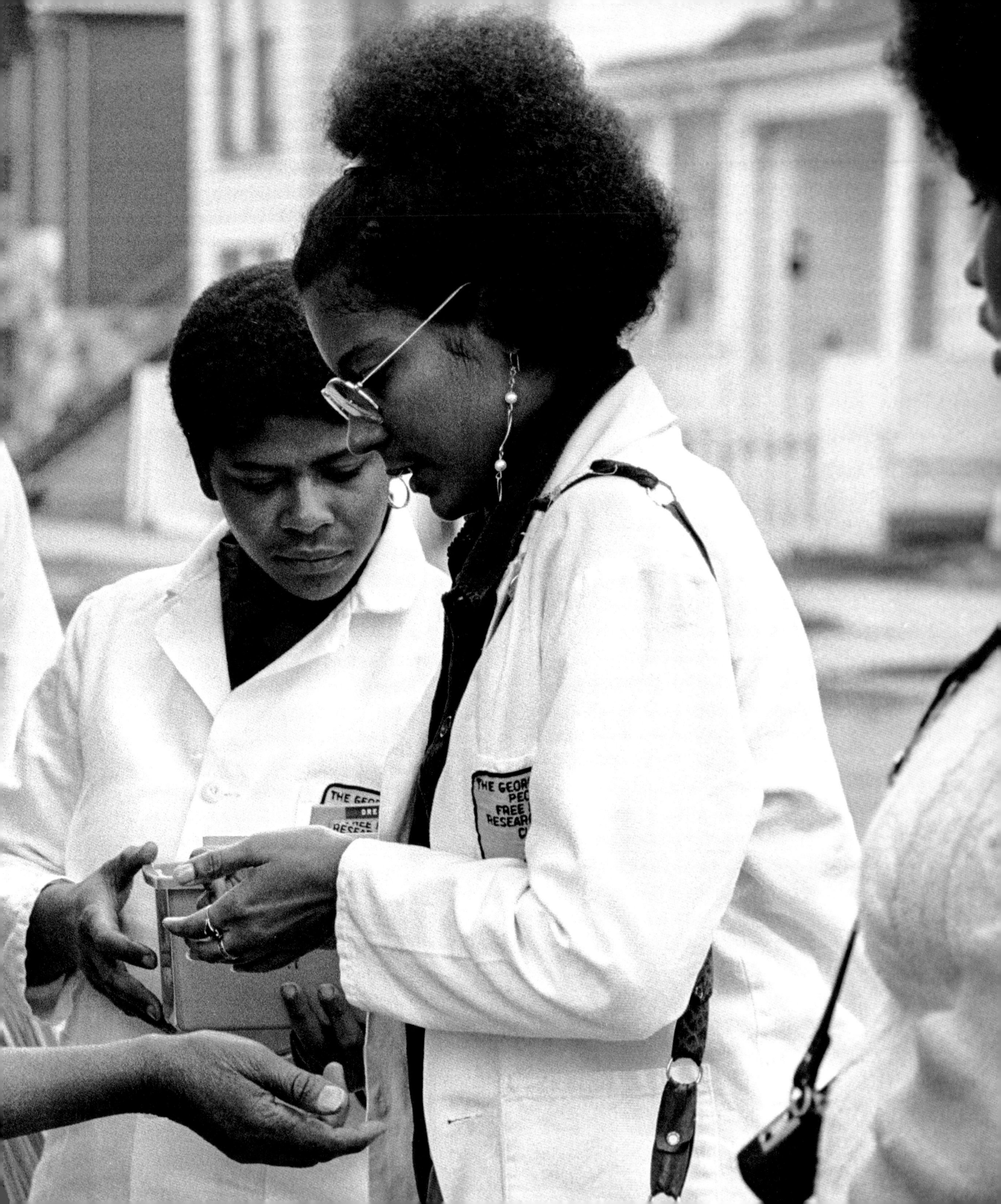
THE GEOR[GE]
BRE[...]
[...]CE [...]
RESEAR[CH ...]
THE GEOR[GE]
PEO[...]
FREE [...]
RESEAR[CH ...]
C[...]

What drew me to the party was the raid on the office in Los Angeles, December 1969. Al and I were married. I'd been resistant to the idea of becoming a member. I was a student at Cal State LA, I had my little boy, my little Al, and we were just like the song say, *movin' on up*.

After the SWAT raid, when they beat Al so bad and put him in jail, that got my attention. I understood what Al was trying to explain to me. This country ain't all it's cracked up to be. I started working with Russell Washington, officer of the day, at the LA office. I did typing and helped out at the bombed-out, beat up office on 41st Street. I was majoring in physical education and minoring in math.

Soon, Elaine Brown knew that I had the most information about health, and so I became the coordinator of the Alprentice "Bunchy" Carter People's Free Medical Clinic at 3223 South Central Avenue.

What do I want women of all ages, and girls to know about serving community?

My dad used to tell me I reminded him of his mother. They owned a farm, and during the Great Depression and afterwards, people down south were hungry. If you didn't have a farm with food growing on it, you were probably in very tough shape. Dad said his mother would have them hitch up the old blind mule, Sally. She would put vegetables and stuff on that wagon, and they would go around to the neighbors' houses and give it out.

My dad said, "You remind me of mama. I guess it's in the blood."

That's who I am, that's what I do, and that's what I will continue to do. That's my job. You know, it's not always about money. You want to make sure that you're paid your value—don't undersell yourself—but know that service is important. Sometimes you don't have money to give, but maybe you have some time and some talent.

We got to live together. We got to help each other if we're going to make it through this.

Norma Armour Mtume
Los Angeles and Oakland Chapters, CA

1973 Oakland, California: Norma Armour Mtume, George Jackson People's Free Health Clinic cadre, attends to a young girl in Oakland during the Bobby Seale for Mayor campaign.

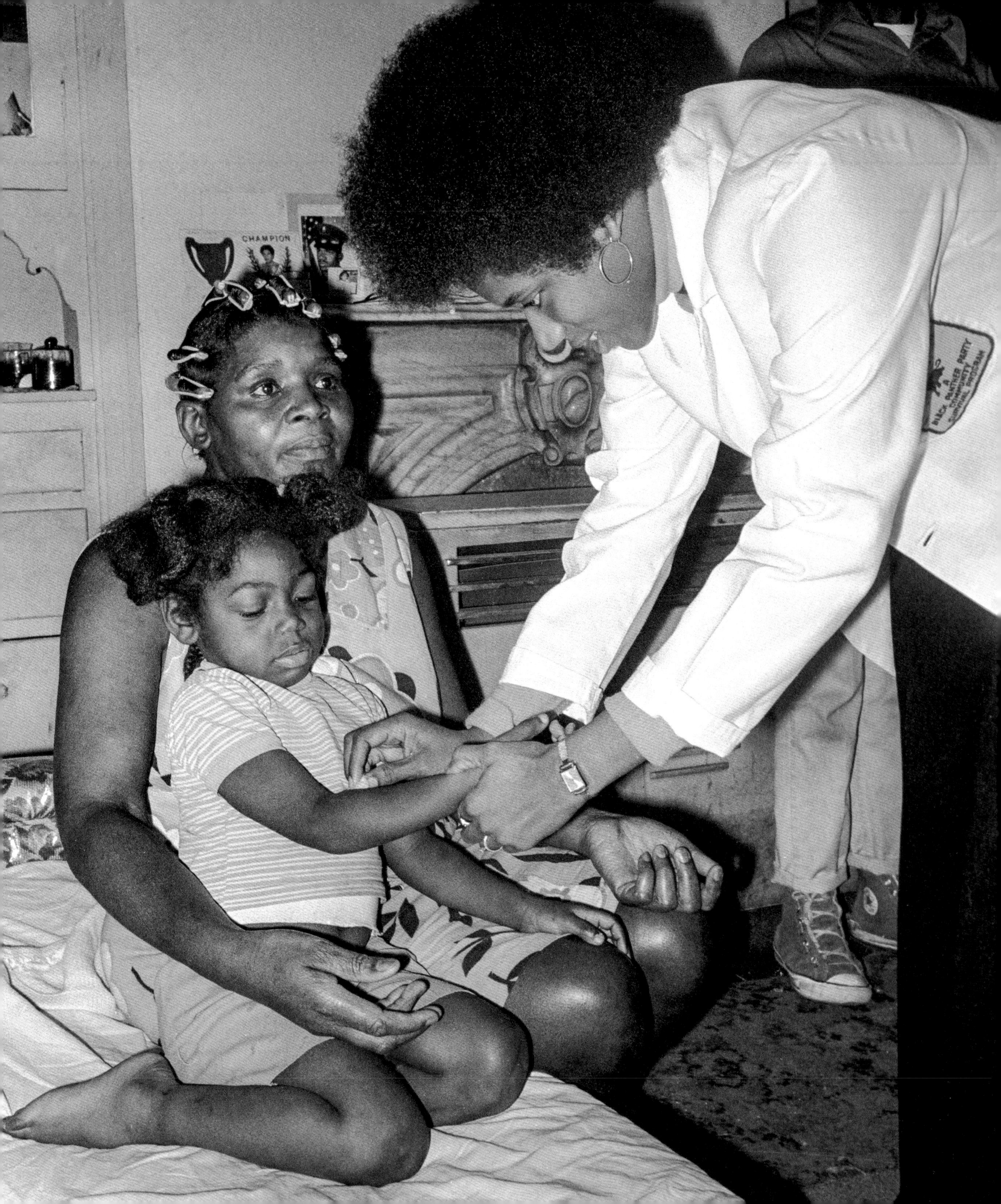

BLACK PANTHER PARTY
A COMMUNITY SURVIVAL PROGRAM

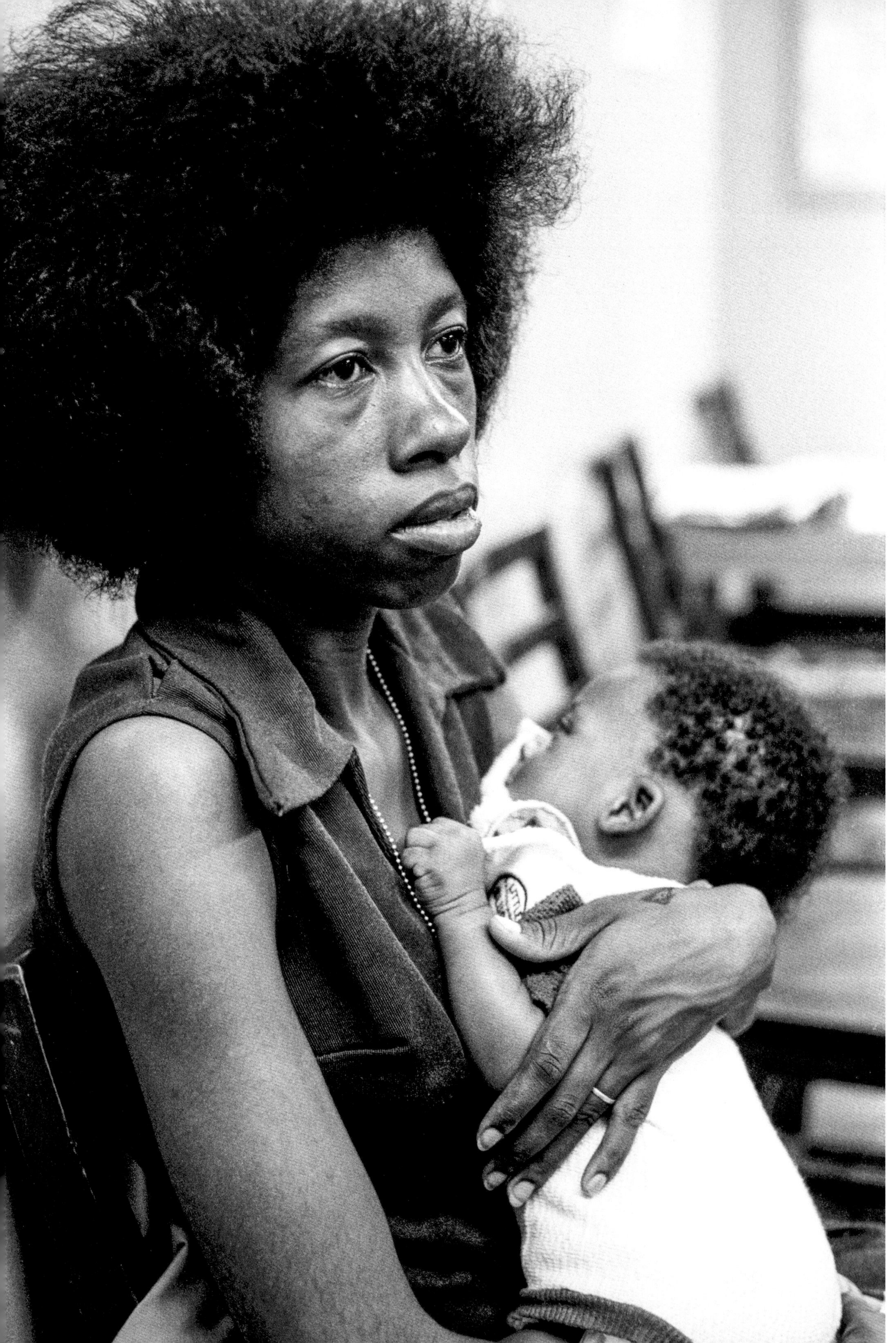

After working in the Party's Alprentice "Bunchy" Carter People's Free Medical Clinic in Los Angeles, I was assigned to the George Jackson Free Clinic in Berkeley, in February 1972. Shortly after, Jody transferred from Detroit and was assigned to the clinic. Joceiter Donzella Weaver, although very young, quickly became my right-hand lady, exceptionally gifted in working with children. We developed a collaboration with Children's Hospital Oakland and established a pediatrics program on Thursdays at the clinic. That collaboration grew to include the operation of one of the first Women, Infants, and Children Programs (WIC) in the East Bay.

WIC paid Jody, and with our combined incomes, we rented an apartment together. She was my Comrade Sister, my roommate, my children's aunt, their caretaker in my absence, and the best secret keeper a girl could ever have.

Jody was reassigned to the Oakland Community School in 1974 as the children's health officer, attending to their every healthcare need. After separating from Party service, Jody returned to Detroit; I moved to San Diego. We found each other, reconnected, and she moved to San Diego. We resumed our relationship as the family we had become during our time in the Party. My children Al, Leilah, and Bryan, were happy to have their Auntie Jody with them again. I'll never forget her shy demeanor—but you didn't get her riled up, because then Detroit would come out!

Just writing this remembrance, I'm crying. I still love and miss my little sister. She left us in 2000, much too soon.

Joceiter Jody Donzella Weaver
Oakland Chapter, CA *(a remembrance by Norma (Armour) Mtume)*

1970 Chicago, Illinois: Mother and baby at the Black Panther's Spurgeon "Jake" Winters Medical Center.

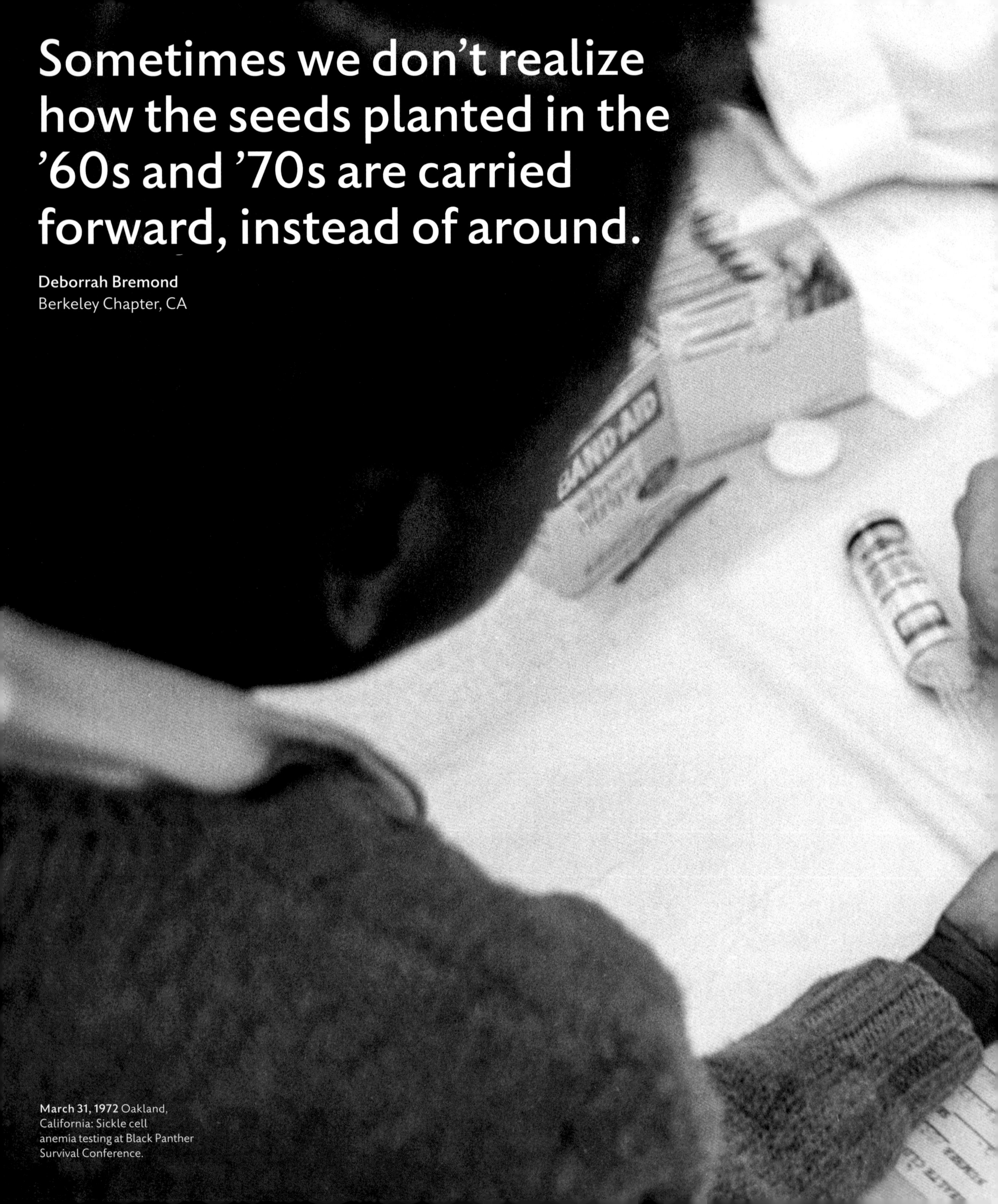

Sometimes we don't realize how the seeds planted in the '60s and '70s are carried forward, instead of around.

Deborrah Bremond
Berkeley Chapter, CA

March 31, 1972 Oakland, California: Sickle cell anemia testing at Black Panther Survival Conference.

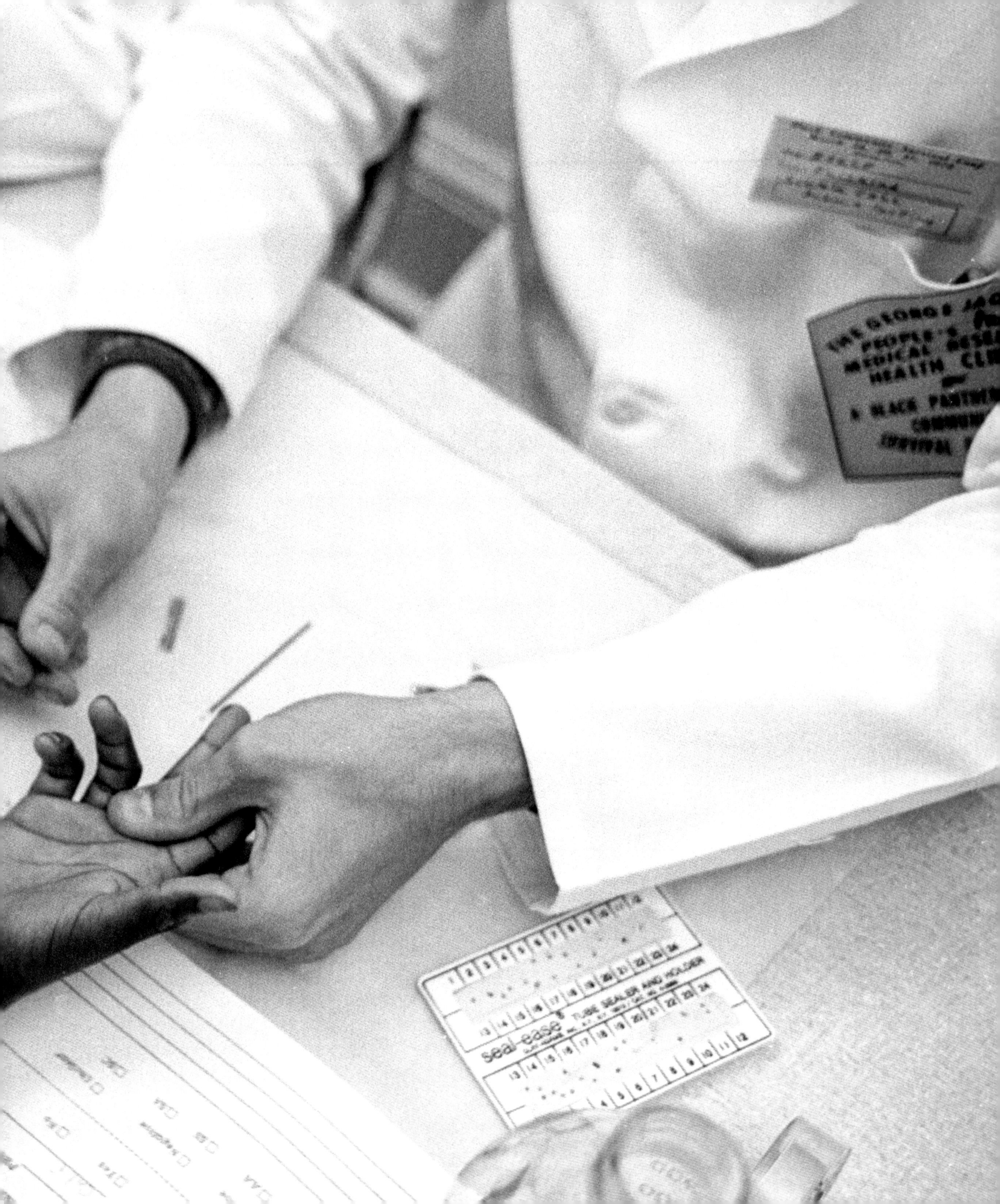

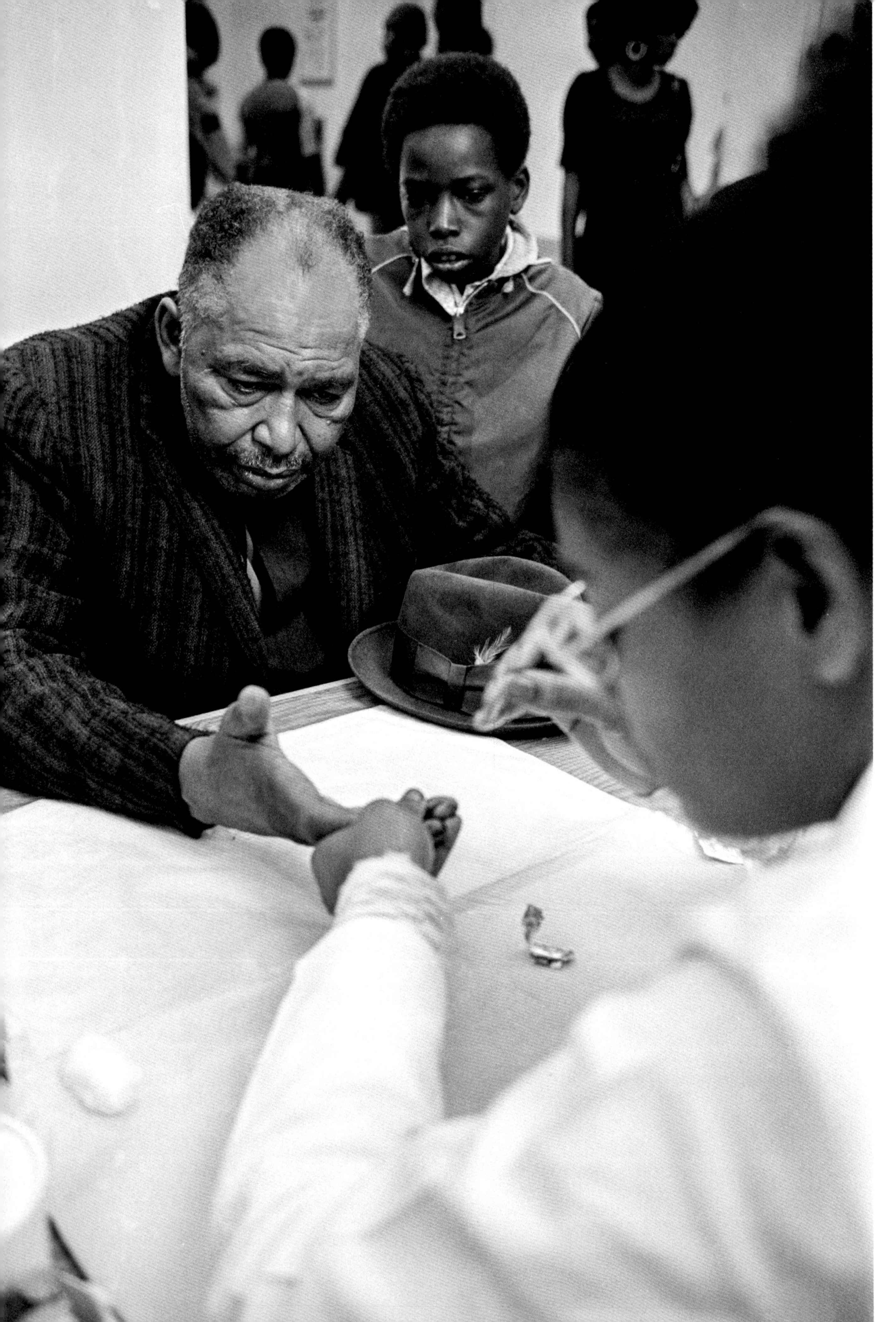

I met Adrienne Shankari Humphrey in my early childhood at the Oakland Community School (OCS). She worked in the offices, as a bookkeeper. Adrienne grew up in Cincinnati, Ohio. Once she was accepted to Harvard University, she moved to Boston, MA. A year later, she told her parents: "I am quitting school, staying in Boston, and joining the Black Panther Party." She made a choice to help people of color several years after the Civil Rights Act was ratified. Adrienne found her way to Oakland, California, and the Oakland Community School, from the Boston Chapter of the Party.

When I was five years old at OCS, Adrienne was "the pretty lady who worked in the office." She didn't have much interaction with the children. One of my earliest memories of Adrienne, is the day I discovered the water hose on the side of the building. I liked how the water would sheet down the glass when I sprayed the window with water—so, I kept doing it. Adrienne eventually came out to the playground, a place she rarely visited. I remember watching her walk directly toward me. She asked me if I was mad at her, "Is that why you were spraying the window with the water hose?" She was kind and curious. I wasn't mad at her. I didn't know it was her office window. I just enjoyed the physics of the water sheeting down the glass.

The Party was fighting against race-based violence. The school was educating children and adults, a punishable offense in the early years of Africans living in America. By 1979, due in part to the impact of FBI COINTELPRO's destructive pursuit of liberation movements, many women and families close to our family were making exits from the Party. When my family left the Party, it was a scary time for all of us: an over-night lifestyle change. Auntie Adrienne moved in with my mother, my sister, and me. She stayed with us from when I was nine to when I was 13 years old. As a child, still having some connection to members of the Party and families who attended the school helped with the transition. Living with Adrienne for those years helped provide me with the consistency and normalcy a child needs.

A more recent memory of Adrienne is the day she reached out to tell me she was at my mother's house. She invited me over. We enjoyed laughing together. We always had a laughing relationship.

In 2018, months before she retired, Auntie Adrienne purchased a condo, with a lake, ducks, and a fountain off the balcony. While helping her move from the rental to her new home, my Auntie Adrienne asked me if I would take care of her estate when she passed.

I said, "Of course. Why would I not take care of my auntie?" I didn't know any other option. She started to cry.

My Auntie Adrienne Shankari passed peacefully less than a year later; I handled her affairs as she asked. There was no other way!

Adrienne Shankari Humphrey
Boston Chapter, MA / Oakland Chapter, CA,
(a remembrance by her nephew, Zachary Killoran)

1972 Oakland, California: Ruby Moore, sickle cell tester, pricks a man's finger to test for sickle cell anemia during Bobby Seale's campaign for Mayor of Oakland. The man's son watches.

My mother was born in Brooklyn, where I grew up. She was responsible for
the Breakfast Program in New York. She was a regular contributor to the Party
newspaper, and she worked diligently to free the Panther 21.

Her first job was the people. She had a heightened sense of analysis, and she
was searching for her kin, for her people. She found them in the Black
Panther Party. For her the Party was one of the only places where a vision for
the economic base for revolutionary change was articulated and discussed.

My mom loved the Community Survival Programs because she knew the Party
wasn't filling in for the state. It was building a beloved community, the kind of
community where you're bringing food to families and teaching kids.

My mom had sickle cell anemia. The Black Panther Party was the only national
political organization that took on the issue of sickle cell anemia. At the time,
there was no research. There were no treatments, except blood transfusions.
My mom died from repeated blood transfusions at the age of 59. Now people
are living longer. Children are being healed from sickle cell anemia with
new treatments.

My mother was also drawn by Fred Hampton's idea of transracial alliance
along the lines of class. She learned about white resentment, the relationship
between the Black struggle and the class struggle of the white working
class. She also felt that the Black Panther Party was one of the most explicitly
feminist Black organizations that she participated in. It's the reason why
she could openly support me as a queer person, coming out at age 12. The
party was the only Black organization in the country at that time that had
a commitment to dealing with, and working with queer people.

My mom was a firm fighter for Black liberation, and she was also a humanist.
She loved people. She was sensitive and empathetic. She was the most loyal
person I've ever met. When I was a child, I didn't understand her loyalty. My
mom explained it to me in a very clarifying way. She said, "If you are enslaved
and there is a slave revolt coming, and some of the people in the slave revolt
are people that have harmed you, do you decide not to participate in the slave
revolt or do you participate?"

Memories are kept alive by keeping the memories alive. I love talking about
my mother, and I appreciate the opportunity to do it.

Janet Cyril
Brooklyn and Harlem NYC Chapters, NY
(a remembrance by Malkia Mac Devich-Cyril)

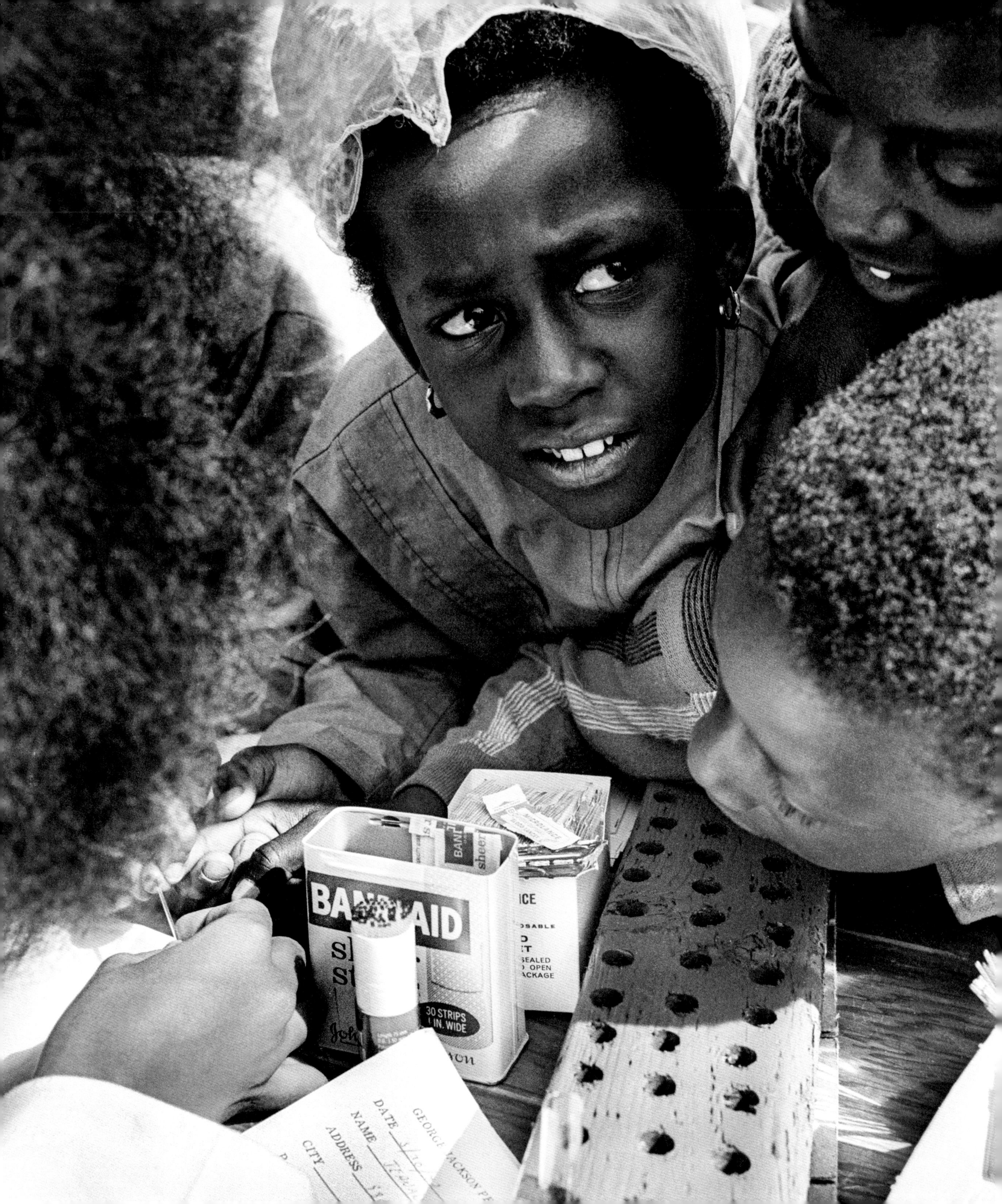

BAND-AID
sheer
strips
30 STRIPS
1 IN. WIDE
John
son
BAND
sheer
ICE
OSABLE
T
SEALED
O OPEN
ACKAGE
GEORGE JACKSON P
DATE
NAME
ADDRESS
CITY

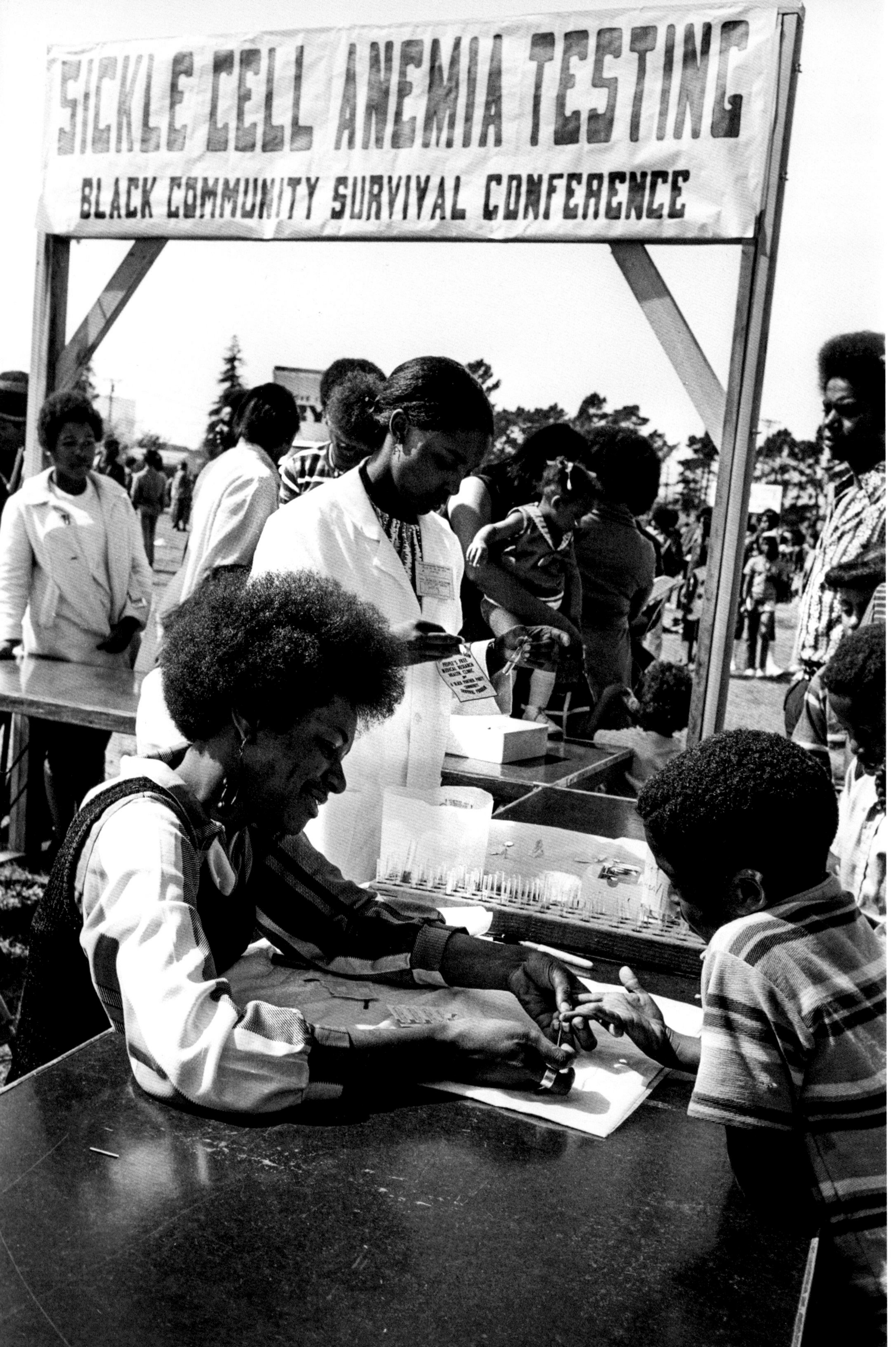

SICKLE CELL ANEMIA TESTING
BLACK COMMUNITY SURVIVAL CONFERENCE

I'm a native of Winston-Salem, North Carolina, where I started volunteering with the BPP as a 17-year-old while attending Winston-Salem Business (Rutledge) College. I worked full-time with the Party's Community Survival Programs after completing school. What comes to mind, amongst so many services and social issues, was our chapter's Joseph Waddell's People's Free Ambulance Service, which was one of a kind in the country.

During this time, Forsyth County did not have a price ceiling on the ambulance ride during health emergencies. People were literally dying on their doorsteps. Without cash in hand ($75 or a health insurance card) low-income Blacks were left on their doorsteps. Having a job did not automatically ensure one had health insurance coverage; thus, many were denied transportation to the emergency rooms.

Party members obtained certifications as Emergency Medical Technicians from Surry Community College. Our focus was not on monetary compensation. We possessed a desire to impact the basic human right to healthcare. Larry Little, Chairman of the Winston-Salem Chapter, tells the story of how the Director of Surry County Community College had been approached and asked to deny Party members from attending class. The director replied that the Panther classmates were the best students in that class. We were young, we were serious, and we loved the community. The community loved us.

We received a grant from St. Paul's Episcopal Church of New York for $75,000, so that we could purchase the ambulance. I was a communication dispatcher at the office. My parents did not want me doing this work, but it so happened that one of my mother's friends had to be rushed to the hospital and was denied county transportation. Later, my mom's friend told her how the Panther's ambulance service had saved her life. Everyone realized the power of what we were doing. The ambulance service was named after Joseph Waddell, a Panther who died under suspicious circumstances while incarcerated in one North Carolina's notorious penitentiaries.

We exemplified that in order to serve the people, we have to love the people. And we had to love the people to do what we did. We have within us the power to change lives. We have such a history of Kings and Queens. Our chapter was the first in providing many services, including but not limited to a Free Breakfast for School Children Program, a resource for human injustices, sickle cell anemia testing, free clothing, free food and other programs. In October of 2013, the Forsyth County Historic Resources Commission unveiled a historic marker in honor of the Black Panther Party's contributions before an enthusiastic crowd of supporters.

I encourage girls and women to take care of themselves. Take care of your bodies, minds, and spirits in your younger years, and experience getting to know yourself.

Cynthia Norwood
Winston-Salem Chapter, NC

March 31, 1972 Oakland, California: A woman of the Black Panther Party tests a child for sickle cell anemia at Community Survival Conference rally.

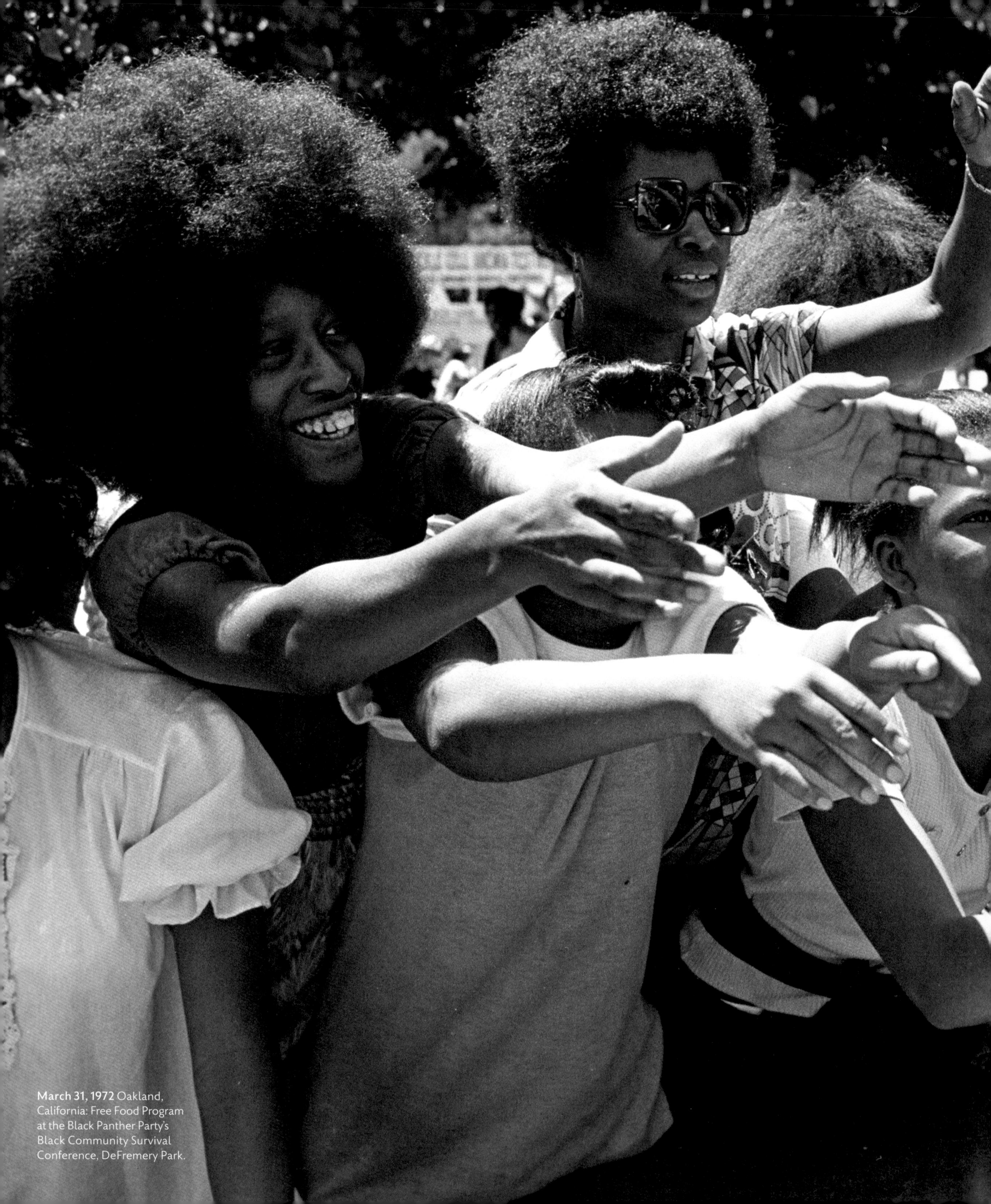

March 31, 1972 Oakland, California: Free Food Program at the Black Panther Party's Black Community Survival Conference, DeFremery Park.

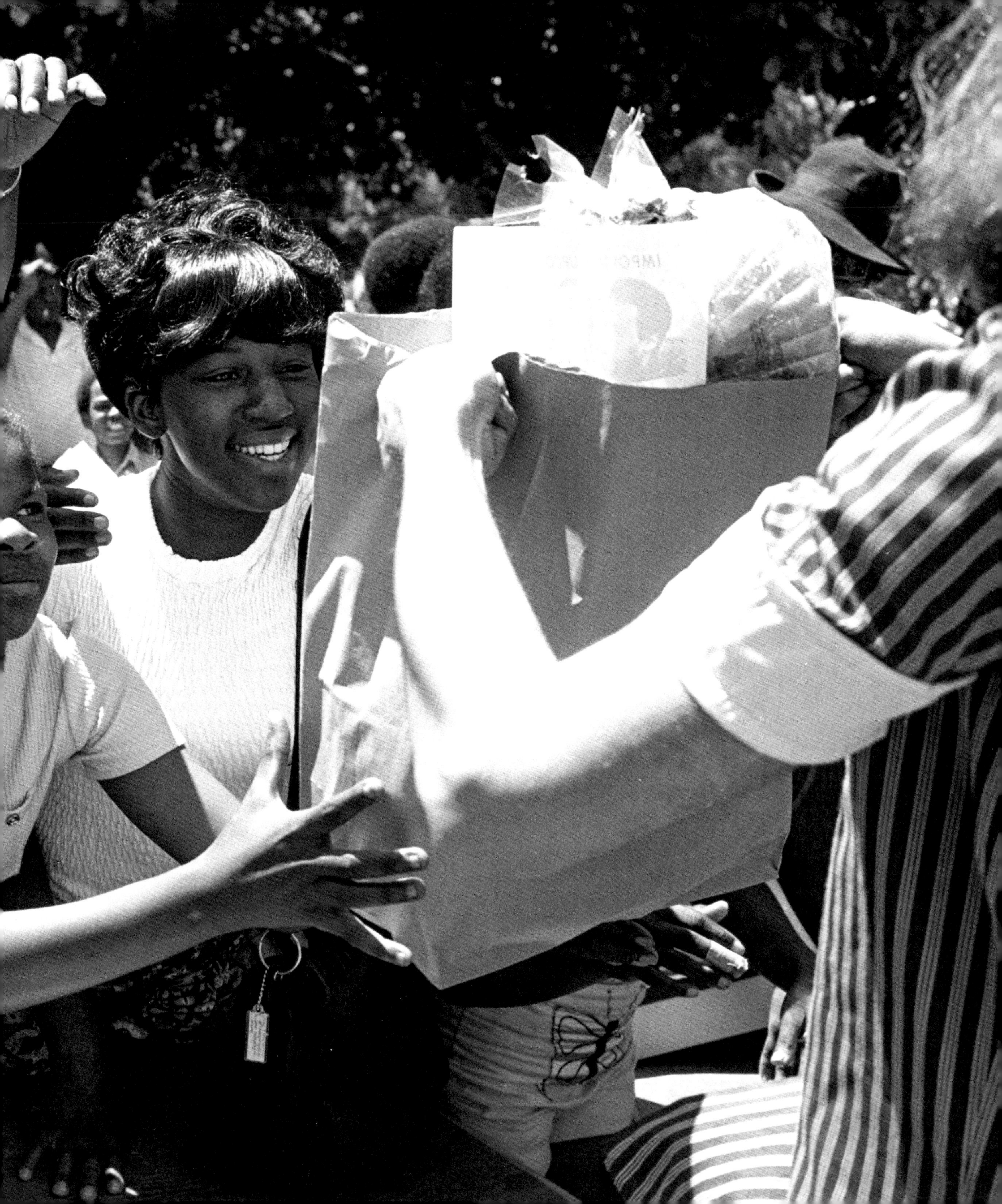

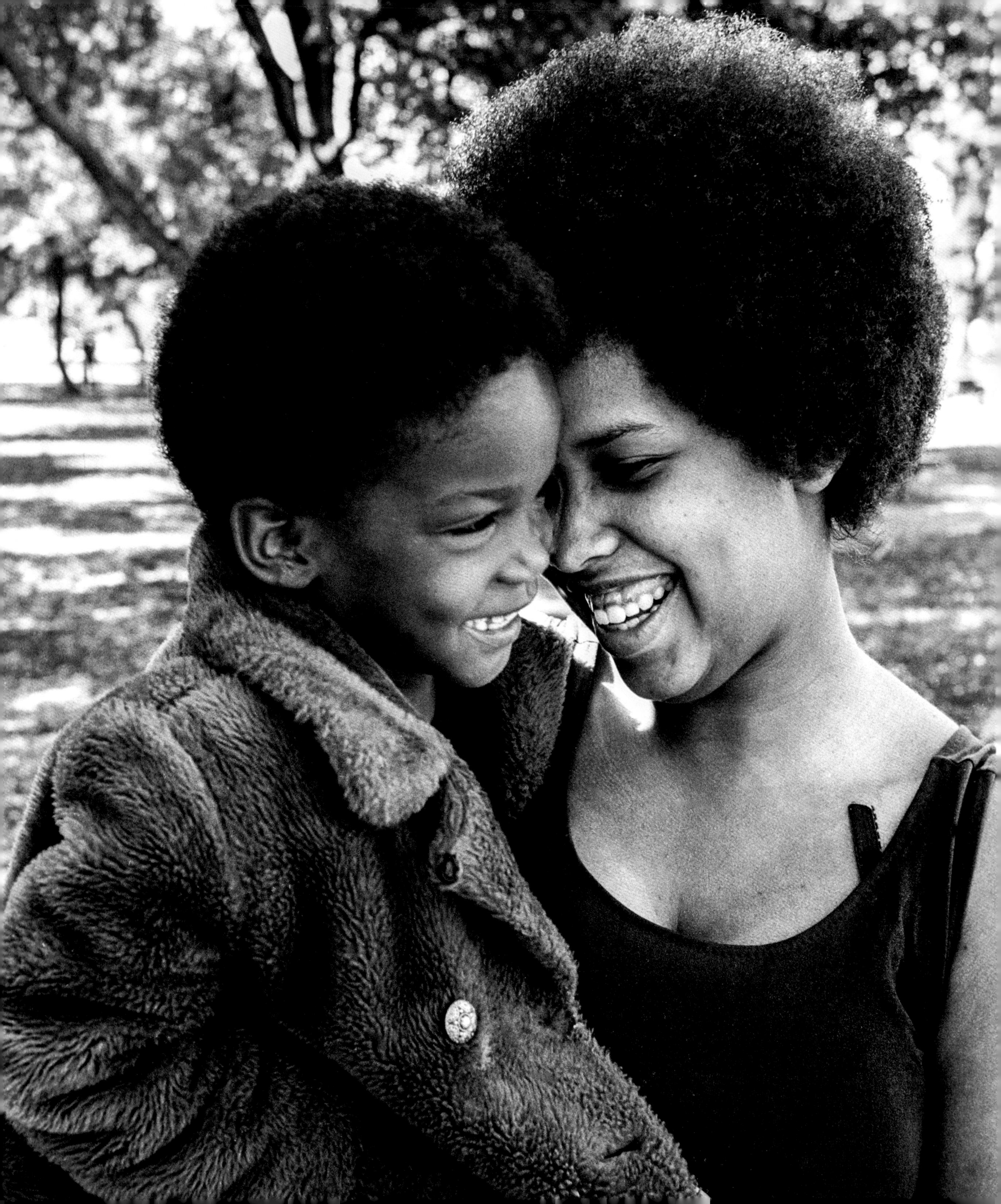

I had many roles in the Party. I volunteered to pick up Bobby Seale's wife (Artie) for a meeting and ended up driving all the time. I loved driving the Oakland Community School children on excursions. A favorite trip was the drive to Marin County, where a communal farm group would invite the children for lunch. I enjoyed being a typist for *The Black Panther* newspaper, and I was the first female Party photographer. Working at the school was really a highlight. At their former schools, the children from the community were considered 'bad'. At our school, the children were considered as smart, with potential. I was reminded that their behaviour changed because we really cared.

I'll never forget the 10,000-bag food giveaway. Bobby Seale first told us we were going to pack 100 bags, then 500, then 1,000. Eventually we packed 10,000 bags. I had no concept of how it would happen, of what 10,000 of anything looked like. Luckily, because of Bobby's background as a draftsman and engineer, it was a beautiful program. When I think about it today—that we gave out 10,000 bags, with chickens in every bag! —that memory brings me so much joy. The thing is, we were all so young. We were a youth organization.

Young women today, you need to understand your history. Get your education but also make room for self-care. Joy comes with having family, friends, and connections in your community. You can't do 'everything' by yourself. You need others to live a healthy life.

Lauryn Williams Jackson
San Francisco Chapter, CA / Oakland Chapter, CA / Queens Chapter, NY

1969 Berkeley, California: "Free Huey rally" in Provo Park. The official name of the park was Constitution Park, but it became Provo Park, in honor of the Dutch Provos. In 1983 it was re-named Martin Luther King Jr. Civic Center Park.

1972 "10,000 Free Full Bags of Groceries," Black Panther Party, courtesy of Lincoln Cushing and Lisbet Tellefsen.

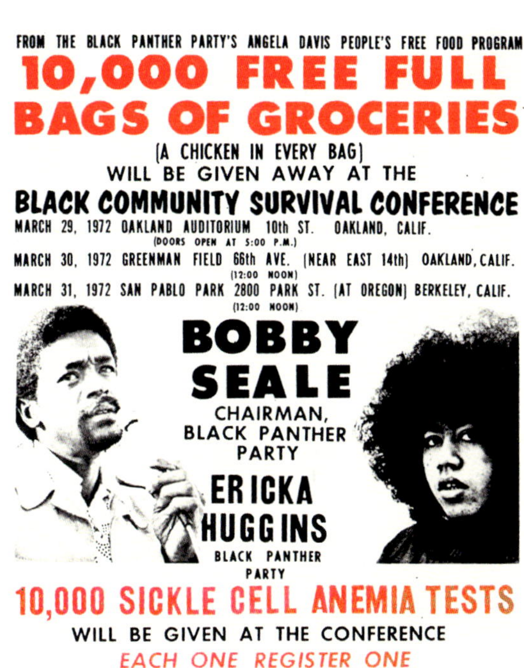

I first heard about the Black Panther Party because the Panthers would meet at the Malcolm X Community Center. When I joined the Black Panther Party, I was 14 years old. I worked in all of the Free Breakfast for School Children Programs—Corona, Harlem, Brooklyn, and the Bronx—with my buddy, Sam Napier.

He was my brother, forever. *Forever*. I still get sad every time I think about him.

I worked in the Bronx with the paper distribution. We also went to the moratorium held in Washington in protest against the war, to sell papers and organize.

Women and young girls: I would like you to have a connection to your community. You should take care of the elderly in your community; we did that when we were younger, before the Black Panther Party came along. We'd check on the senior citizens on our block and have conversations with them on a daily basis. Don't be selfish and think about just you. Your wants and your needs are not the only important ones. Don't get tunnel vision. You have to understand that there's more to life.

Young women, be independent of your partners and your significant others. You don't have to depend on your mate. Say *no* as many times as you want to. This life is serious; it's no game. We have to have fun, though. We have to stop and smell the roses; we have to make time for family. And education is important. I quit school at a very, very young age. I'm just now back—I started three years ago!

Thelma Bunny Davis-Legare
Brooklyn, The Bronx, and Harlem offices, NY / Jamaica Chapter

March, 1972 Oakland, California: Panther Free Food Program. Earlene Coleman, Black Panther Party member, prepares bags of food for distribution at the Laney College student center for the Black Panther Community Survival Conference at the Oakland Coliseum where the Panthers gave away 6,000 bags of groceries. Bobby Seale announced his run for Mayor of Oakland that night.

June 5, 1972 *Let It Shine … Let The Power Of The People Shine!*, artwork by M. Gayle Asali Dickson.

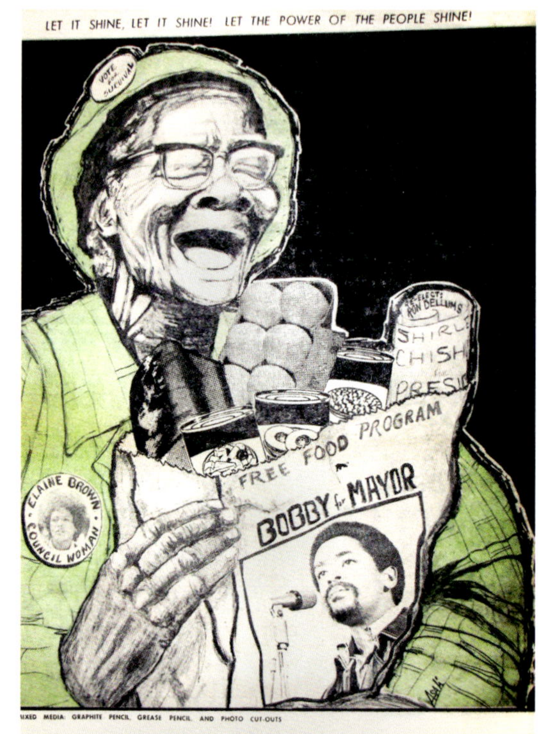

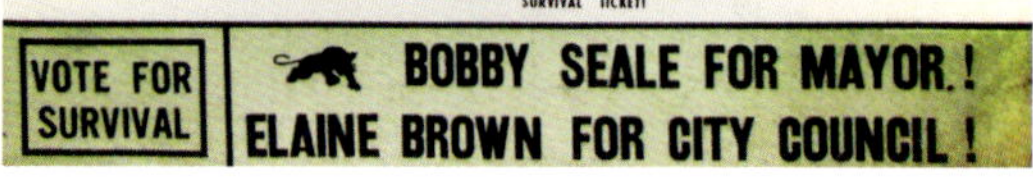

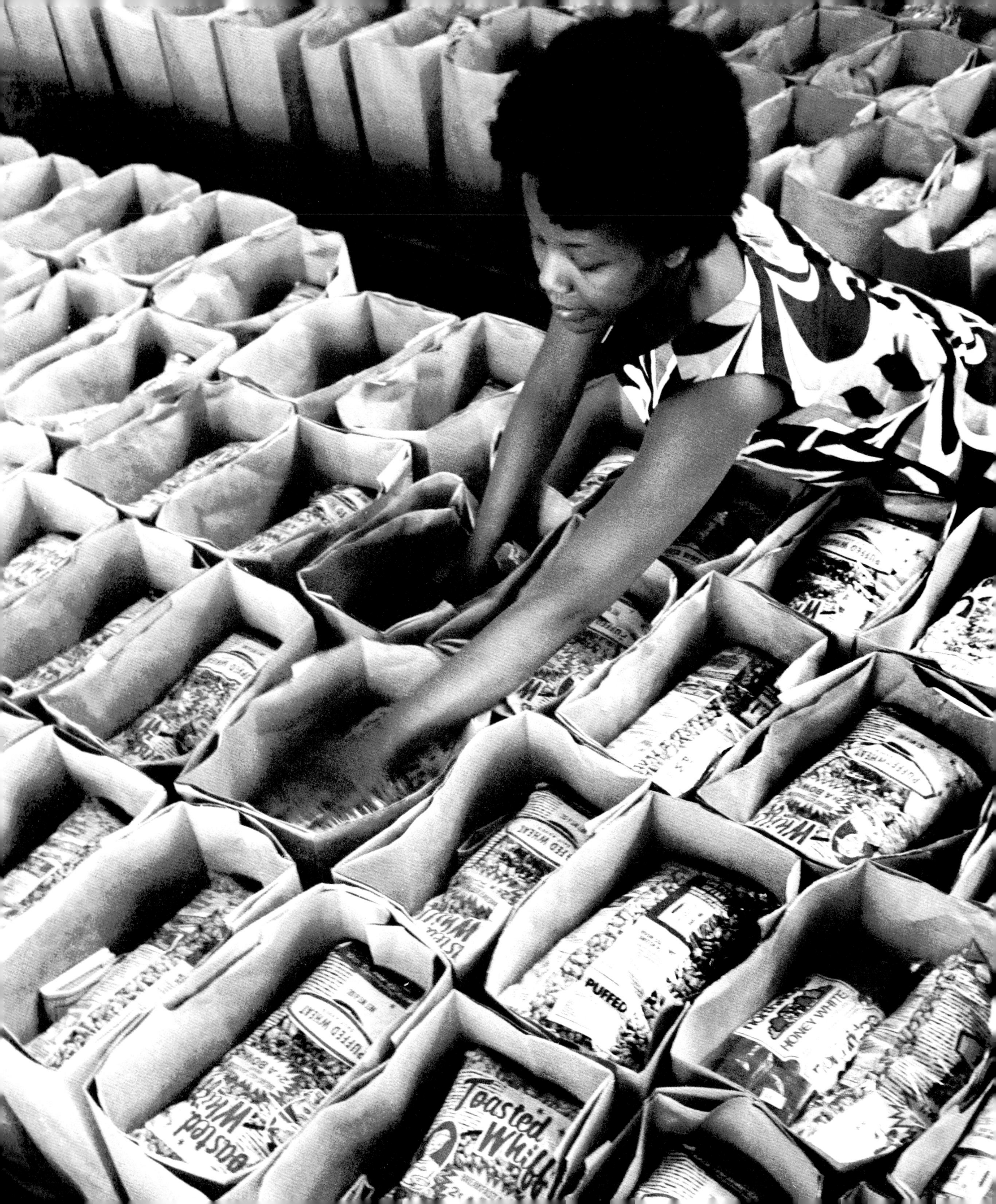

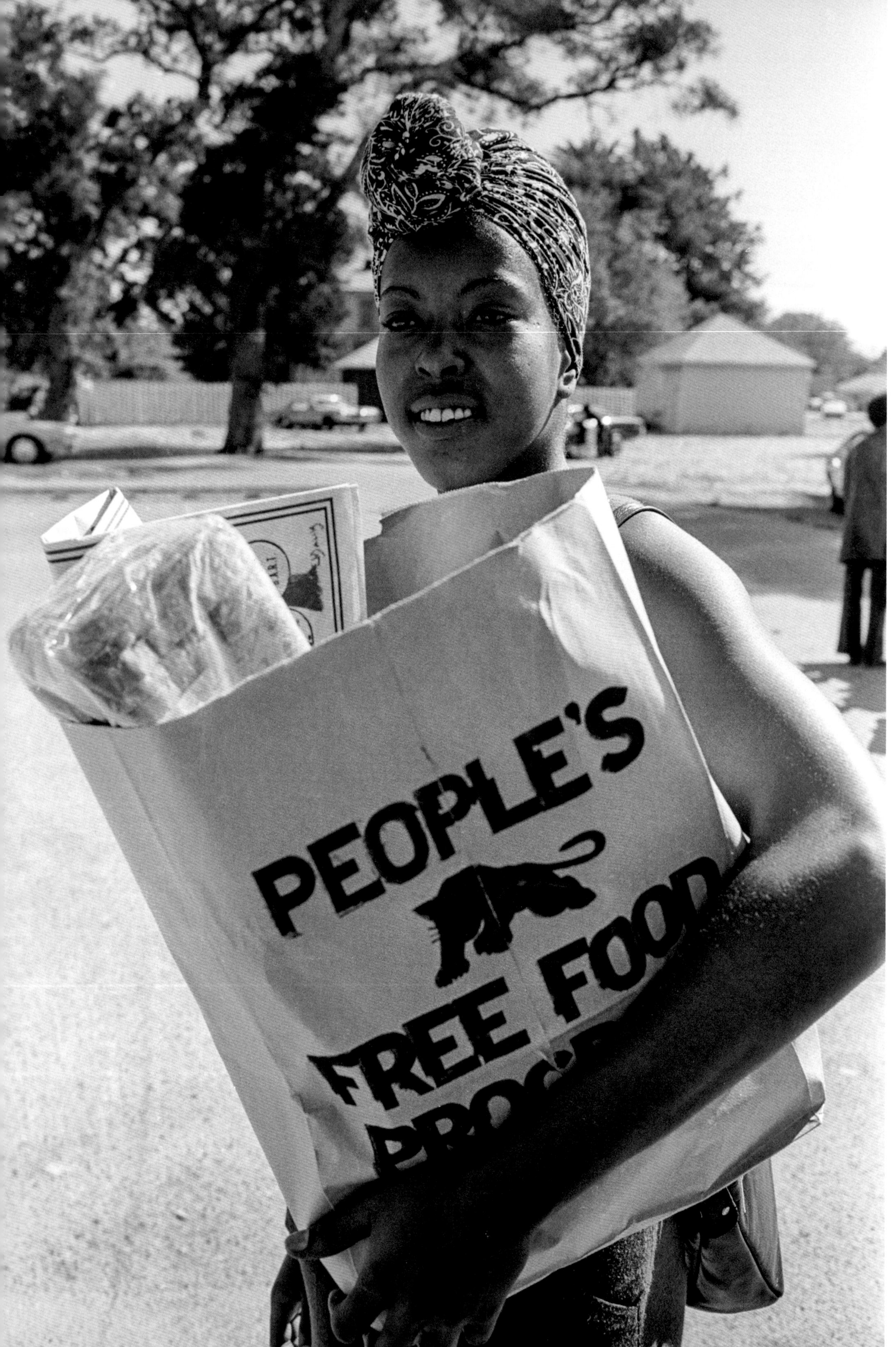
PEOPLE'S
FREE FOOD
PROG

I now live in Atlanta, Georgia, but I miss Oakland fiercely. Oakland is home. I came to the Party with a rebellious nature and a stifled reality. What drew me to the Party was my need to be the Black woman that I knew I was, but didn't have the courage to be. In California, in Oakland, in Richmond and the Bay Area, a beautiful freedom began to come out of me.

I realized I had a Black son, and at some point, his number was going to come up. What would I be able to do on that day?

When Elaine Brown ran for councilwoman, in 1973, she had an office in downtown Oakland. I went over there to volunteer, and I found out about the senior's program. My grandmother was in a convalescent hospital, and that very Sunday I brought her over to learn about Seniors Against a Fearful Environment. I loved that because I saw everyone on television going out, helping the seniors.

The commitment to feeding the kids and the community was an absolute priority to the Party. Recognizing that kids learn better when they are not constantly hungry, they began the Free Breakfast for School Children Program, the precursor to today's state and federal school programs. Along the same lines, efforts to provide free bags of groceries to community families was vital. This eventually evolved into a major event where 10,000 free bags of groceries were given out over a weekend. Procurement of the food was essential to those endeavors. Being part of the procurement process was probably my most gratifying experience.

I didn't think I was brave in the beginning, but the community was behind us. The community supported us. I was proud to be a Panther. In the early days, we were looked at as healers, rescuers and soldiers: everything that the community needed. We were the answer to the violence against us, the lack of power in our communities.

I want to say to all the young ladies out there: women are not your enemies. Sisters are not your enemies. We need to love each other and embrace each other; there is no *me* without *we*. And as far as service goes, *Each One Teach One.* We must look beyond ourselves and go back to the community, and the community is much broader than it used to be. It's not just my street. It's the whole Black community that we need to embrace and to teach, and we teach by example. We must love one another.

Osa Russell-White
Oakland Chapter, CA

1972 Palo Alto, California: Woman with a bag of food at the People's Free Food Program, one of the survival programs.

We were in the West Berkeley branch. We opened the chapter in 1970 and between 1970 and 1971, there was a lot going on in Berkeley. It was an education in community organizing. I was there for two years when I was 18 and 19 years old.

We worked coordinating the Free Breakfast for School Children Program. We had a free after-school program, and a free clothing program. On the weekends, we went door to door in the community, building relationships with families. During the week we went to the UC Berkeley campus. We would sell over 3,000 Party newspapers.

One of the things that I remember most is meeting Jonathan Jackson, the brother of George Jackson [author of *Soledad Brother* (1970)]. Jonathan would come to the house in Berkeley and he would spend the night. I think he was just 16. I remember sitting with him on the front porch. He and I would watch my son play. Jonathan told me, "Your baby reminds me of how I was, when I was a baby."

A week later, Jonathan was killed in Marin County.

Life is one way in one moment, and then it can be totally something else in another moment. I will never forget meeting and getting to know him.

I want women and girls to know that in serving the community, it is important to understand that community is the social safety net. The most important aspect of serving the community is the significance of an individual to quietly observe, to listen attentively, and to offer connection. Community is made up of individuals; their strength lies in coalescing into units of being and doing. Those who serve must make sure that it has heart and meaning, both for them, and those they serve.

Sometimes we don't realize how the seeds planted in the '60s and '70s are carried forward, instead of around. I now understand the significance and importance of this early commitment and experience. It laid the foundation for the person I grew to be.

Deborrah Bremond
Berkeley Chapter, CA

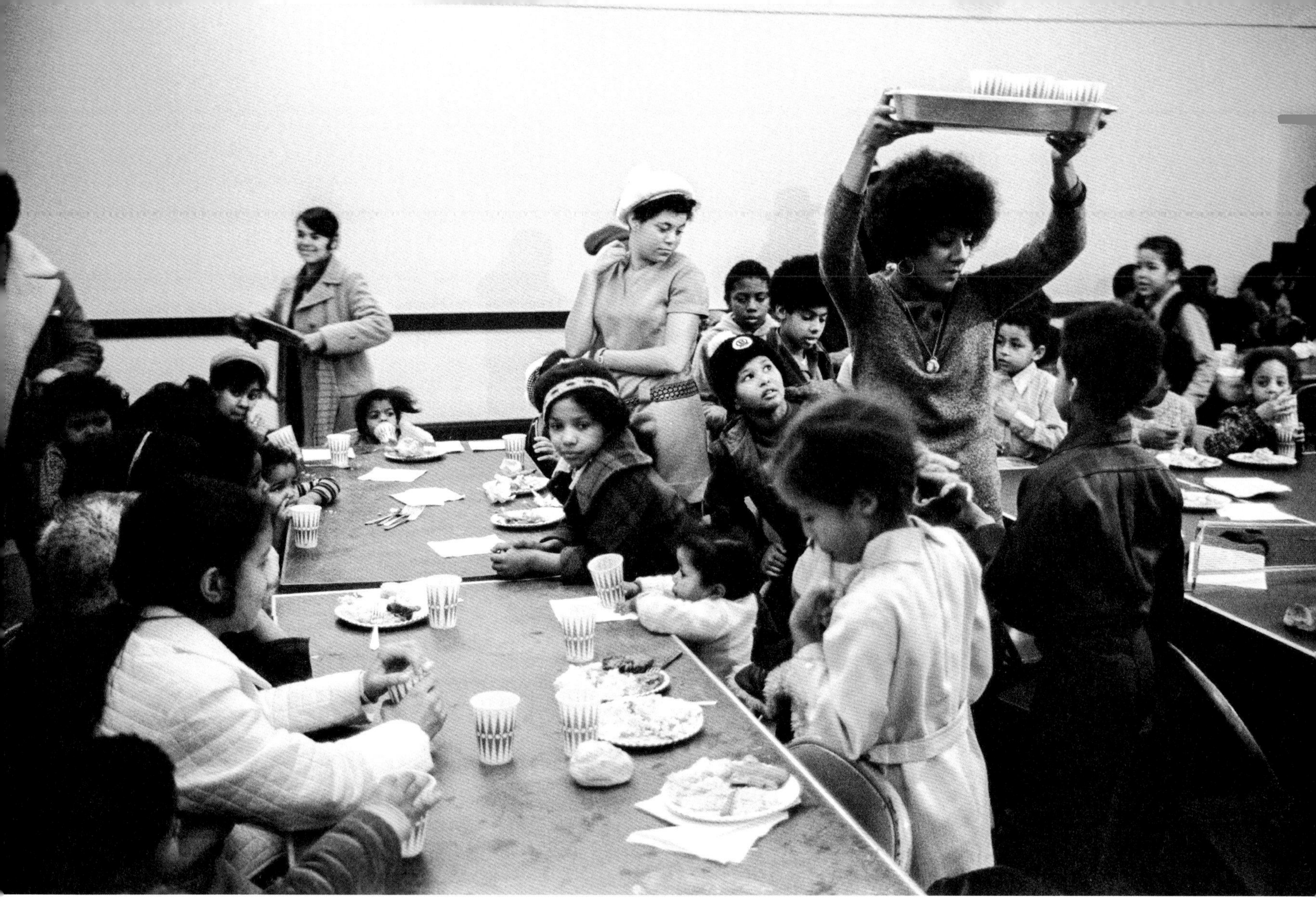

1971 New York, New York:
Black Panther Free Breakfast for
School Children Program.

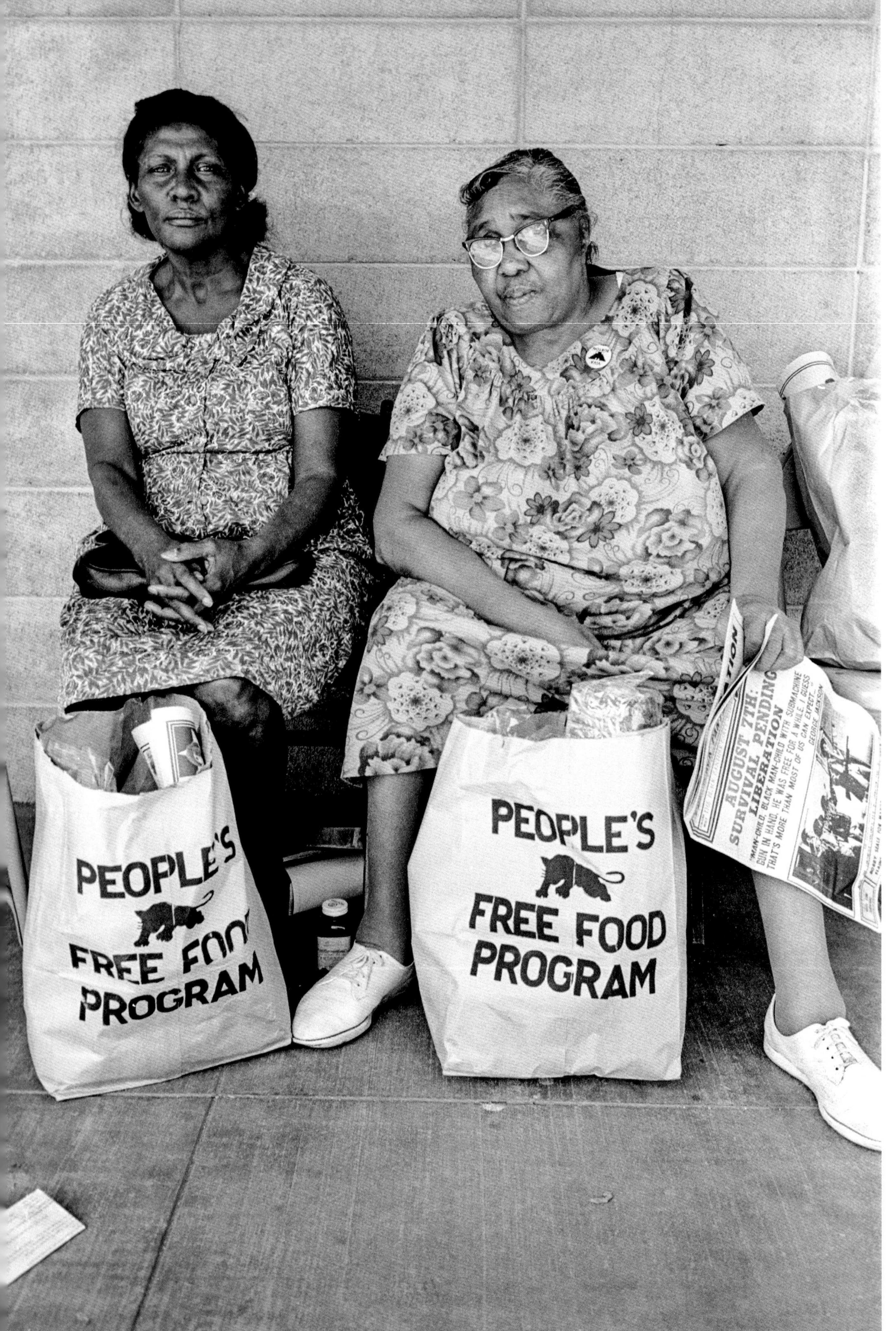
PEOPLE'S
FREE FOOD
PROGRAM

PEOPLE'S
FREE FOOD
PROGRAM

AUGUST 7TH:
SURVIVAL PENDING
LIBERATION

I was born and raised in Kansas City, Kansas, and I joined the Kansas City Chapter of the Black Panther Party when I was 18 years old. I left the U.S. with my husband, Pete O'Neal, when I was 19 years old, and we've been living in Tanzania since 1972. Some folks say a cute guy brought them to the Party. Well, that's what happened to me—and 52 years later, I'm still with that cute guy!

At that time, we were all watching what was going on across the country on TV. I remember seeing images of Brother Pete O'Neal announcing the formation of the Kansas City Chapter, cutting out newspaper articles and pasting them on my bedroom wall. When I joined the Party, Pete was on tour. He was visiting the Omaha Chapter, the Des Moines Chapter, and maybe Oklahoma. He was gone almost a month before I met him.

In the interim, I was experiencing actual community service, feeding breakfast to the children, interacting with mothers—mostly welfare mothers, who couldn't get transport to see their incarcerated family members. We would arrange transport for them. We started the Little Bobby Hutton Medical Clinic. There was such camaraderie. We were a family.

Being a Panther taught me how to work hard, and to this day, if I'm not doing community service, I get right on it, 'cause that's in our blood and it's in our bones. My experiences gave me a global perspective. It gave me pride in myself. I just kept increasing that perspective. I feel so blessed to be carrying that Panther woman inside me, as I know all of y'all do. It's a blessing.

Mama Charlotte Hill O'Neal
Kansas City Chapter, KS / Tanzania, Africa

1972 Palo Alto, California: Two women with bags of food at the People's Free Food Program, one of the Panther's survival programs.

October 5, 1974 *Sleep Long, Be Strong Little One For Tomorrow's A New Day,* artwork by M. Gayle Asali Dickson.

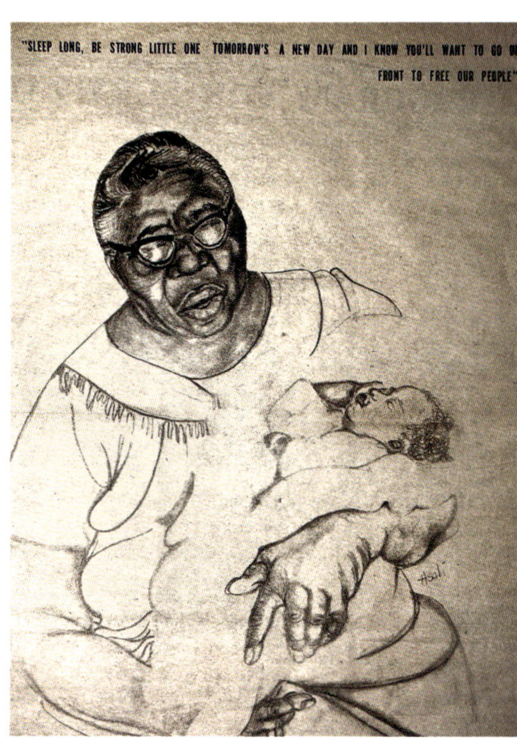

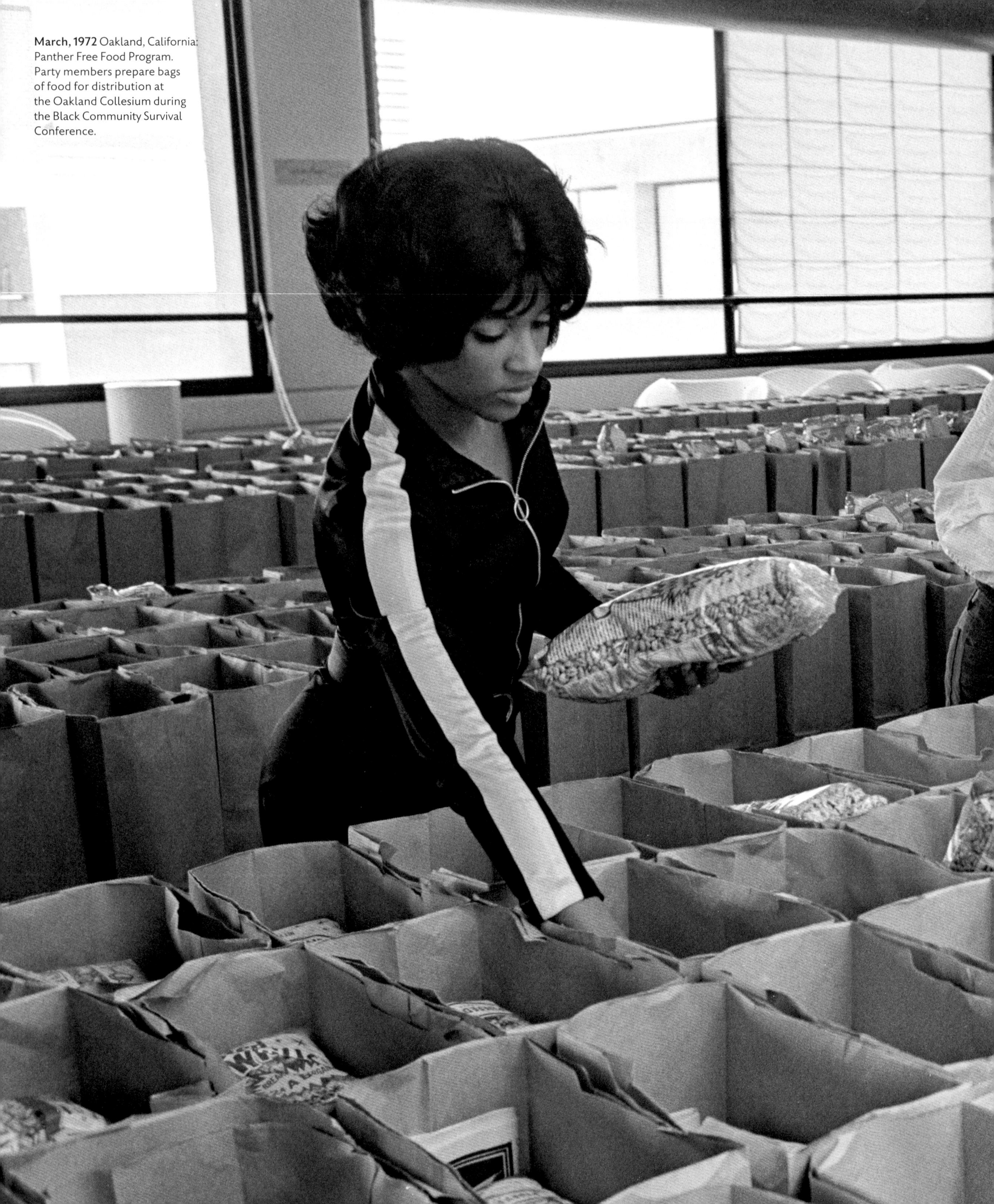

March, 1972 Oakland, California:
Panther Free Food Program.
Party members prepare bags
of food for distribution at
the Oakland Collesium during
the Black Community Survival
Conference.

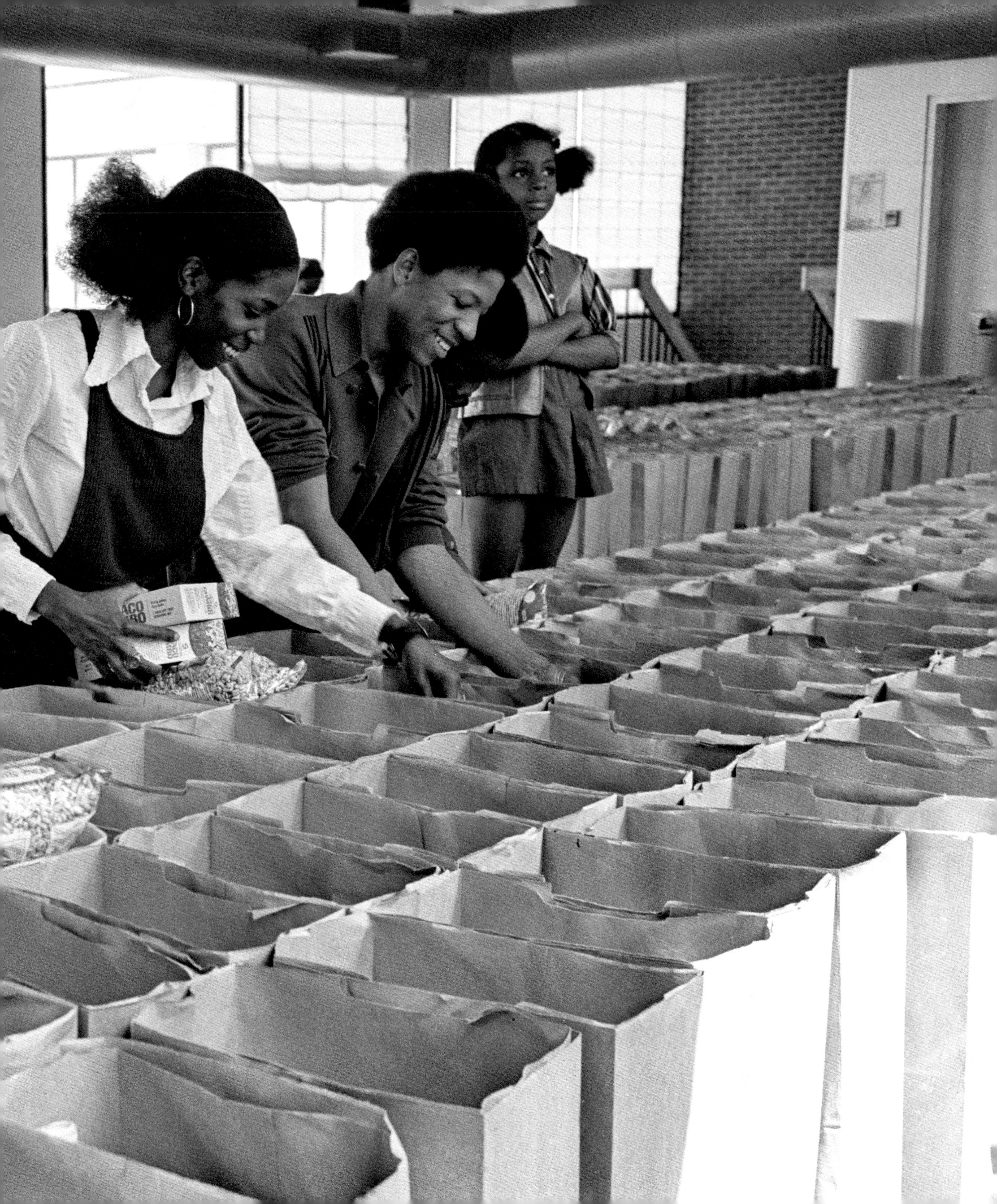

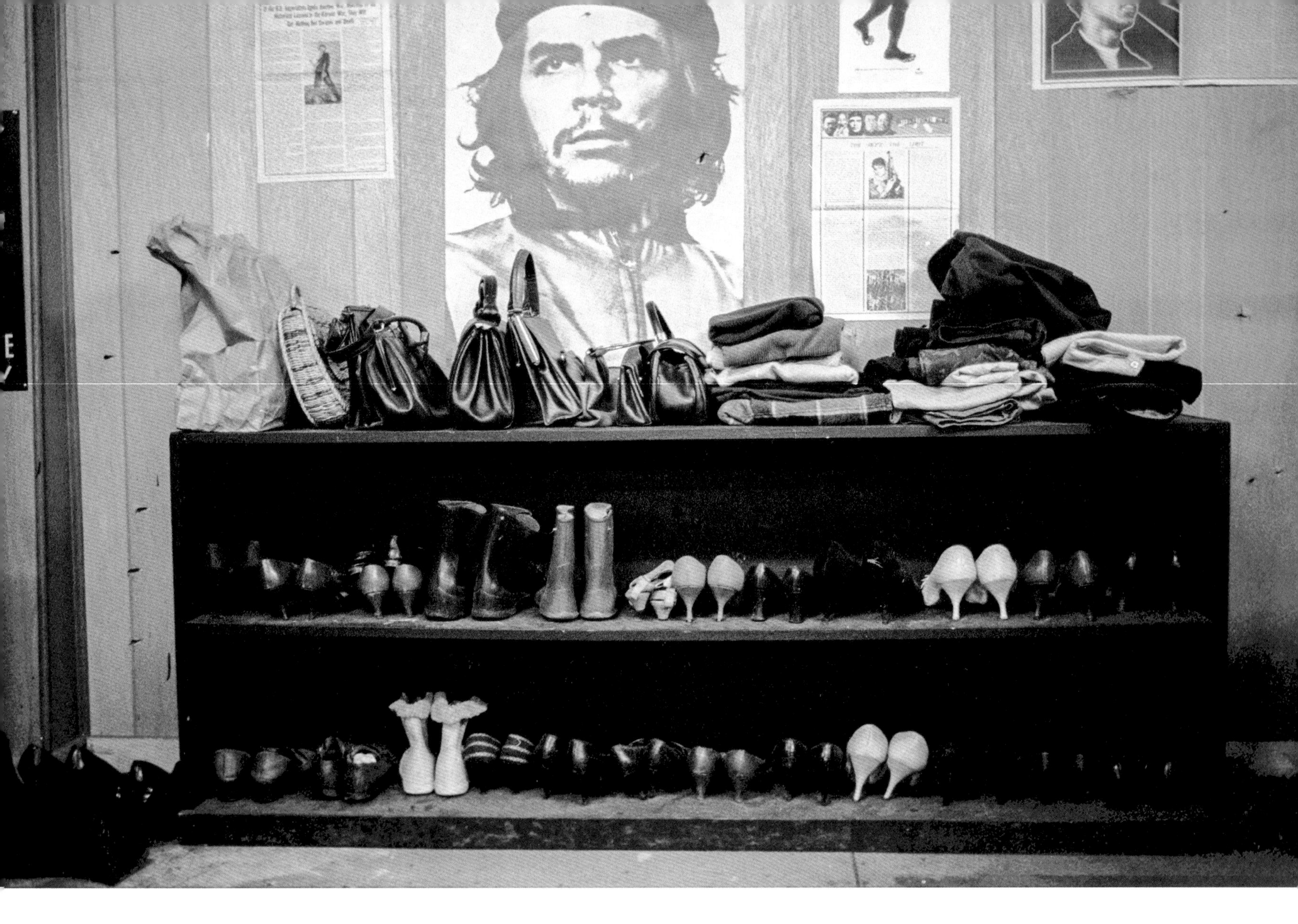

1970 Toldeo, Ohio: Black Panther
Free Shoe Program.

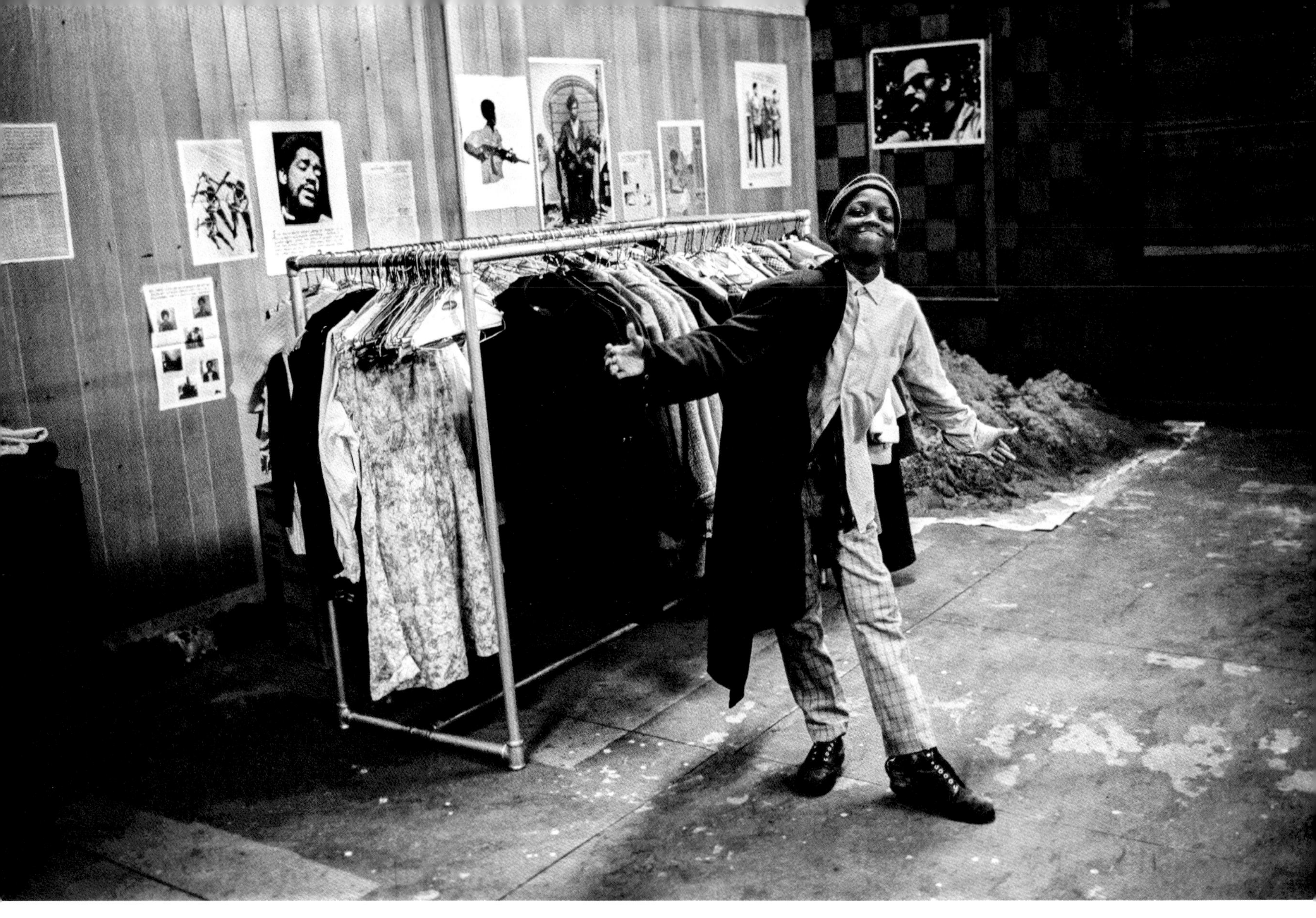

1970 Toldeo, Ohio: Free Clothing Program, one of the Panther Party's Community Survival Programs. A proud young boy tries on a winter coat to take home.

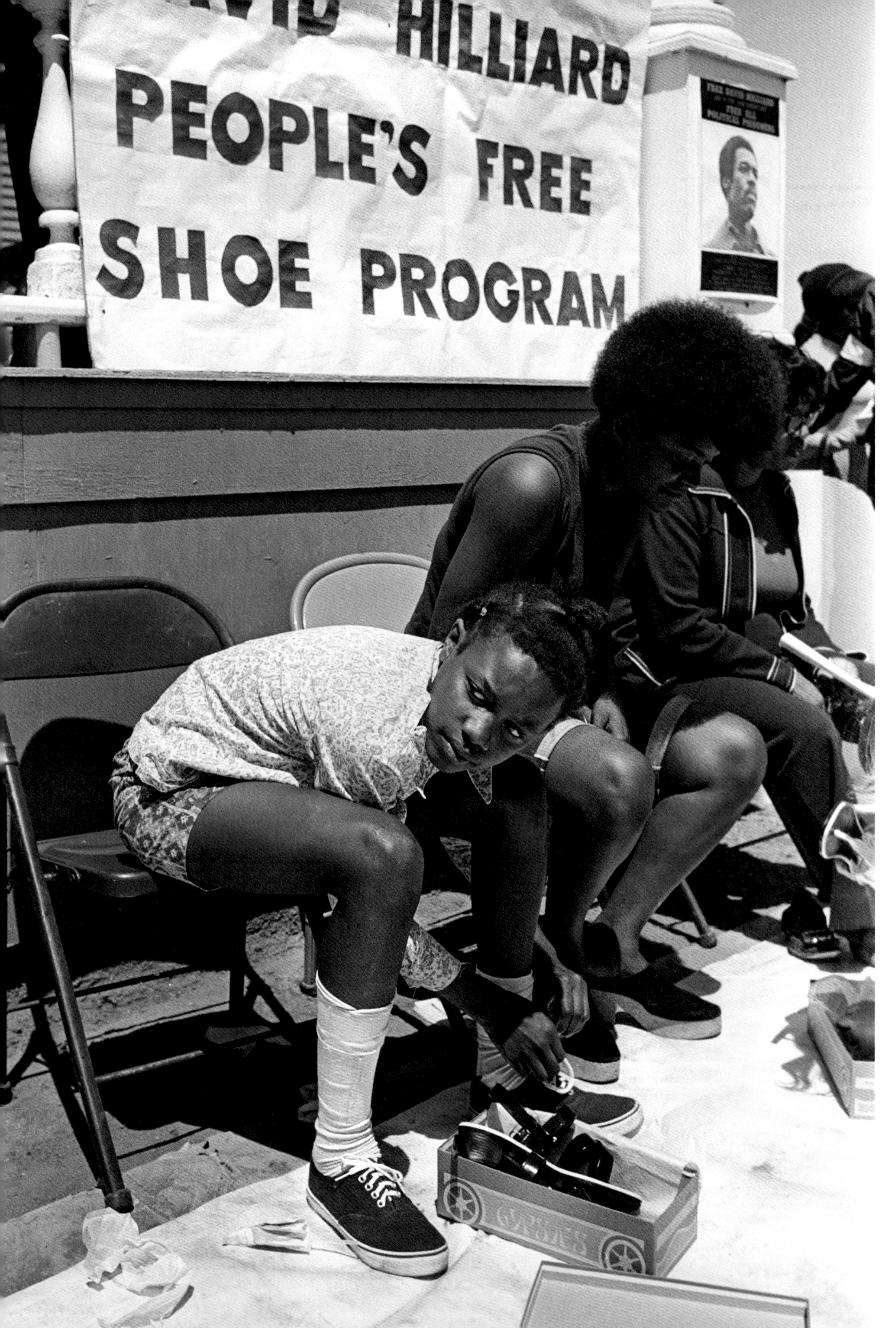
HILLIARD
PEOPLE'S FREE
SHOE PROGRAM
FREE DAVID HILLIARD
FREE ALL
POLITICAL PRISONERS

My mother was 21 when she joined the party. She often worked out of the main office in North Philly and at the People's Free Medical Clinic in North Philly. Most days, however, Mama Aisha was at the West Philly branch, where she helped set up and run the Free Breakfast for School Children Program and the Free Clothing Program.

When my mother heard about the BPP's food program for children, she said that it would be a labor of love for an organization to commit to feeding children every single day. Skeptical, she went to see for herself, and saw BPP members feeding children. Thinking it wasn't a daily thing, she returned a few days later and then, she joined. She saw that the BPP members were absolutely committed, and she joined them to help make the BPP's vision for Black children's wellbeing a reality.

She loved the self-determination, the BPP's Ten Point Program, and the political education classes. Aisha also appreciated the historical, economic, and political education that came to her via the BPP. She shared this knowledge and these resources openly for years.

My mother's most memorable work was her contribution to the Free Breakfast for School Children Program. She loved the children and they loved her back. This love for the people required sacrifices and she was a person beyond reproach. Aisha would want girls and women of all ages to know that, historically, women have always been an instrumental and integral part of our fight for justice.

My mother would often quote a Ghanian proverb: "If you educate a man, you educate an individual, but if you educate a woman you educate a family, a nation."

Saundra Dickerson, also known as Aisha El-Mekki
Philadelphia Chapter, PA *(a remembrance by her son, Sharif El-Mekki)*

March 31, 1972 Oakland, California: Free Shoe Program. Black Panther Party's Black Community Survival Conference in DeFremery Park.

I was born in Oakland, California. I've lived other places, but I keep coming home to Oakland.

As scrappy as Oakland is, I just love it. I was 19 when I joined the Party in Berkeley. I started working with what was called the Samuel Napier Intercommunal Youth Institute. My mother did real estate work for the Party. She invited Huey over to our house for lunch. I had just come back from college —even though I came from an activist family, I never internalized it till I went to college. I met Huey at that lunch. He definitely was "the older man," plus, he was this iconic figure at that time. Our relationship developed really quickly, like that night.

That was my introduction to the Party. I never went back to school in Oregon. I worked at the Food Co-op in Berkeley. The children came to the lunch counter there. They had collection cans. They were getting donations for the Free Breakfast for School Children Program and selling newspapers. They told me they were at this school on Shattuck Avenue. I started going down to the school, though I hadn't connected the dots that the school had anything to do with Huey. And then, of course, I started working in this school for children of Party members. I remember telling Huey, *That's my school. That's the Samuel Napier Intercommunal Youth Institute.*

It was Huey who introduced me to the Party, but it was the kids who really drew me in. It was the children.

I want women to know that it's so important to use your voice. And we must take care of ourselves emotionally and spiritually. It's all about balance; we can't serve our community if we don't take care of ourselves. Start serving the people by taking care of yourself, and being in balance. Know that you have a voice.

Fredrika Newton
Berkeley Branch, CA / Oakland Chapter, CA

1969 Berkeley, California: "Free Huey" rally in Provo Park. The official name of the park was Constitution Park, but it became Provo Park, in honor of the Dutch Provos. In 1983 it was re-named Martin Luther King Jr. Civic Center Park.

September 28, 1974 *Birth Gave Me A Right That No One Can Claim … We Hold The Power of the World in Our Hands!*, artwork by M. Gayle Asali Dickson.

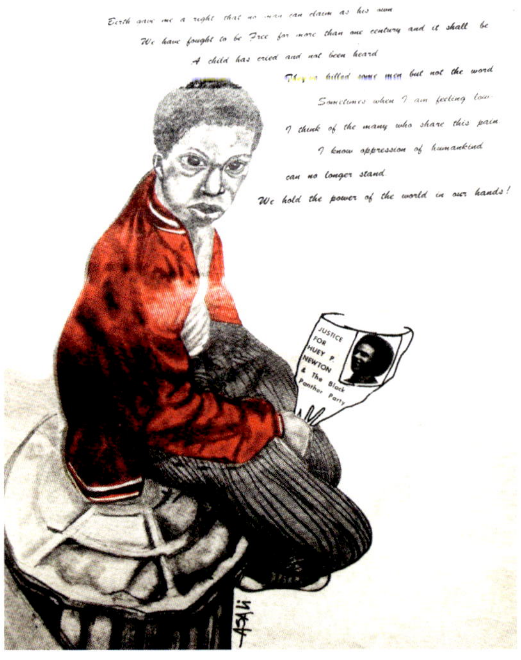

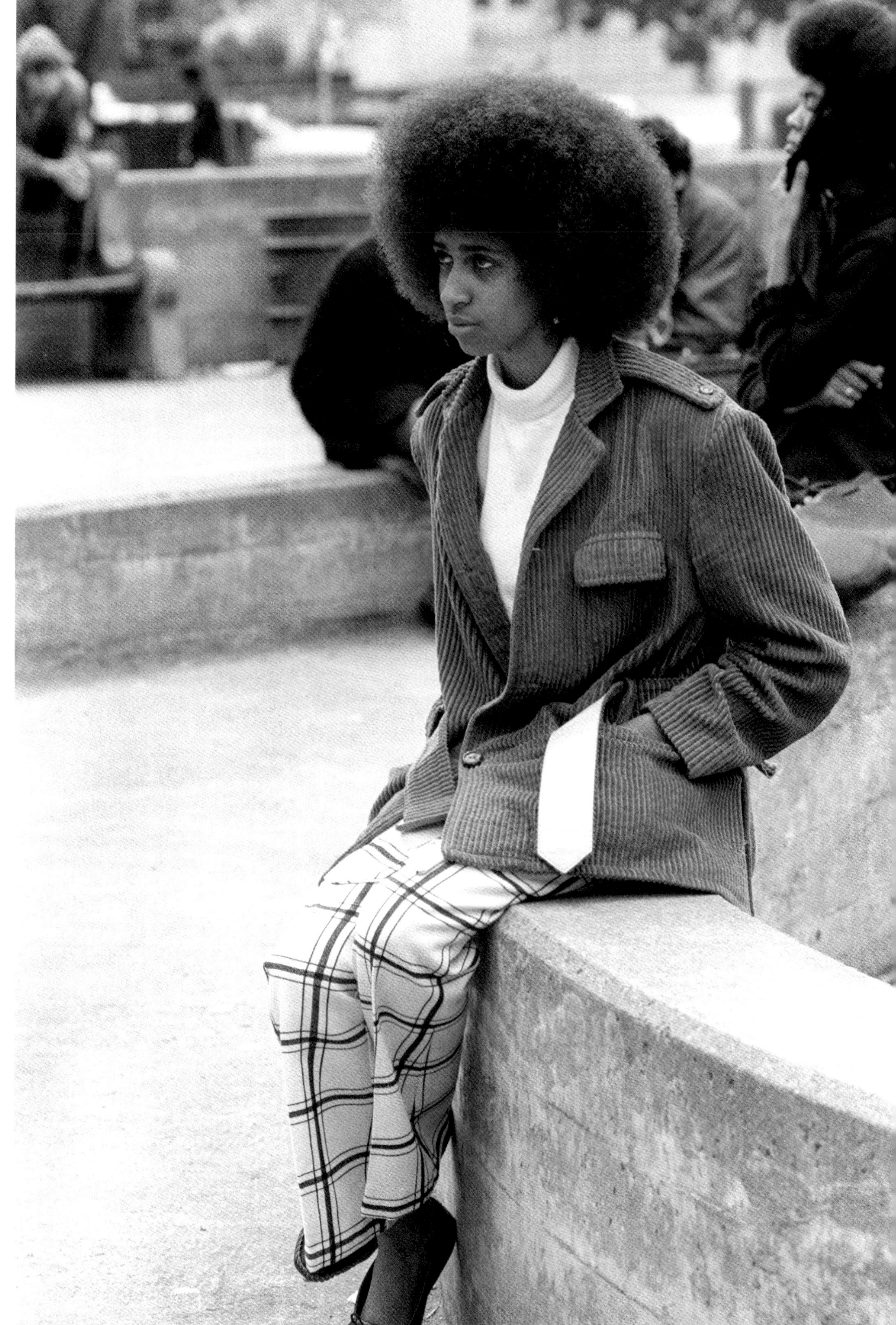

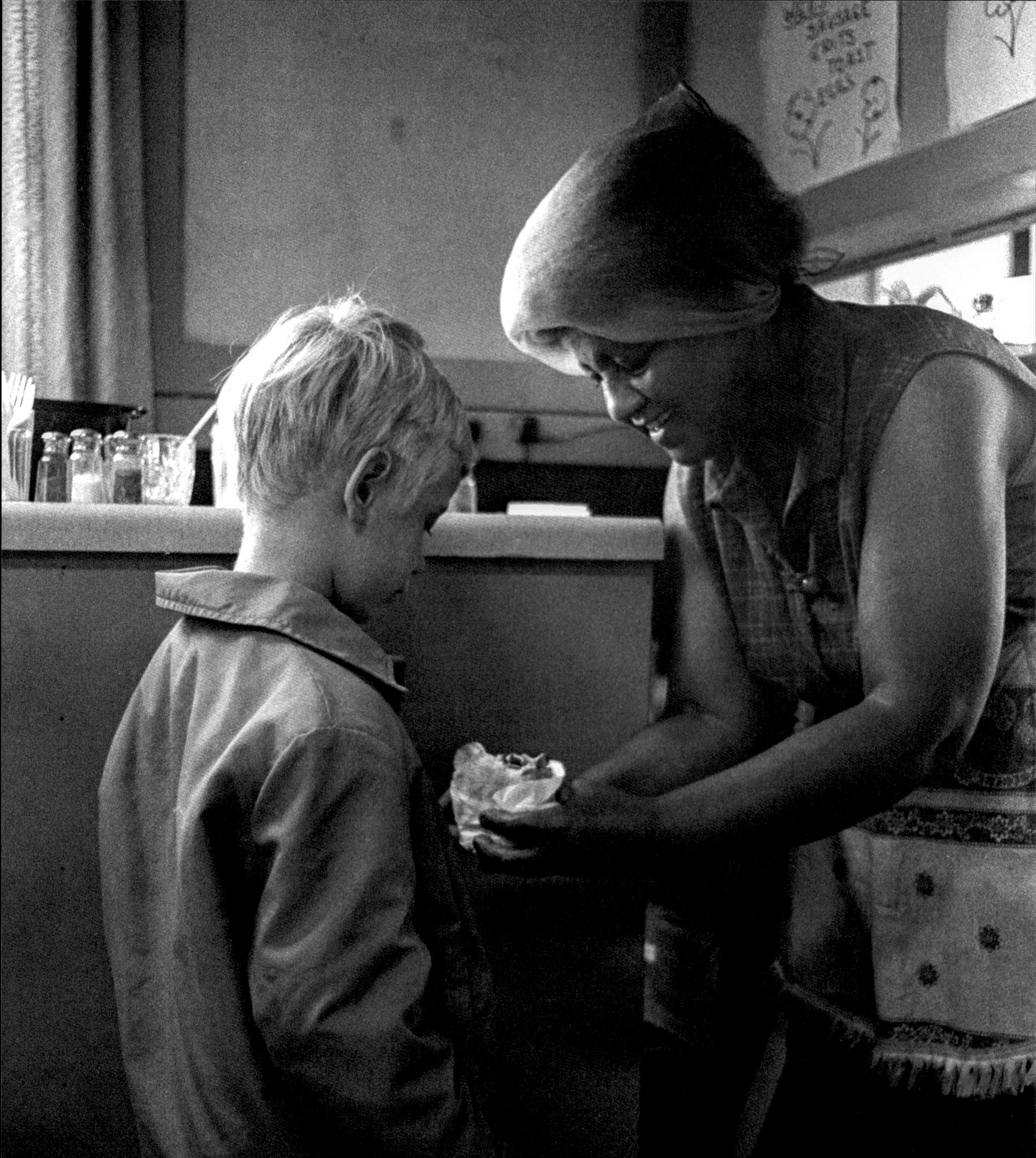

I joined the Party in the first chapter to form outside of Oakland: Seattle. I was 20 at the time. What really drew me to the party was the Survival Programs. It was the opportunity to do something, everything, from free breakfast programs to medical clinics.

My most memorable work was waking up early and going to serve at one of our five breakfast locations, selling Party newspapers on a regular basis, working in the medical clinic, and helping with the Free Busing to Prisons Program for families of incarcerated women and men. I absolutely loved working with the community members who would come and volunteer to feed the children hot breakfast every day. Seeing those beautiful faces come and eat and then go to school… I knew that was going to make for a better day for them, because they were fed a warm breakfast.

Our children should not go to school hungry. Our children need to have their brains and their spirit nourished.

I played a central role in the Free Medical Clinic in Seattle also. It is interesting how the party would recognize your skills and leverage them. My skills were administrative and organizational so I was able to help set up the medical clinic, and coordinate the volunteer nurses and doctors from the University of Washington Medical Center.

Around the time that the comrades were reassigned to Oakland, Elmer Dixon, second in command, was set up on false charges and jailed, I was given Elmer's leadership role until Elmer was released.

Young women, educate yourselves! *Knowledge is power.* Educate yourselves about our history, about our innate skill to survive. We have been doing what we've been doing for years. We *learned* by doing. Young folks, carry the baton and move forward. Seek out and appreciate your elders while you're educating yourself. While we're still here, download our brains, our souls, our spirits, and our experiences. Carry this forward for the next generation.

Rosita Holland Thomas
Seattle Chapter, WA

1969 Oakland, California: Free Breakfast for School Children Program at St. Augustine's Church. Ms. Woods gives loving care to a child.

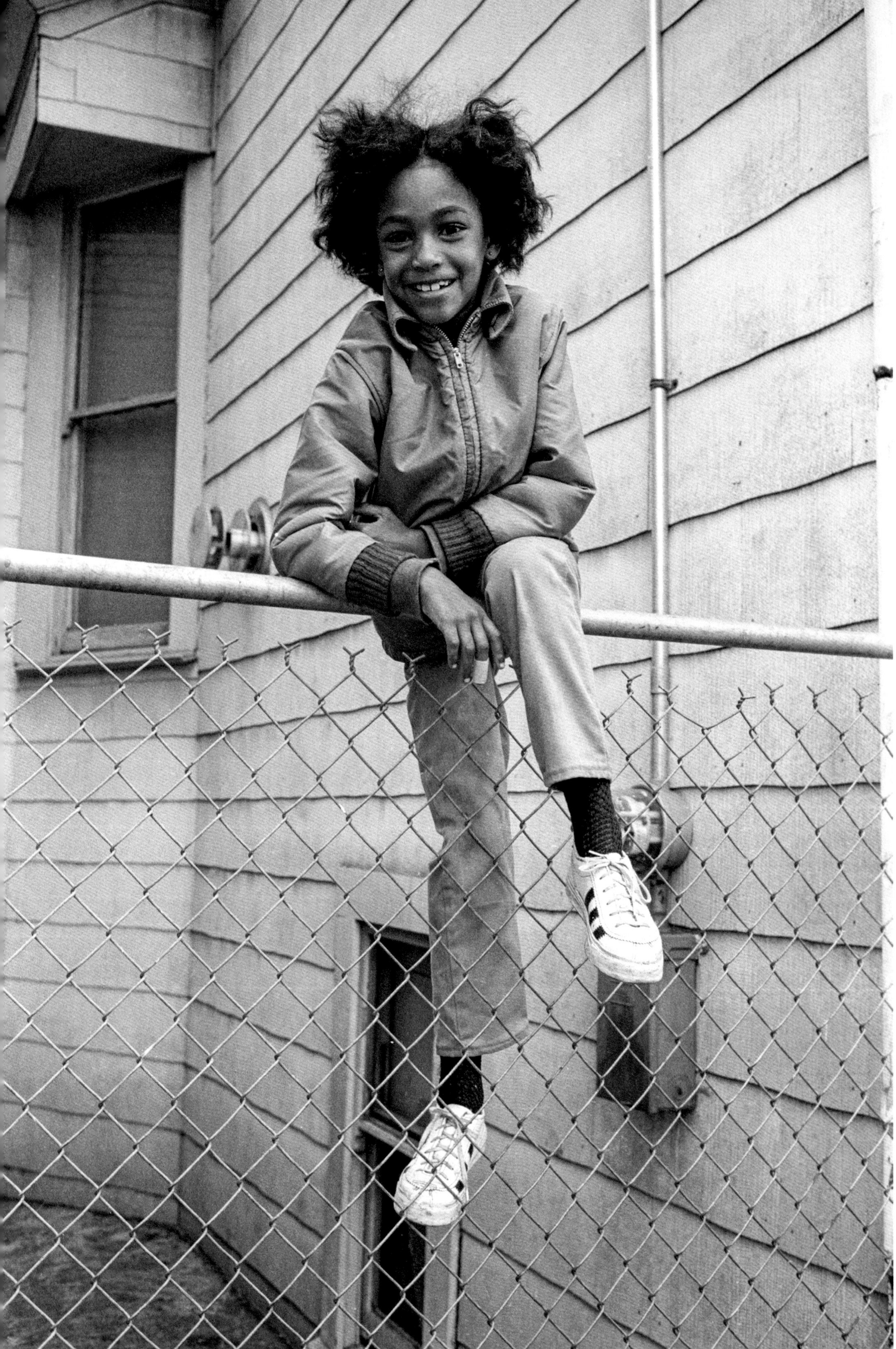

What drew me to the BPP? I was, what, 17? I went to Temple University in Philly, to the Revolutionary People's Constitutional Convention, and Huey was speaking. I'm looking around and I said, "Damn, how do they know how to do all this?" That impressed me: talking about rewriting the Constitution.

I started going to the office in Philly. It was right across the street from my high school, West Philadelphia High. Then I served in Richmond, VA, Winton-Salem, NC, and then I was asked to move to Oakland, where I worked at the Oakland Community School for years. Because of the school, I became an educator.

Haven Henderson
Philadelphia Chapter, PA. / Winston-Salem Chapter, NC /
Oakland Chapter, CA

One of my most memorable experiences is the Free Breakfast for School Children Program. No question. I mean—the whole idea of it!

When our captain would pick us up, it was still before dawn. When we got into that van, I remember that the sky was doing that beautiful thing it does, before nighttime turns to daylight. I remember the way those children looked at me and all of us Panthers who fed them. It was love. I will never, ever, ever forget that.

The breakfast program was at Father Earl Neal's church, St Augustine's, in North Oakland. We were able to address the needs of hungry children, to see them smile, laugh, and just be happy. Sometimes their parents would be there too, and we would feed them, of course. I wouldn't have been able to say it then, but now I know I was doing something wonderful for my people.

One thing I want women to know, especially at this time, is that you don't have to be hard, you don't have to be like a man, to have courage. The combination of taking care of yourself and exhibiting courage allows you to be a thinker, a doer, and a giver.

Recently it occurred to me what givers we were; how spiritual it was for us to get up in the early morning to feed children. Nobody paid us. If we're on this Earth, we are here to serve. I don't think that we were sent here randomly.

Regina Jennings
Philadelphia Chapter, PA / Oakland Chapter, CA

1971 Oakalnd, California: Sadiqa, daughter of Brenda Bay, scales a fence at the Children's House, a dormitory for children of Black Panther Party members.

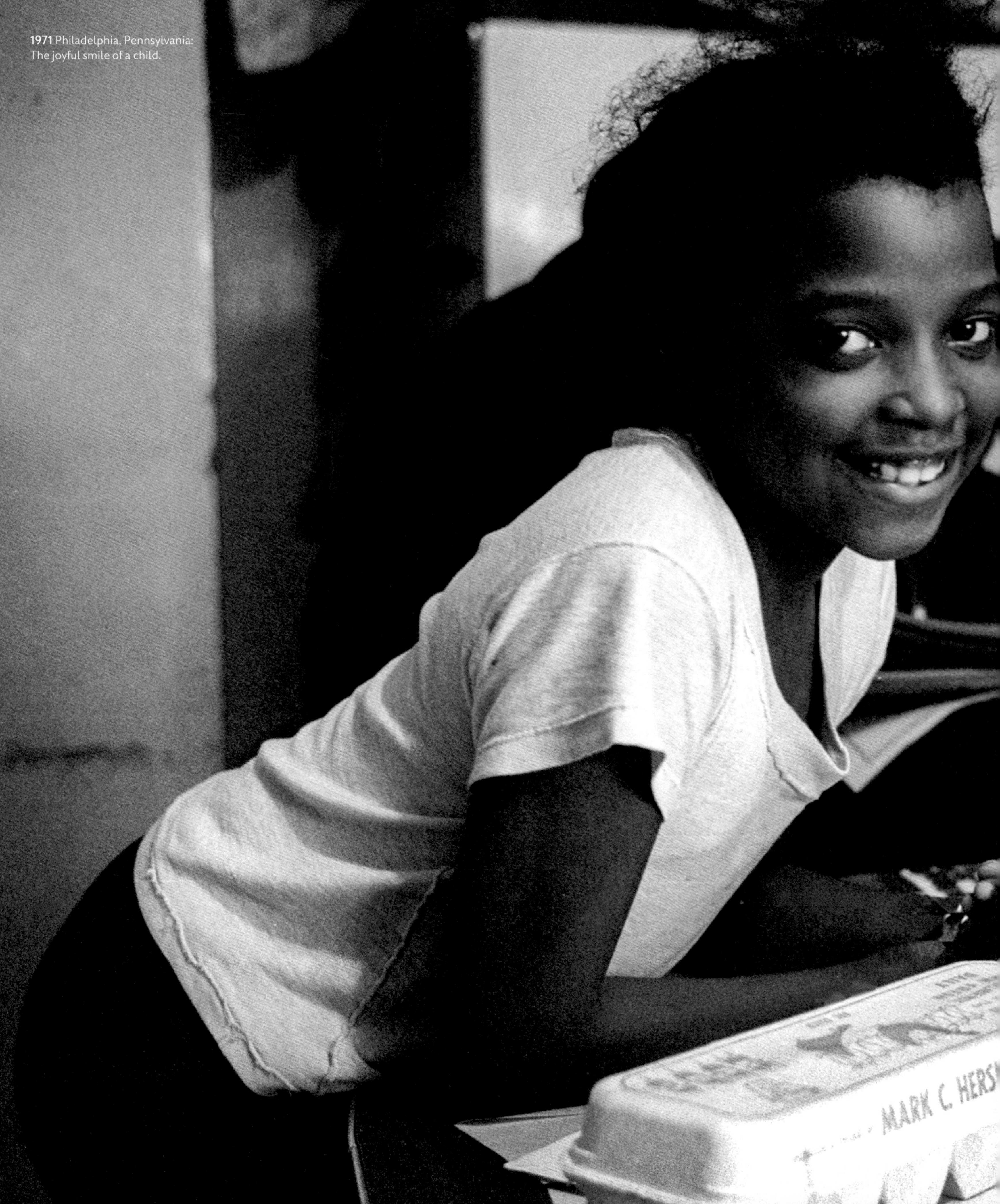

1971 Philadelphia, Pennsylvania:
The joyful smile of a child.

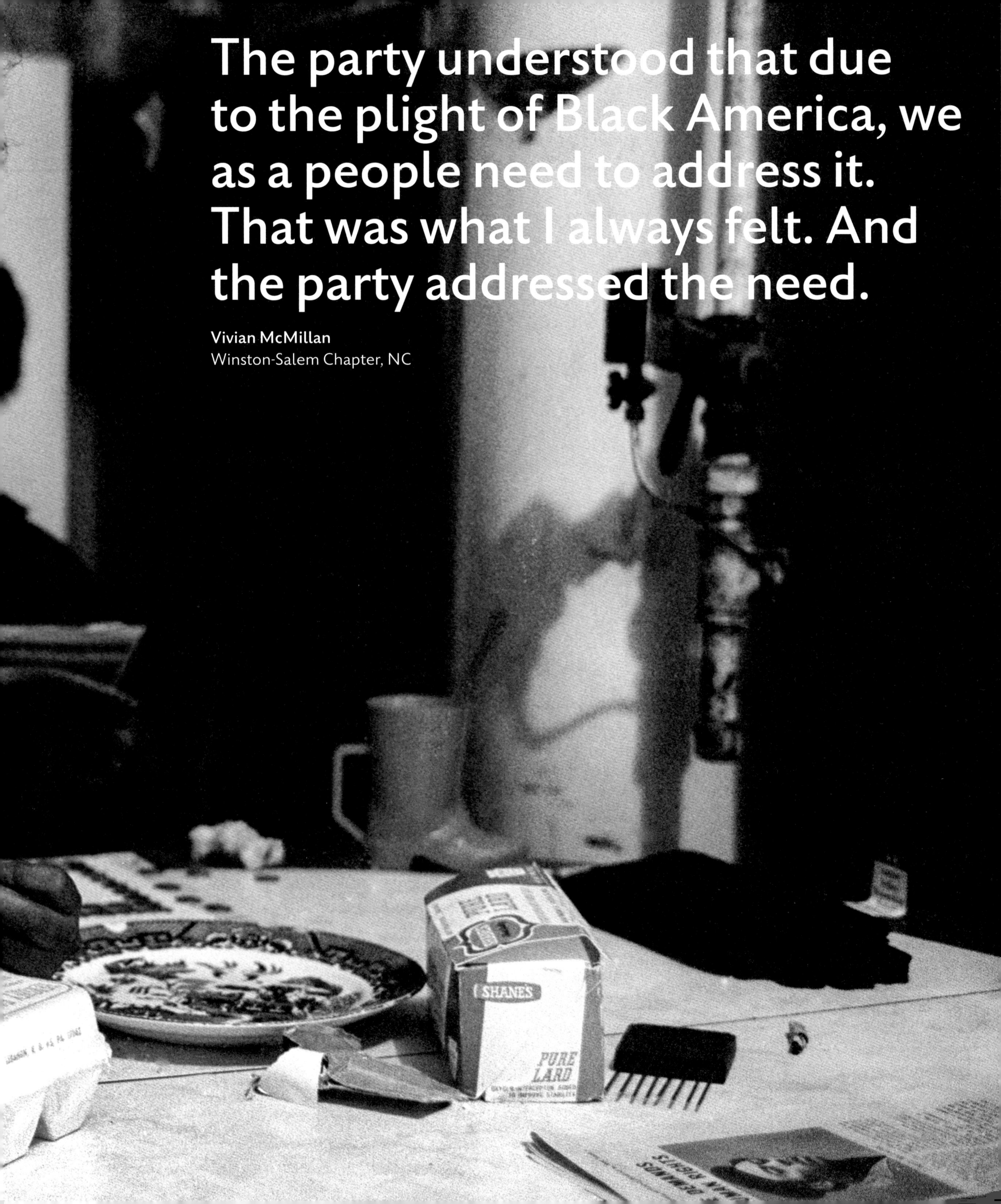

The party understood that due to the plight of Black America, we as a people need to address it. That was what I always felt. And the party addressed the need.

Vivian McMillan
Winston-Salem Chapter, NC

My mom joined the Black Panther Party after participating in the free breakfast program; she was 15. She was sneaking to do it. She was pregnant with me when she started living at the house of the Black Panther Chapter in Berkeley.

I think that was one thing about my mom. She was really resilient. Her life went full circle. She started in the Black Panther Party serving in the free breakfast program. She ended up being a chef, but doing it with the sense of service. For 35 years, she cooked food for people who struggled during the holidays. She would actually make a full meal for the family to eat for a week because she said, "You know, when you have Thanksgiving, you have food, you can eat as much as you want, and I want them to have that experience."

Today, I find myself recalling what my mom taught me: even if it's not what's popular to do, it doesn't mean that it's wrong. She gave me that confidence, and now people are thinking about and doing things that she was saying years ago.

Evelyn Cheatham
Berkeley and Oakland Chapters, CA
(a remembrance by her daughter, Erica Parker Alabi)

1969 Oakland, California: Children eat a nutritious meal at the Black Panther Free Breakfast for School Children Program at St. Augustine's Church.

August 19, 1972 *Vote for Survival*, artwork by M. Gayle Asali Dickson.

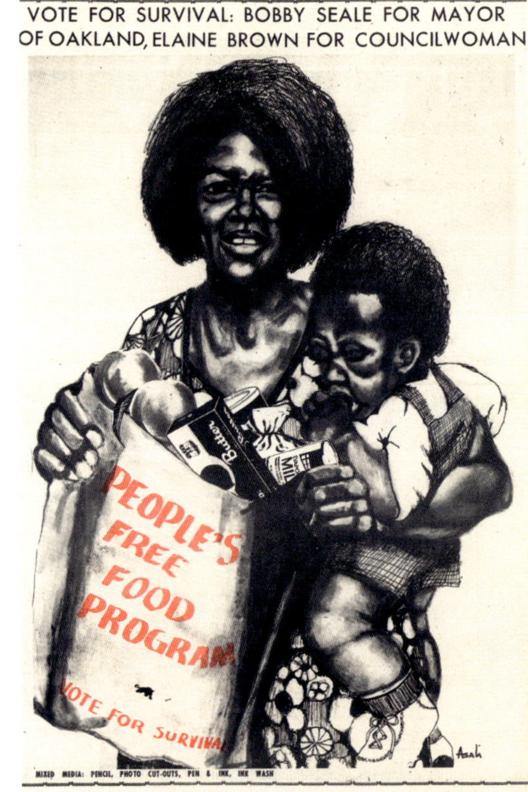

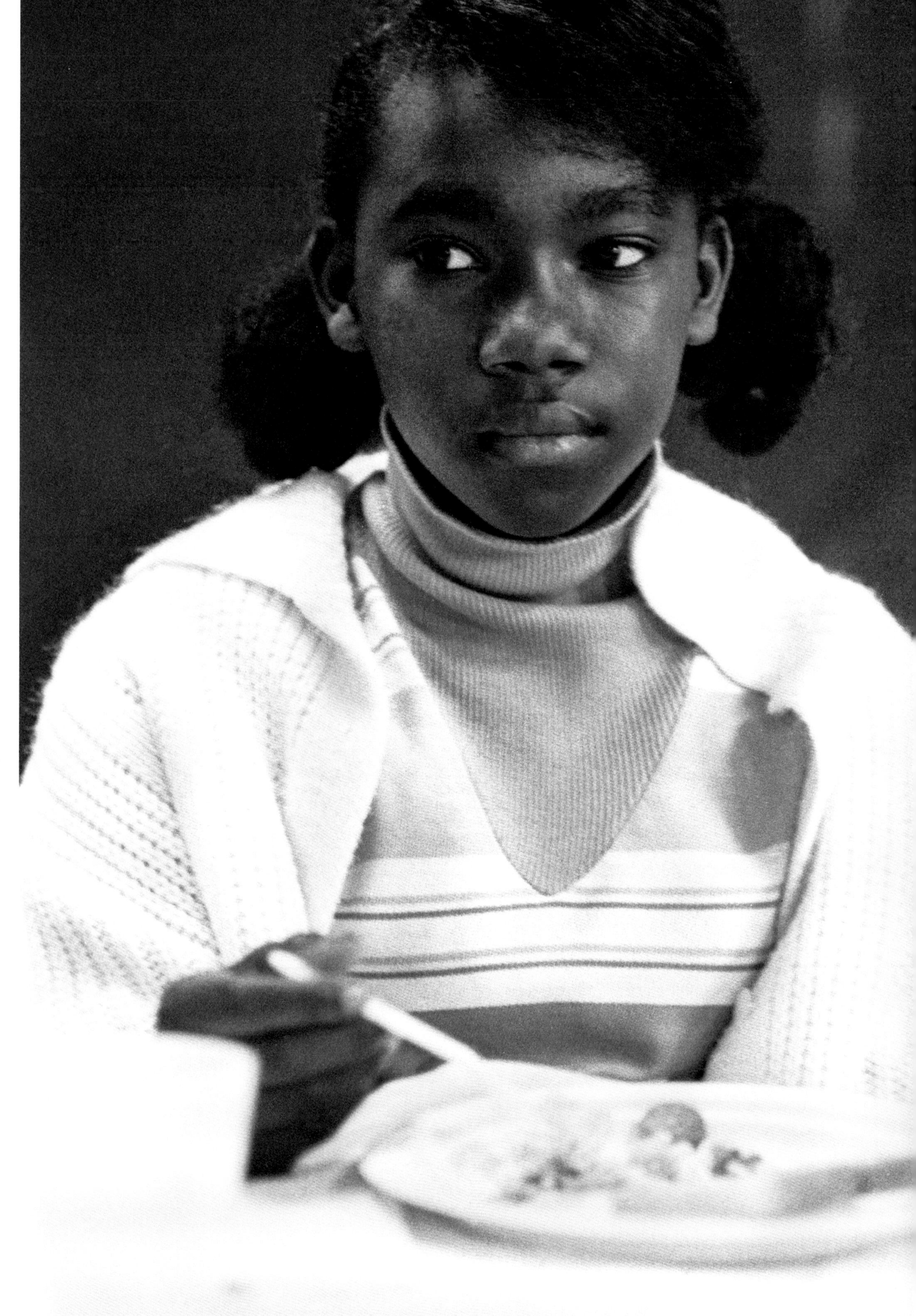

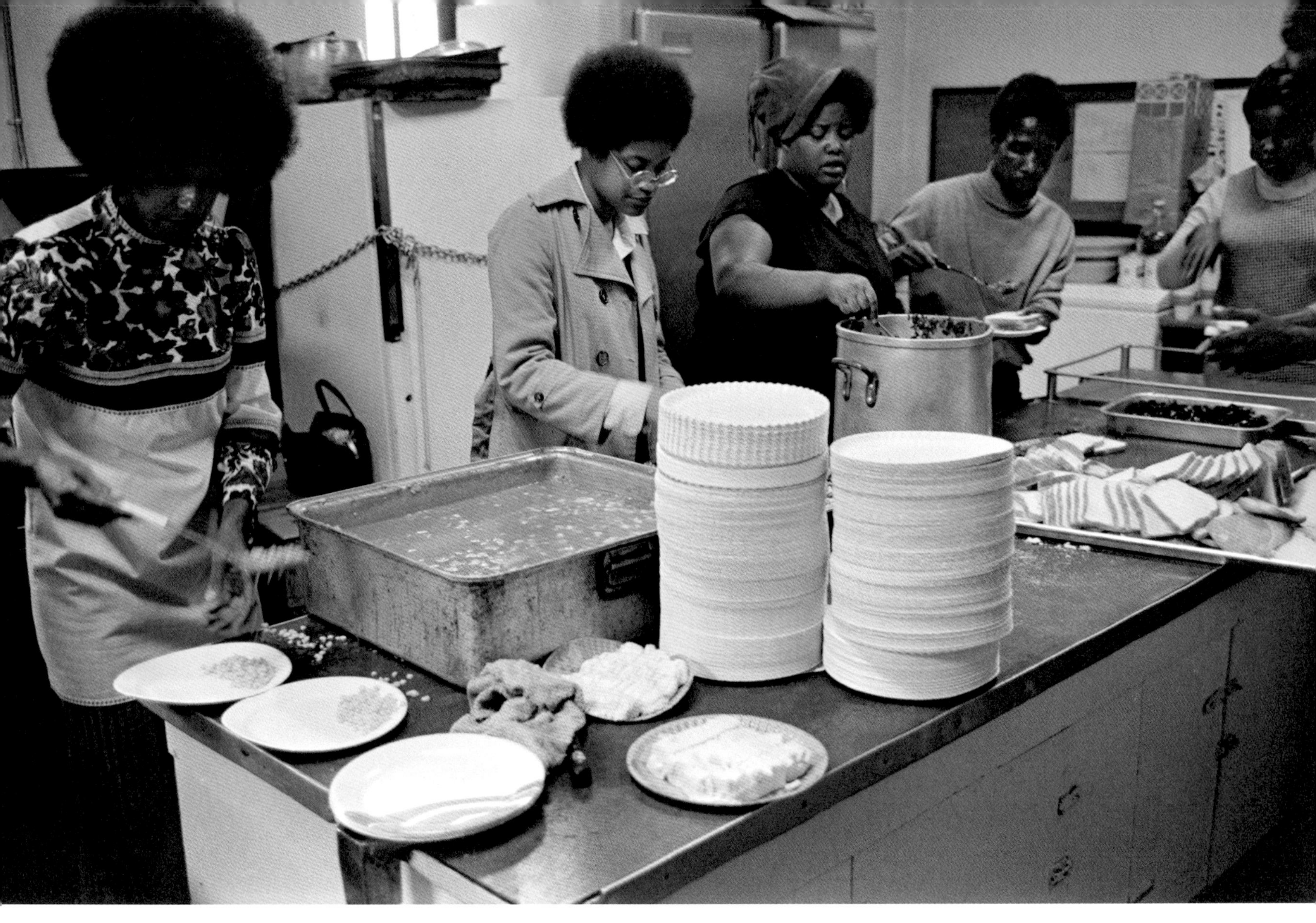

1970 Washington, DC:
The Revolutionary People's
Constitutional Convention
(RPCC) was a conference
organized by the Black Panther
Party (BPP) that was held in
Philadelphia from September
4–7, 1970. The RPCC represented
one of the largest gatherings
of radical activists across
movements and issues in the
United States.

1970 Washington, DC:
Women of the Black Panther
Party prepare food during
a rally for Black Panther's
upcoming constitutional
convention.

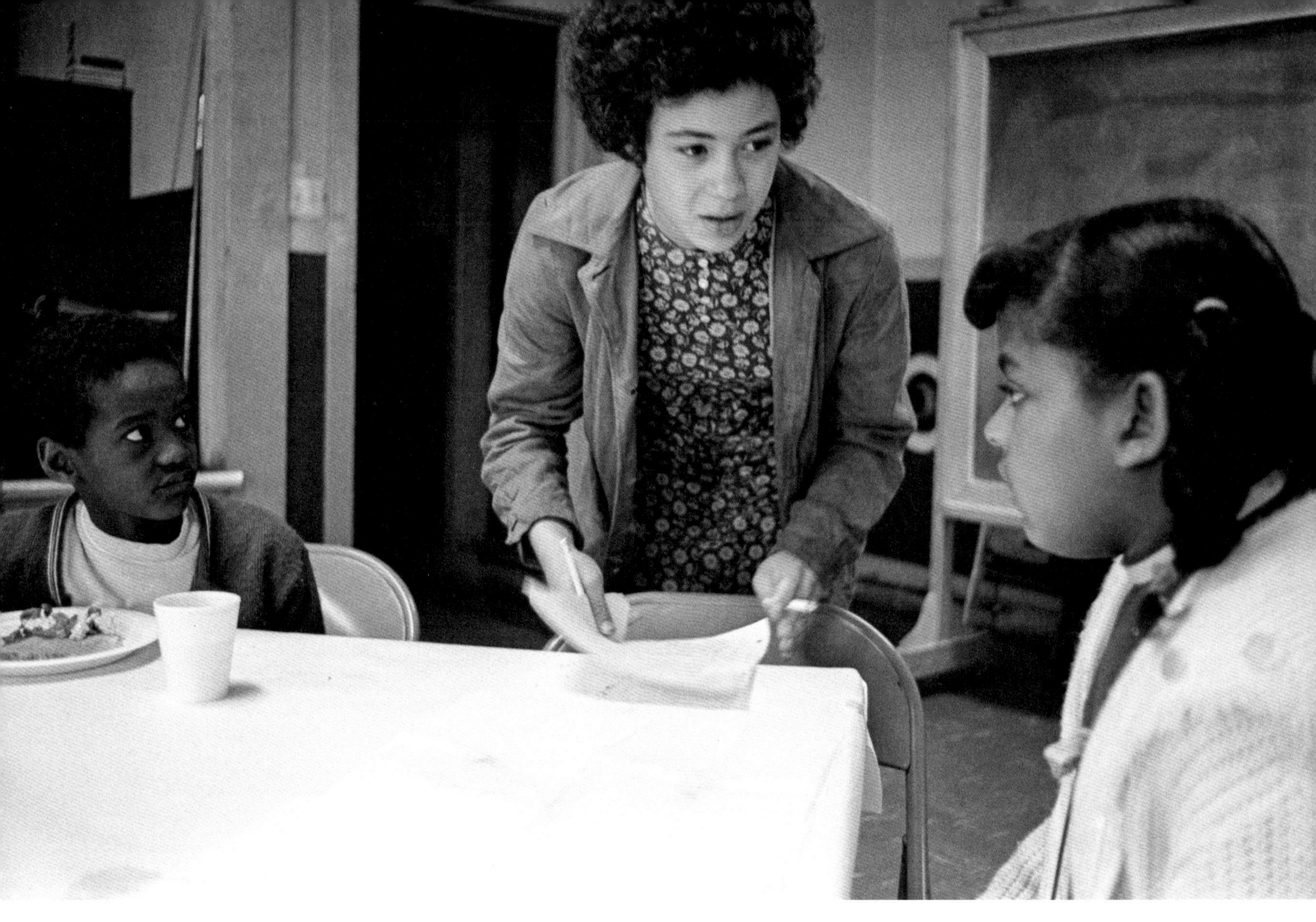

1969 Oakland, California: Party member Shelly Sanders serves food to children at the Black Panther Free Breakfast for School Children Program at St. Augustine's Church.

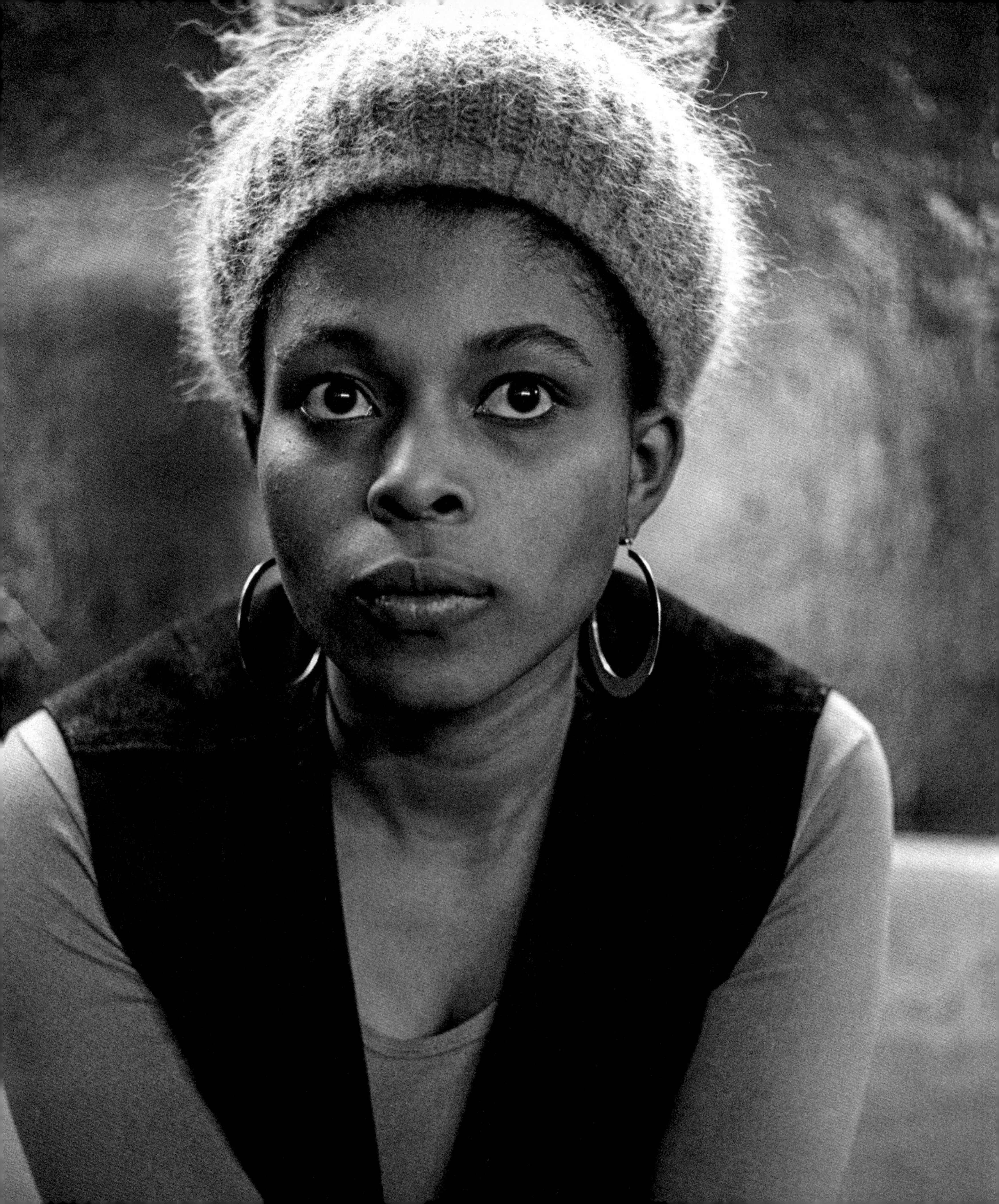

Before we began sickle cell testing and education, the doctors said it was a Black disease and therefore there was no funding for research. They really didn't care. Marie Roper, a sister in the Party, lived with sickle cell and died from sickle cell. She was a Panther in Harlem who went on to serve in Oakland. So, we knew the pain of this disease first-hand because we saw it, sitting at the hospital with her.

My most memorable work was the political education classes. We taught those classes outside of the Harlem office, on the street. These were the most rewarding moments for me. I was about 5'1", 93 pounds. I was little, but I became big when I stepped out of that office onto that sidewalk. I was also scared to death, because people of all walks of life showed up. Jamal Joseph, my good brother, showed me how to find my voice, my strength. Once I did find my voice, well—it was on and poppin'.

One Wednesday night, I was giving a P.E. class and there was a college student. She wore a pleated skirt. She was a girly girl: very ladylike, very soft spoken. This sister morphed into Assata Shakur. She was at one of the P.E. classes I led. I'm not saying that's what made her join the Party. I just hope it was.

It doesn't matter whether we knew it or not, but once our Comrade Sisters left the Party, they still served the people. So many of our sisters went into nursing, into teaching. We are caregivers. When we left the Party, it probably wasn't conscious, but what we learned went with us anyway, because that's what we're still doing. We're serving the people.

I love you, my sisters.

Claudia Chesson Williams
Corona, Queens Chapter, NY / Harlem Branch, NY

1970 New York, New York: Joanne Chesimard / Assata Shakur, at the Harlem office.

I first met Joan in the 7th grade. We were both 11 years old. Together, we attended Carver Junior High and Jefferson High School, on the Eastside, in the heart of South Central Los Angeles; Joan was the student-body president at Jefferson. Before, during, and after our stints in the BPP, we remained very close. So much so that my three kids still speak of her as "Auntie."

Witty, zany, whacky, sometimes corny, she was an easy classmate, colleague, and comrade. Joan was very academic and had a way with words—and, dare I say, she was able to get Bill Cosby to come and do an assembly during our senior year? That was a major accomplishment as, at that time, his career was shooting straight up. Yep, Joan could talk you into doing, giving, partnering, like few others I've known.

And she had connections. A few years ago, I began working on a project in Rwanda, East Africa. I sent out a crowd-sourced email to everyone I thought might have any knowledge of non-profit work in East Africa. Joan was one of the first to respond with two resources with who I was able to connect and who helped me greatly. Joan was always looked up to by her siblings.

Family relations were a struggle, as with many of us, when Joan first joined the Party. That was short-lived, changing after her son Geronimo arrived.

While she was in the Party, Joan worked on the newspaper, in procurement, legal defense, and various administrative capacities. She coordinated many of the programs at the Oakland Community Learning Center. She was always good with words, written and oral, and served as spokesperson for various Party programs and activities. A dedicated, loyal comrade and friend, we miss her.

Joan Alicia Kelley (Williams), my Comrade-Sister friend
(a remembrance by Norma Mtume)

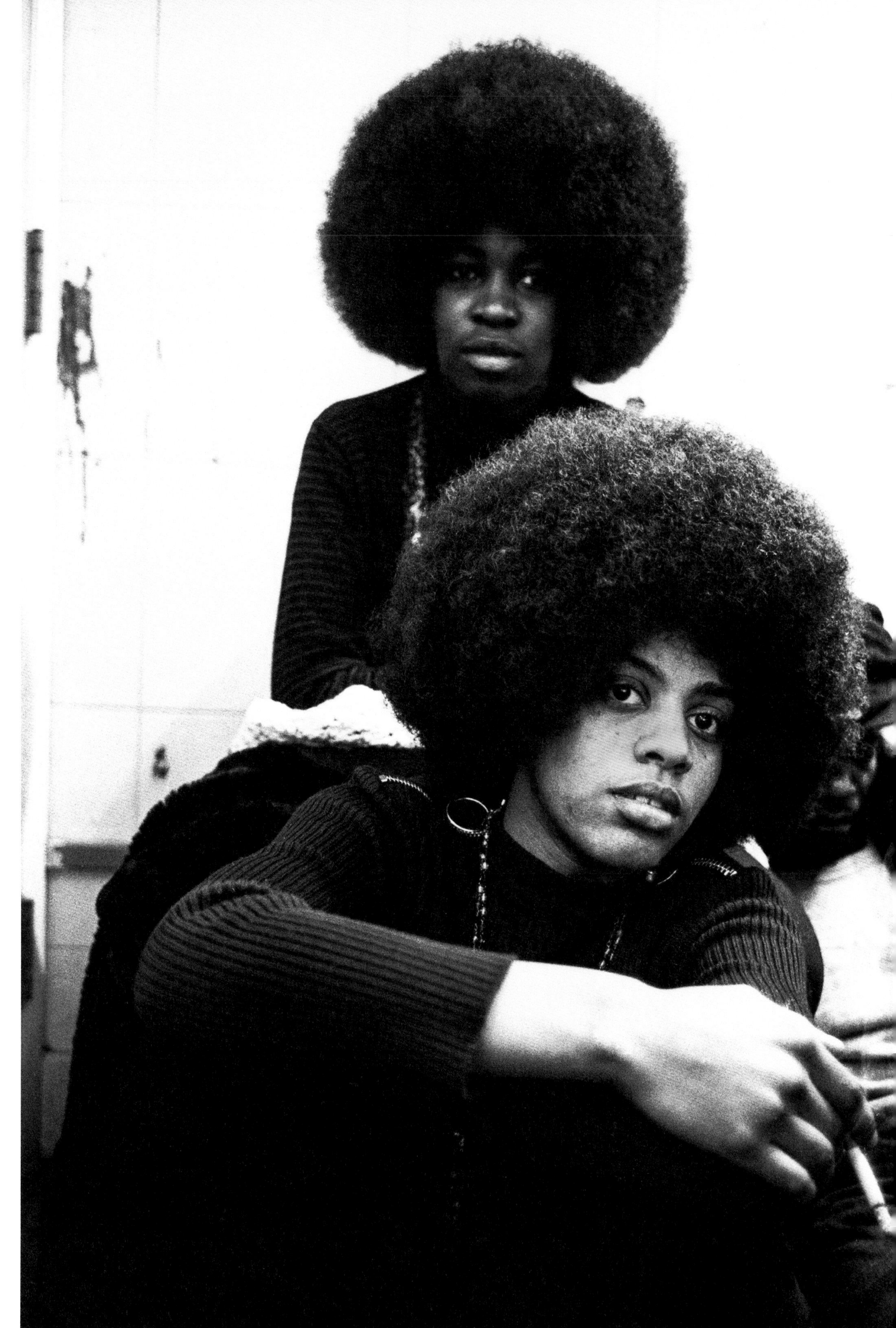

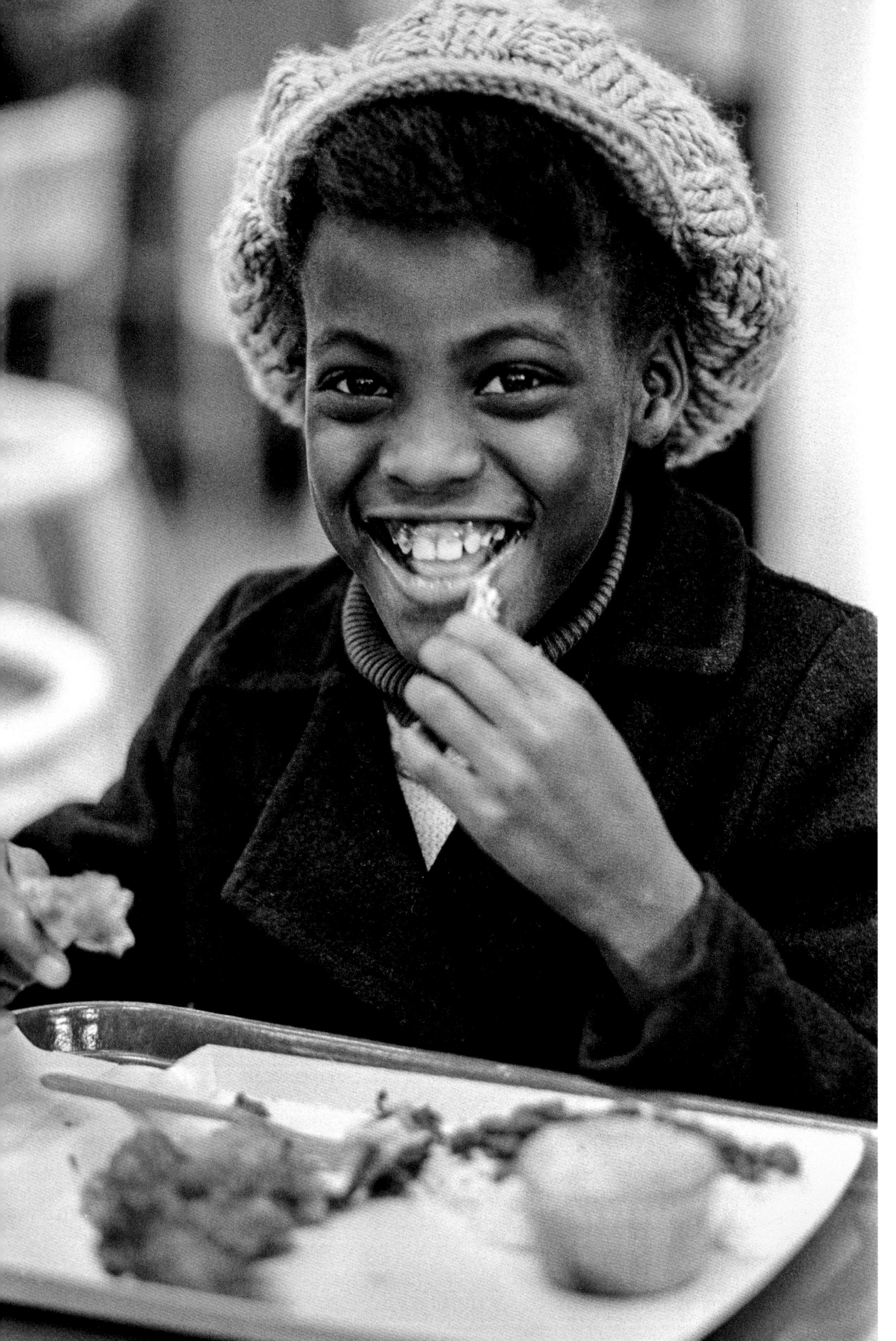

When I was just out of high school, I started going to these meetings with a group called The Black Sisters. Regina Jennings and I went together. These Sisters had afros and braided hair, and dressed in African garb.

One Sister was a teacher. She taught Black history in her basement—it was put together so nice. She had a blackboard, chairs, a desk, and a great big picture of Huey P. Newton in a wicker chair. I asked the Sister who Huey was, and she said he was the leader of the Black Panther Party. She began telling us about the Black Panther Party and the Ten Point Program. I think me, Regina, and Leslie Johnson-Seale were there. We decided that day to join the Black Panther Party. We would save our money, get on a plane, and we out. So, that's exactly what we did: we got on a plane and we went to Oakland.

My best memory is our experience with the Free Breakfast for School Children Program, especially collecting the food for the program. When it started, I was working at a bank in San Francisco. There was an article in the *San Francisco Chronicle* about the BPP breakfast program. I took that newspaper to my job and I said to my boss, "From now on, I will be late because I'll be going to the Breakfast for Children program every day." He said, "OK."

The Black Panther Party brought out something I didn't know I had. I enjoyed serving people, and I loved the people I served, my African-American people.

Ethel Paris
Philadelphia Chapter, PA / Oakland Chapter, CA

1972 St Augustine Church, Oakland, California: Breakfast for School Children Program run by the Black Panther Party. The breakfast program gave nourishment and love to children before school.

2016 *Power to the People*, In commemoration of the 50th Anniversary of the Black Panther Party, this quilt is a tribute to less well-known facts about the BPP, the community survival programs, and the BPP Ten Point Program, artwork by Rosita Thomas.

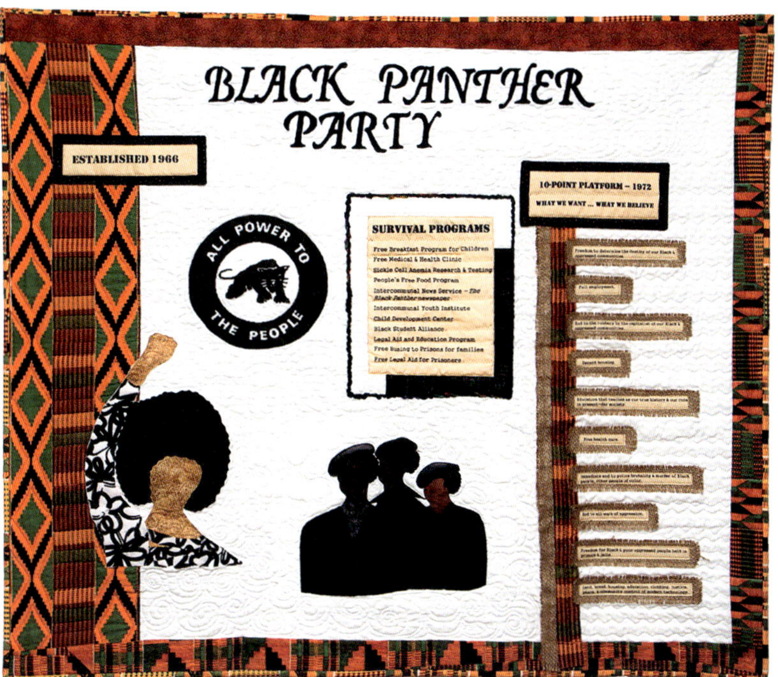

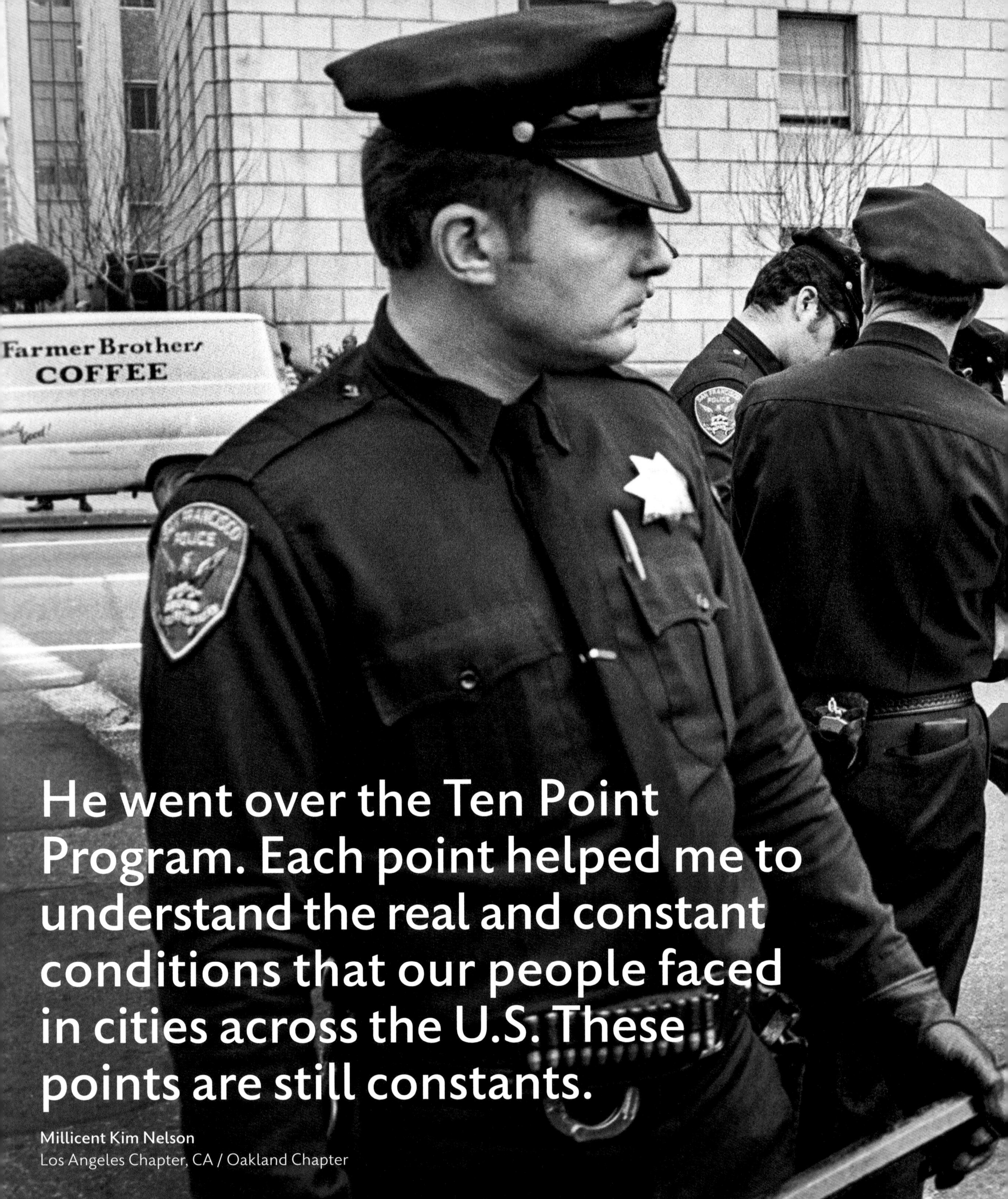

He went over the Ten Point Program. Each point helped me to understand the real and constant conditions that our people faced in cities across the U.S. These points are still constants.

Millicent Kim Nelson
Los Angeles Chapter, CA / Oakland Chapter

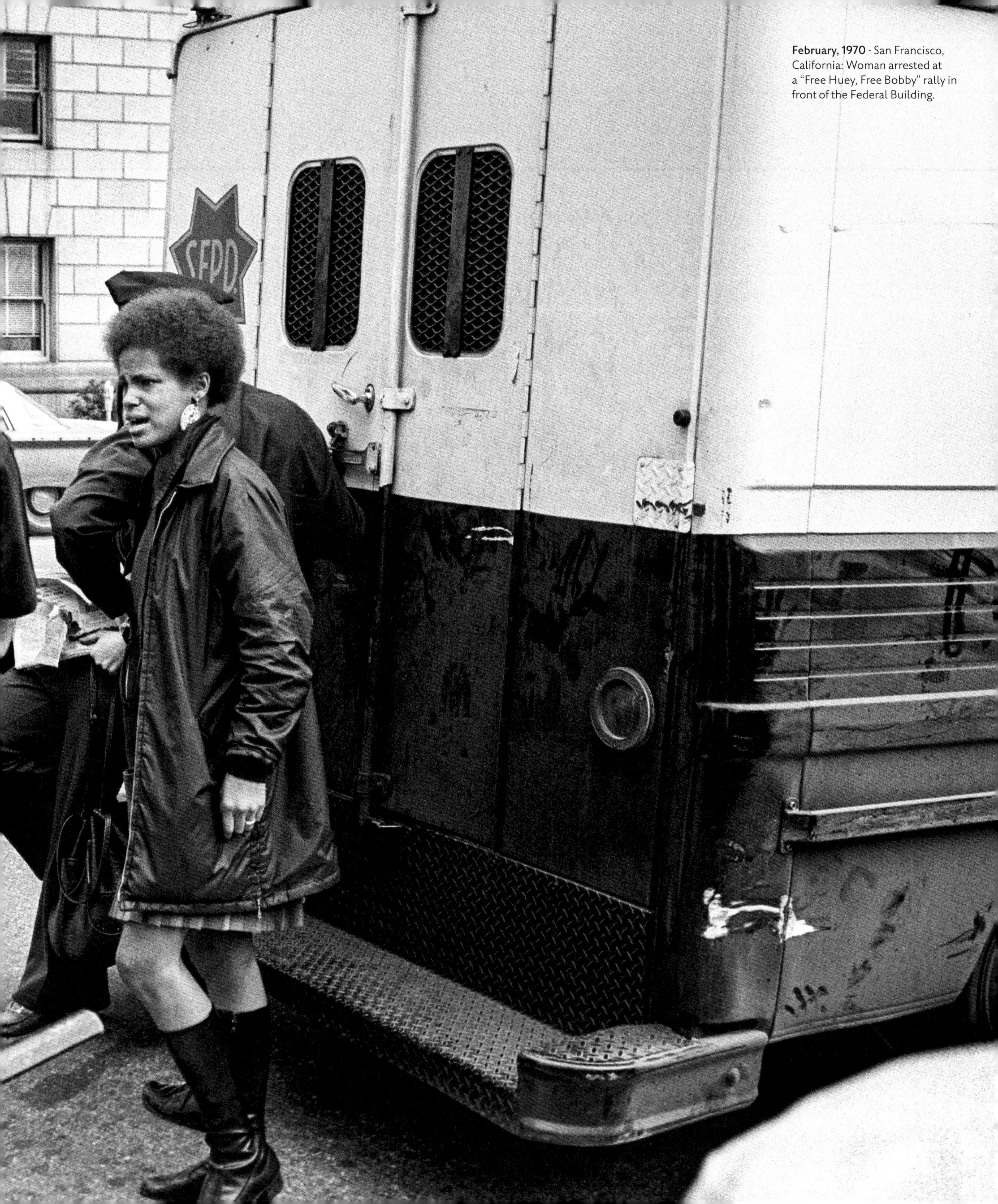

February, 1970 - San Francisco, California: Woman arrested at a "Free Huey, Free Bobby" rally in front of the Federal Building.

My story is somewhat different; I'm not a Black woman. I am an Armenian woman. My grandparents escaped through underground tunnels in Turkey. My paternal grandfather was a master swordsman. They went after him, but he left and finally made it here to the U.S. After he got here, he went back and joined the French Foreign Legion to fight the fascists. I didn't know anything about my history until I was in my thirties.

When I was in high school, I noticed that a lot of people were getting killed. I saved up my little allowance and sent it down to Medgar Evers' family. I was moved to do that. People were falling dead in America, and being sent to fight in the Vietnam War at the same time—I saw these contradictions.

When I was in Cuba, Bobby Seale was on trial in Chicago. In the courtroom they put rags in his mouth; they chained him to a chair. I thought, *What the hell is this? This can't be happening.* It just hit me over the head: I needed to do something about it. It's in my blood.

I want women and girls to know that it's important to concentrate on yourself. Take care of yourself first. Because if you don't, nobody will. So, follow your own heart. Stay true to your own heart. Don't fall for the okey-doke. Look beyond the obvious and question. Question. Question. Don't be afraid to argue. Arguments can result in new awareness and self-growth.

Veronica Roni Hagopian
National Committee to Combat Fascism (NCCF), Cambridge, MA /
Oakland Chapter, CA

1970 New Haven, Connecticut: Woman holds her child at a rally for Bobby Seale during his trial in New Haven.

1969 This image is a reprint of a panting by Emory Douglas, artist of the Black Panther Party. It was featured in the Black Panther Party newspaper.

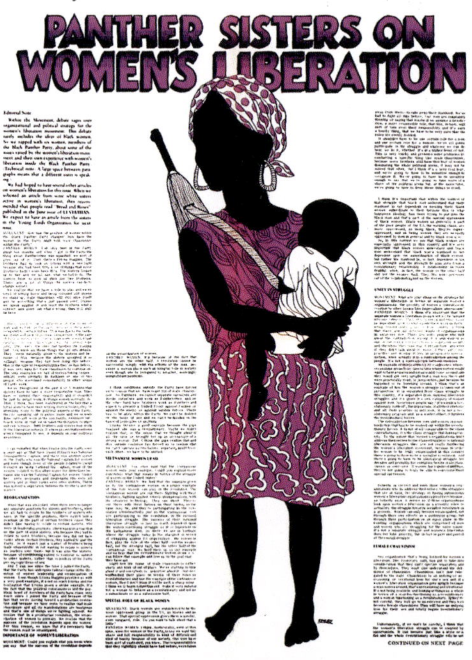

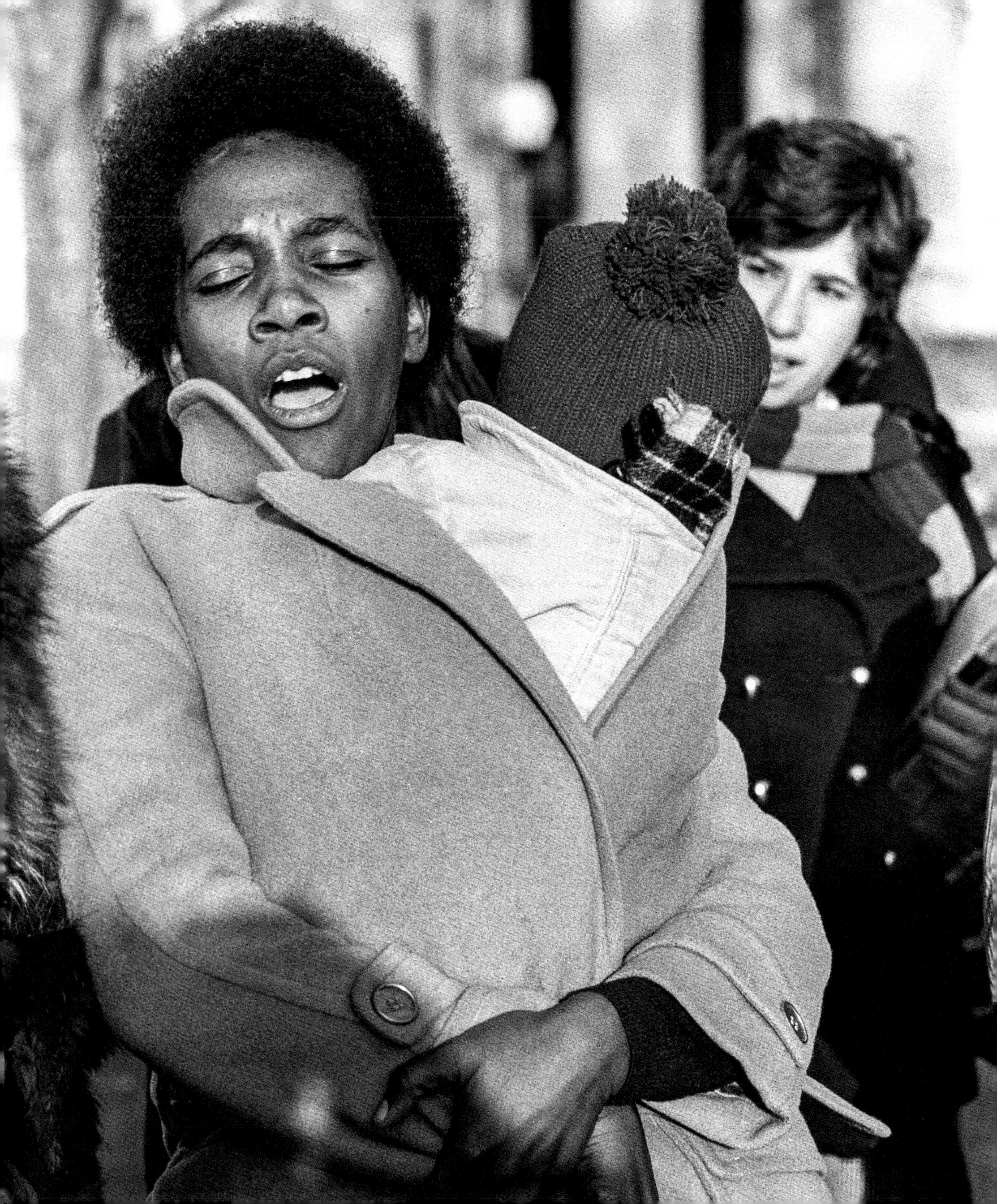

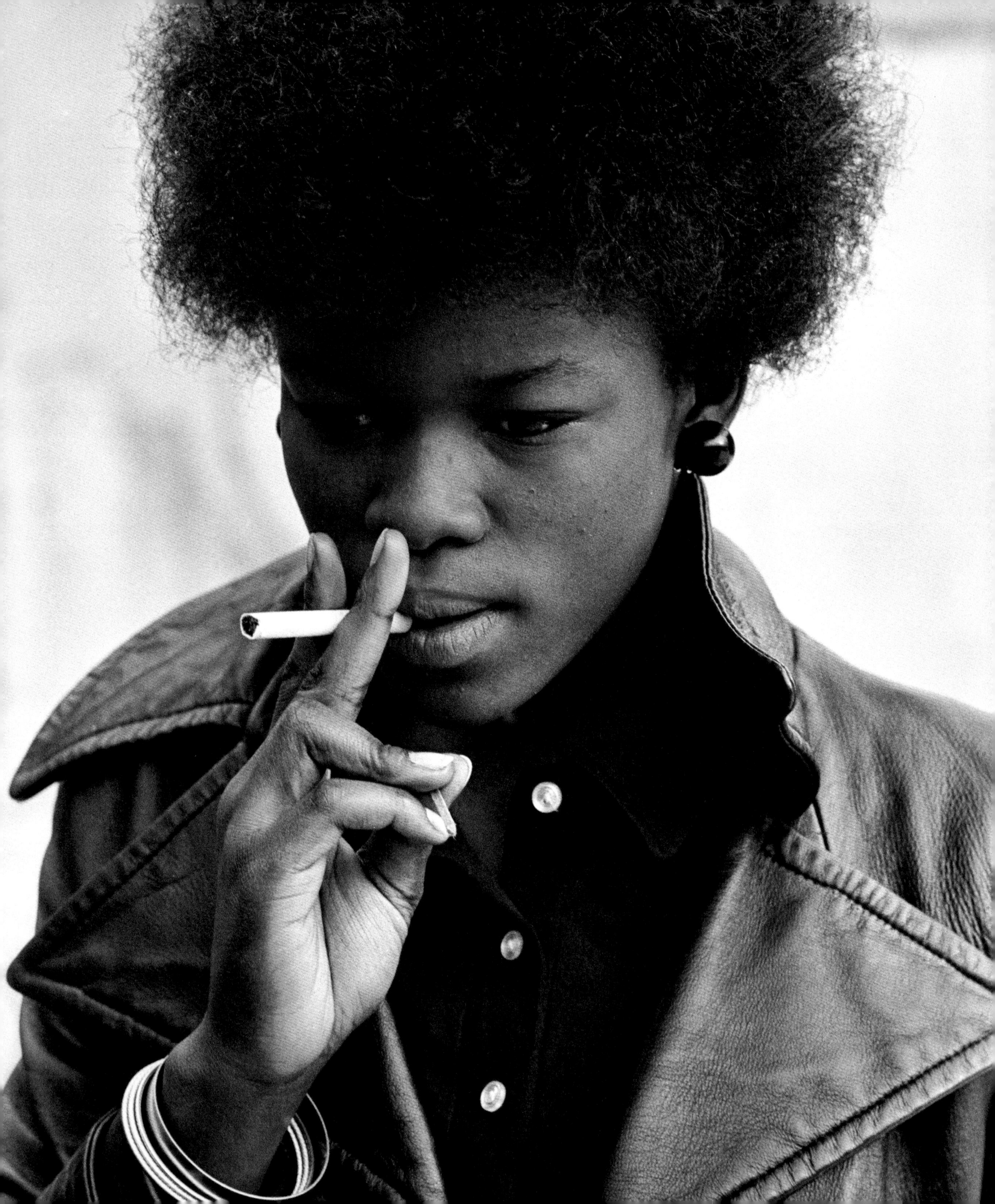

Niue"Ta'alofa lava, my name is Melani Anae. I was born in Ponsonby, Auckland, New Zealand. A lot of us were the first New Zealand-born generation. Our parents were immigrants from Samoa, Tonga, Niue, and the Cook Islands.

When I was 17, in 1971, I lost seven members of my family. Five in a plane crash; my mother and grandmother to illness. I started to question my life, God, everything. If Etta Gillon Schmidt hadn't taken me to the first Polynesian Panthers meeting, I would have gone down a really bad path.

I wanted to do something about the inequalities, the unhappiness in our lives. Our Panther work was done out of love for our Samoa, and for all of our Pacific cultures. We used the platform of the Black Panther Party and reduced it to three points. These points became us.

Point 1: Annihilate all forms of racism.
Point 2: Celebrate Mana Pacifica, our ethnic identities.
Point 3: Educate to liberate.

For the last 11 years, a group of Polynesian Panther women have gone into schools and institutions with our Educate to Liberate Program. We've revolutionized the minds of thousands of Kiwi [New Zealander] students all over the country. We're reaching the minds of the teachers too. If we hadn't been told to read *Seize the Time* by Bobby Seale, we wouldn't exist.

My heart and love goes out to you, our tuakana, our older siblings—the Black Panthers—for starting us on our journey.

Melani Anae
Auckland, Aotearoa (New Zealand)

1970 Boston, Massachusetts: Woman of the Black Panther Party.

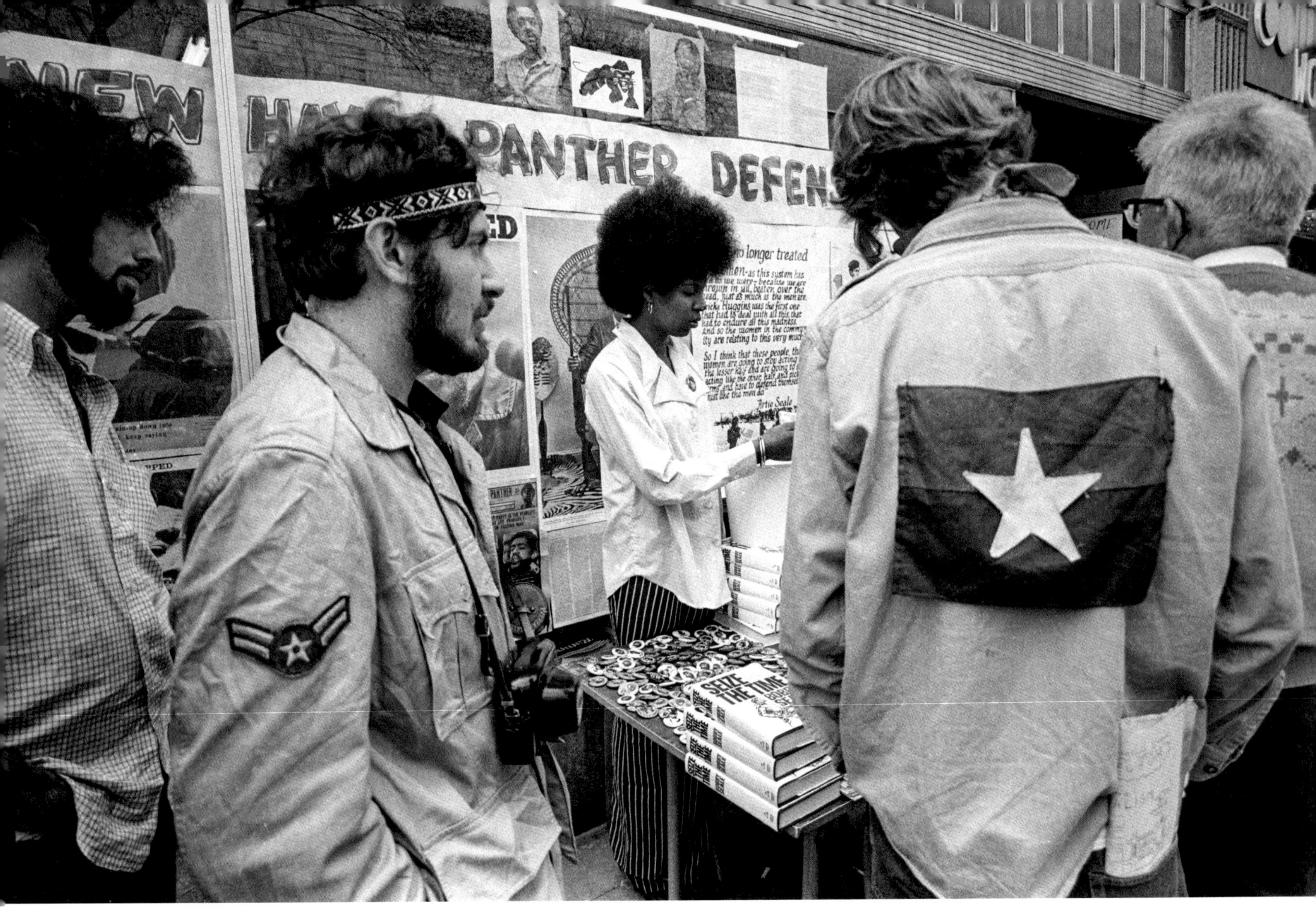

May 1, 1970 New Haven,
Connecticut: A woman
in the New Haven Chapter
of the Party sells Bobby Seale's
book, *Seize the Time*, at Yale
University during the Bobby
Seale–Ericka Huggins trial.

I joined the party in Chicago in 1968. I felt I had finally found a place where I could live into my full potential without apology, and an alternative to the traditional lot in life for Black women.

When Fred Hampton was assassinated, we were all devastated. I was in Cook County Jail, having been arrested in a similar middle-of-the-night raid. We were shot at, beaten, and thrown in jail because the police were actively looking for Fred. The morning of December 4th I was informed by my lawyer that Chairman Fred had been murdered. When I finally got out of jail, the first thing I did was to go to 2337 West Monroe—the site of the assassination. People were lined up. The police hadn't sealed off the apartment, so the Illinois Chapter opened it for everyone to come in and see. We hired our own ballistics experts, who lined up long straws in the many bullet holes so that you could see that all the shots were fired into the apartment were aimed towards Fred's bedroom. We hired our own pathologist, who proved that Fred was drugged before he went to bed. People of all stripes turned out, not just the Black community. There were people from every part of the city because it was so obvious that this was a murder.

The United States government assassinated Fred Hampton. It was just that simple.

It's something that never leaves you; it was traumatizing for all of us. The survivors—my comrades who were in the apartment when the police shot it up—were never the same. I think collectively, the Illinois Chapter still feels that deep pain and anguish. I know that Fred's family, and his close loved ones still suffer from the effects of that day.

Recently, I was invited to be on a panel of women who had been in the Party. I took my daughter, Tania, to Chicago with me. We were at a restaurant having breakfast when I heard someone say the name, Fred Hampton. At the table next to us was this guy who had several young people with him. He was talking to them about Fred: who he was. The man became aware of my eavesdropping. He said to the table, "We'll have to continue this conversation later, because somebody is listening." My daughter got up, went to the table, and said, "Excuse me, I know you realize that we were listening, but I want you to know that the three people at that table knew Fred Hampton and were in the Black Panther Party." It was a lovely moment to see those young people hearing about Fred. Fred is still a hometown hero in Chicago, a native son who people see for the goodness he stood for.

I want women and girls to have the courage to be their best self, and to be true to themselves. Step out and be yourself.

Lynn C. French
Illinois Chapter

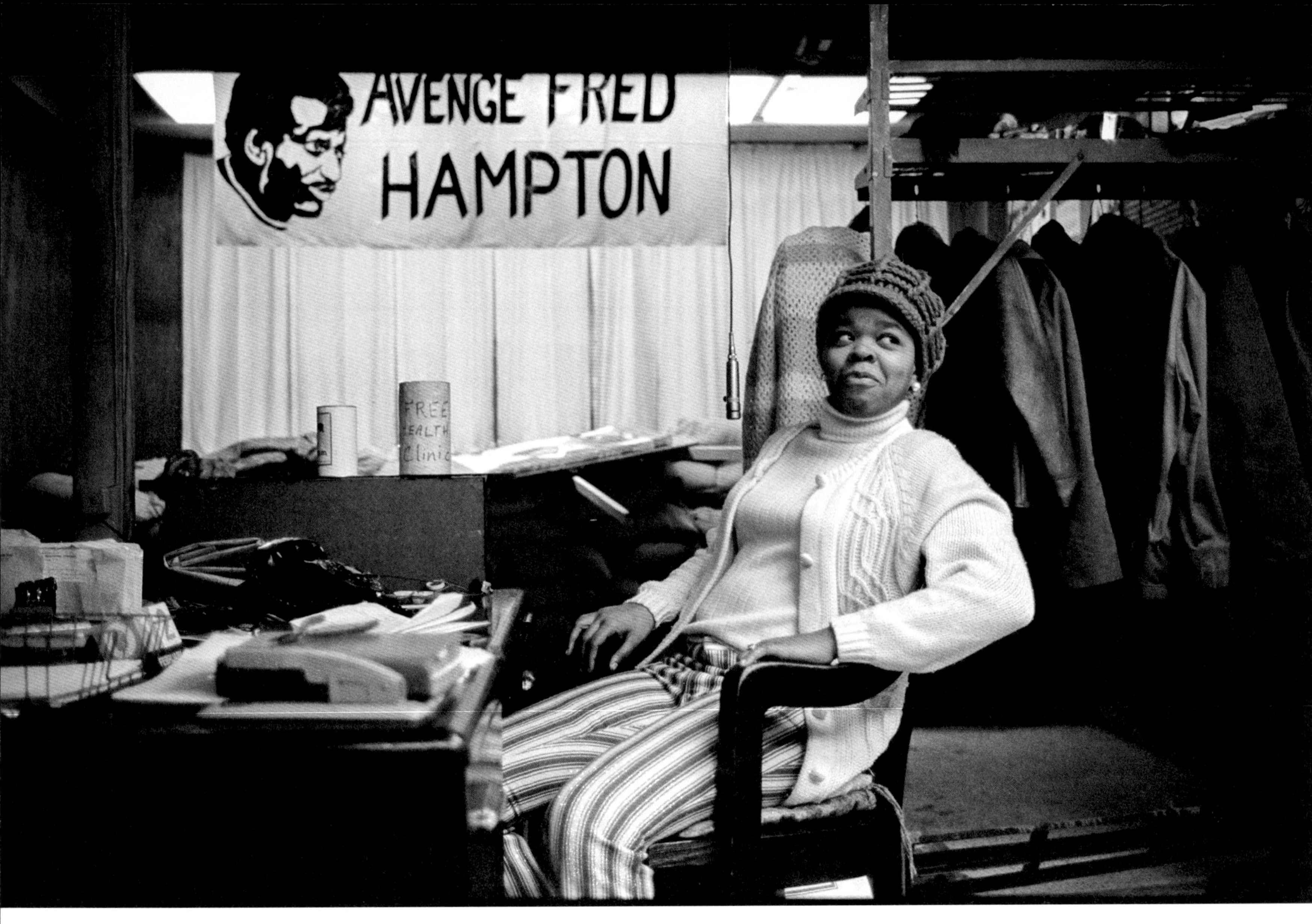

1970 Chicago, Illinois: Woman of
the Black Panther Party inside the
Chicago Chapter office.

164

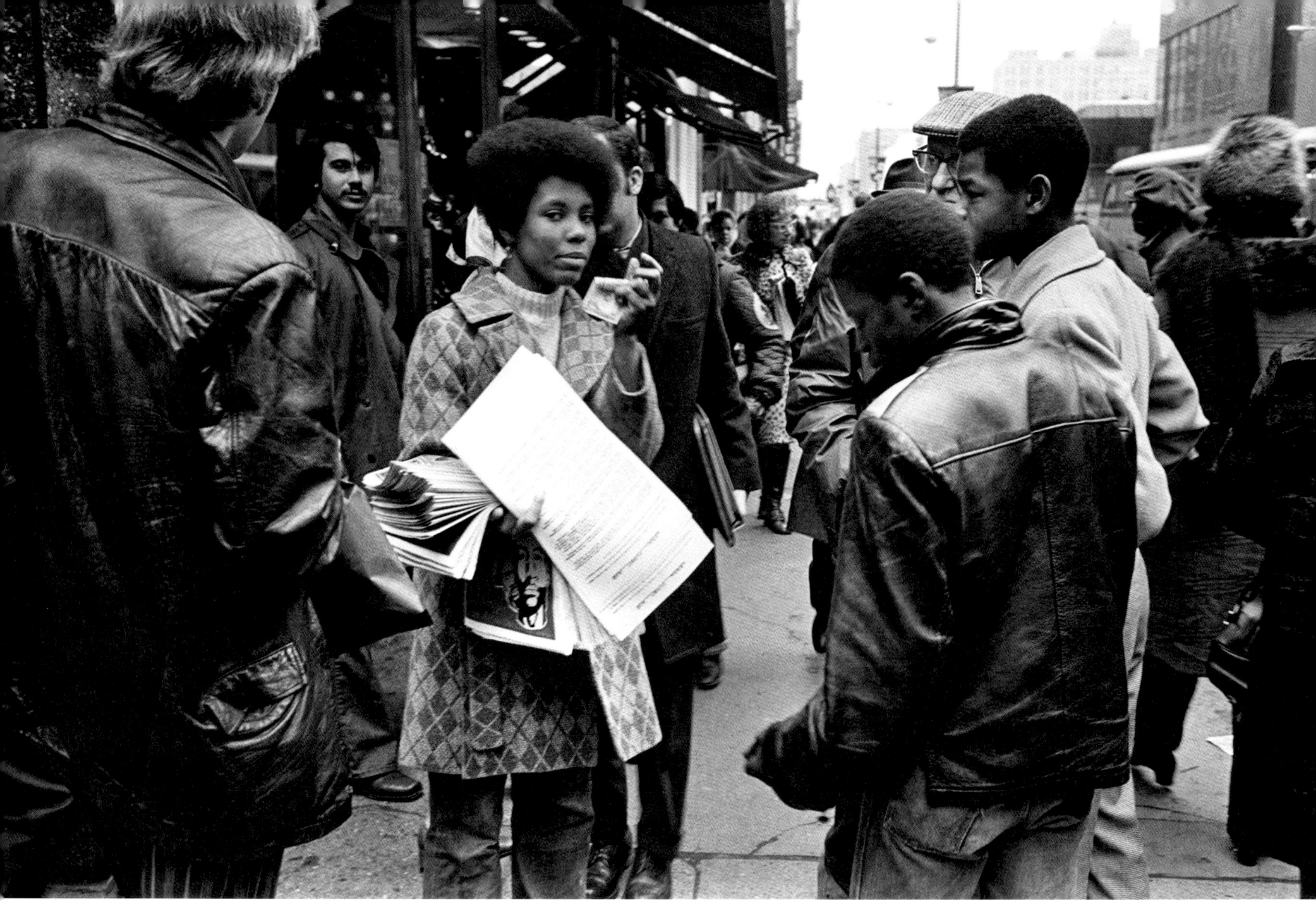

1971 Philadelphia, Pennsylvania: Woman of the Black Panther Party sells *The Black Panther* newspaper downtown.

I was born in Morristown, a small town in East Tennessee. I lived in Detroit. Over the summer of 1972, my fiancé Joe Abron and I joined the Black Panther Party. I was 24.

I can remember working at the Free Breakfast for School Children Program in Detroit, helping to serve the kids' breakfast and realizing how many children went to school hungry every day. Another memory was the Free Busing to Prisons Program. The Detroit Chapter did not have a bus, so I was given a car. We would drive to the Michigan State Prison in Jackson, which, in '72, was the largest prison in the United States. It has since been broken down into several prisons.

I'll never forget the first time I walked into a prison and realized what it was. These people were behind bars, incarcerated. I had never, ever seen anything like it. I had seen the news footage of the Attica Rebellion and I knew what that was about, but I had never been in a prison before, so it was an overwhelming experience. I was in the Black Panther Party, so I made myself suppress the tears and the anguish. By the time I got back to Detroit, I was able to cry.

To see this sea of humanity locked up… I realized that the Black Panther Party was doing something important. Many of those loved ones and family members wouldn't have had a way to visit their family members if we hadn't had those vans and buses. They didn't have transportation, and they would have lost total contact with their families. Knowing that I was doing something that was helping Black people kept me going.

The Black Panther Party served the people, body and soul.

To all the young women activists out there: as you serve, be mindful of taking care of yourself. Save something of yourself, for yourself; remember that you are one of the people, too. The people are not some great body out there somewhere. We're the people. I want girls and women and whoever may read this to remember to take care of yourself.

JoNina Ervin
Detroit Chapter, MI / Oakland Chapter, CA

1972 San Jose, California: After being released on bail, Angela Davis sits quietly in a friend's yard.

Circa 1971 *Free Our Black Sisters* – Soledad Brothers Defense Committee, courtesy of Lincoln Cushing and Lisbet Tellefsen.

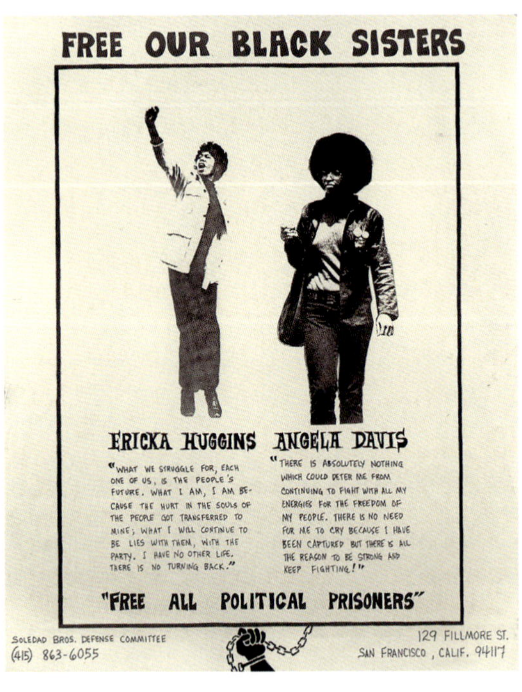

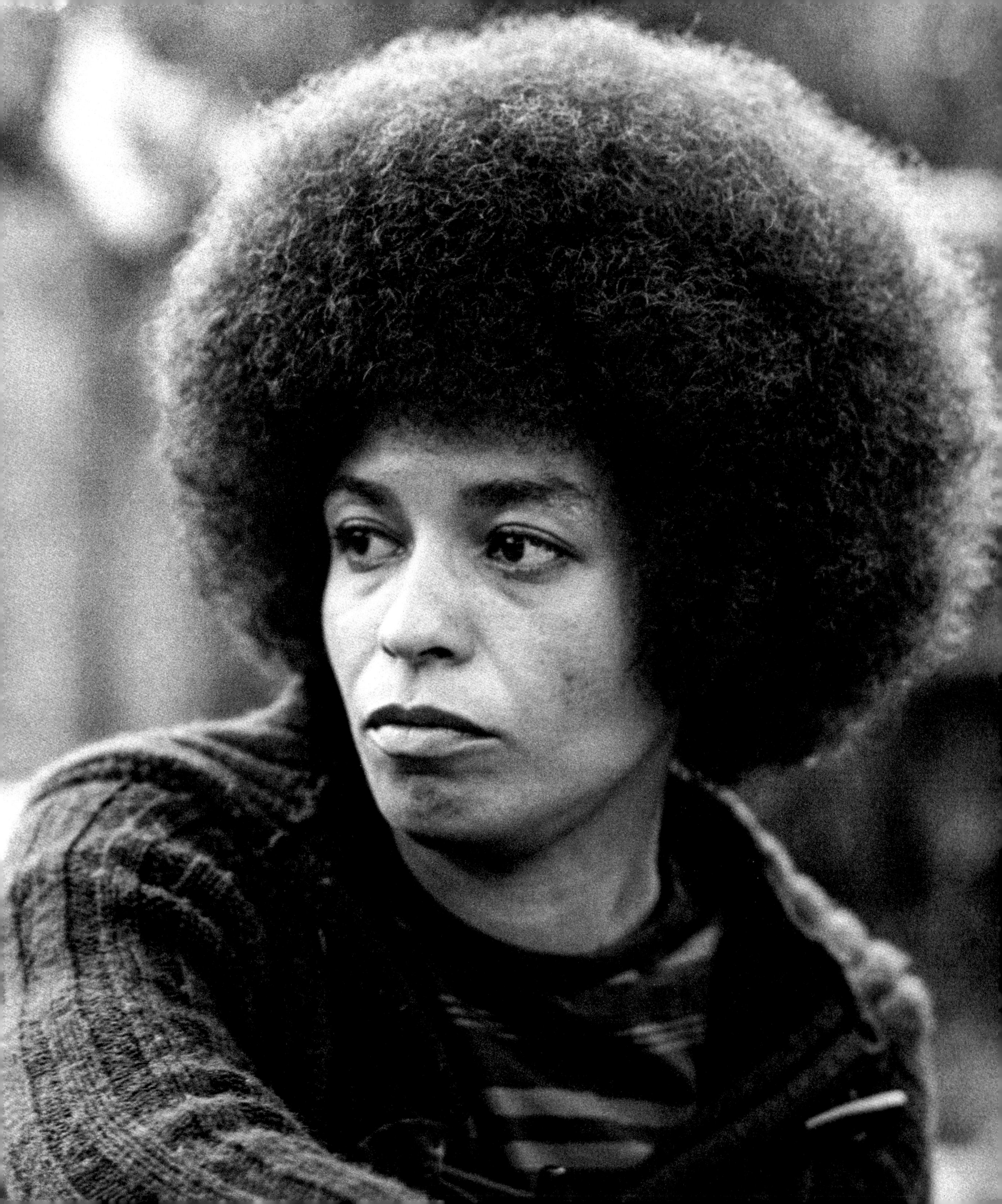

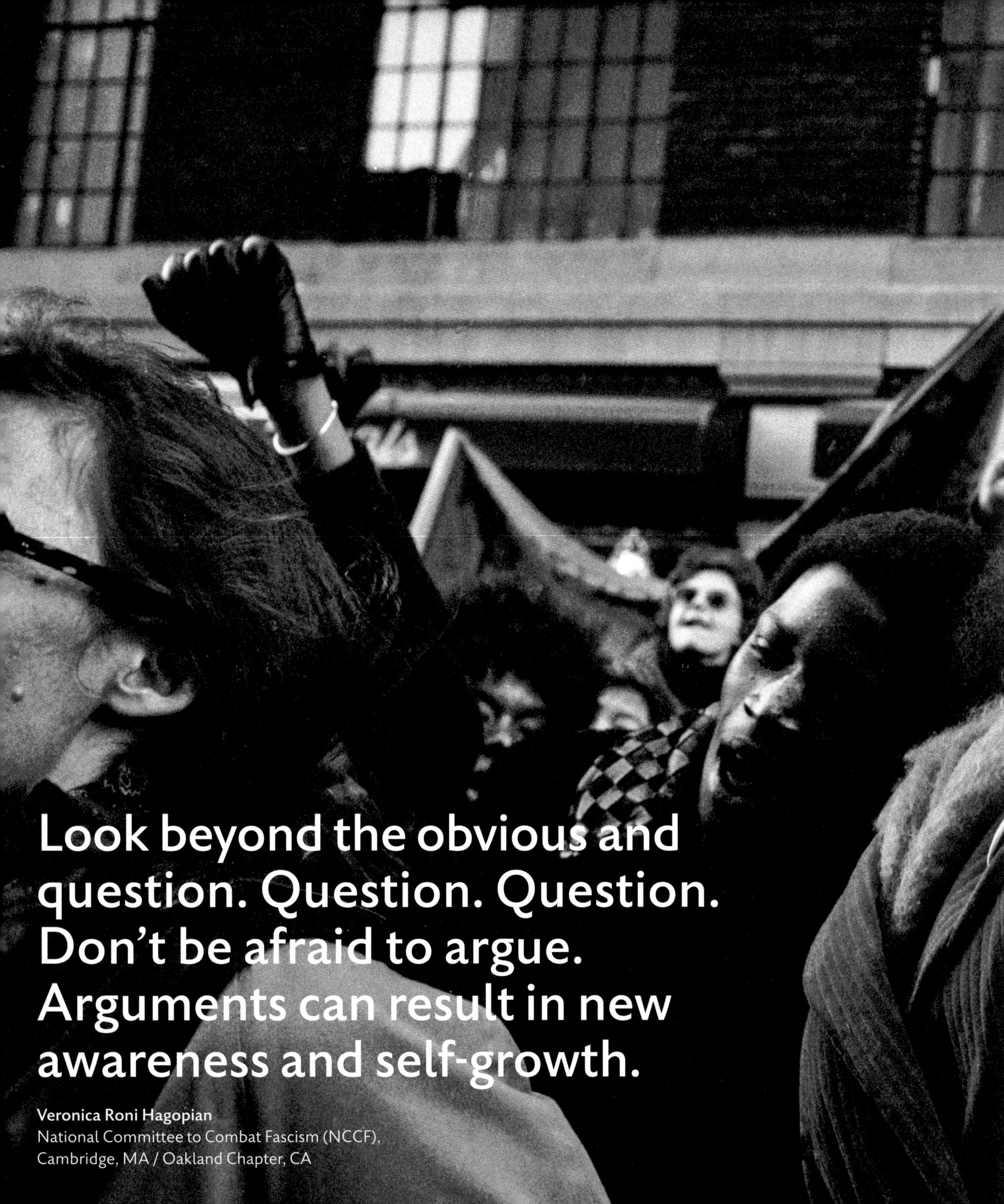

Look beyond the obvious and question. Question. Question. Don't be afraid to argue. Arguments can result in new awareness and self-growth.

Veronica Roni Hagopian
National Committee to Combat Fascism (NCCF),
Cambridge, MA / Oakland Chapter, CA

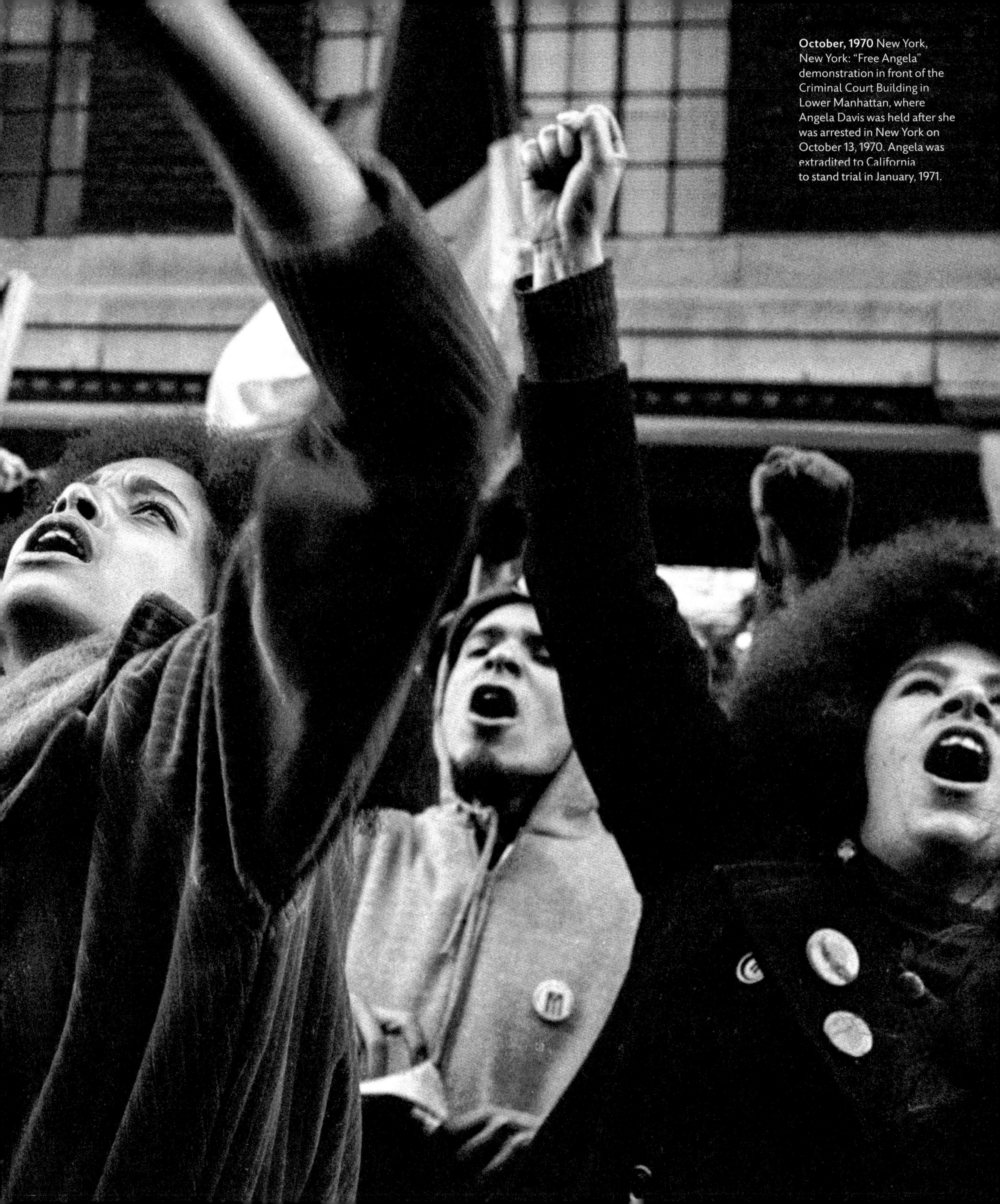

October, 1970 New York, New York: "Free Angela" demonstration in front of the Criminal Court Building in Lower Manhattan, where Angela Davis was held after she was arrested in New York on October 13, 1970. Angela was extradited to California to stand trial in January, 1971.

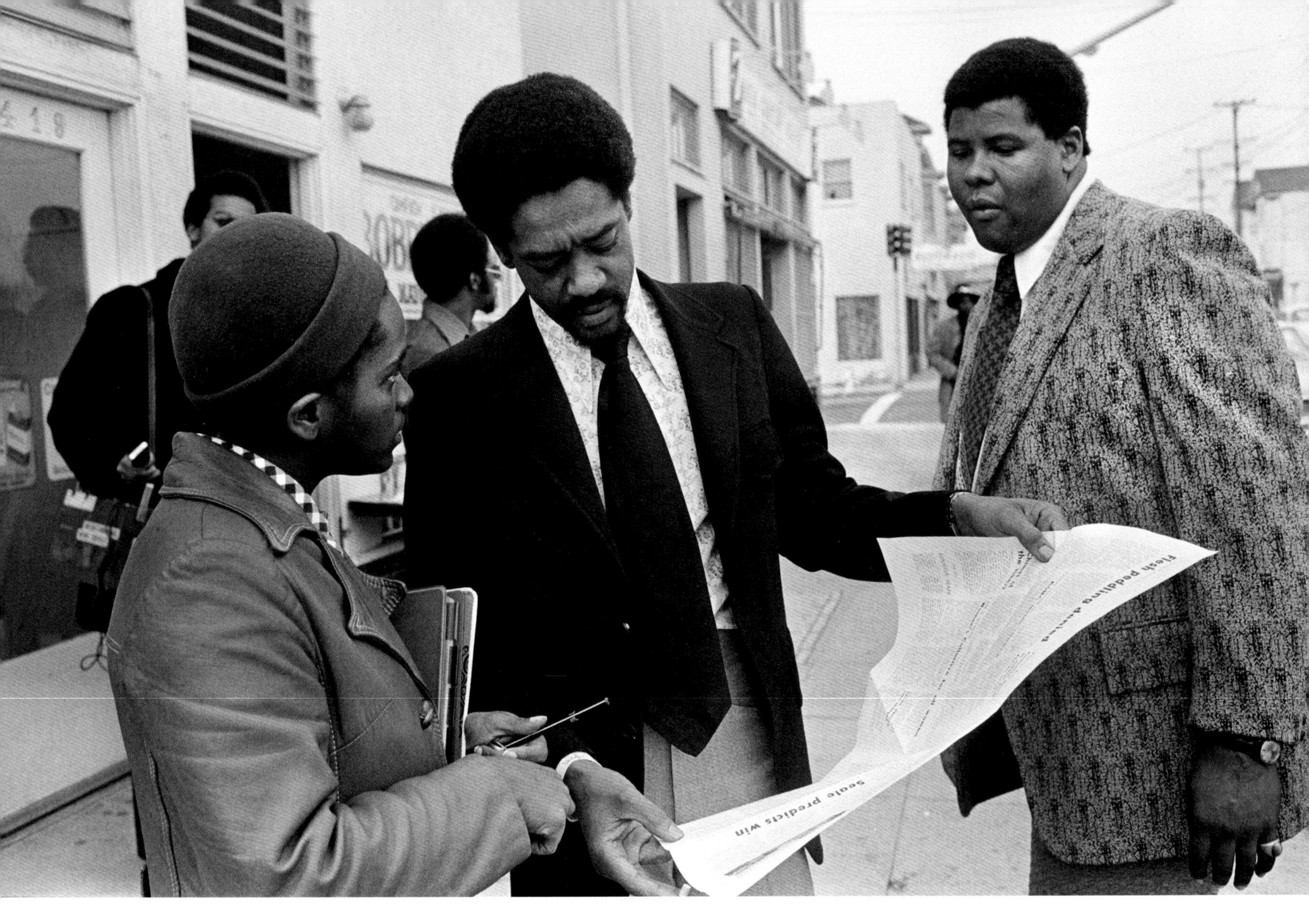

1973 Oakland, California:
Audrea Jones, campaign organizer,
from the Boston Chapter of
the party, speaks with Chairman
Bobby Seale as he campaigns
for Mayor of Oakland. Right:
Campaign Manager Herman Smith,
later known as Sultan Ahmad.
The voter registration drive,
"Bobby Seale for Mayor and Elaine
Brown for Oakland City Council",
helped Judge Lionel Wilson to
become the first Black mayor of
Oakland in 1977.

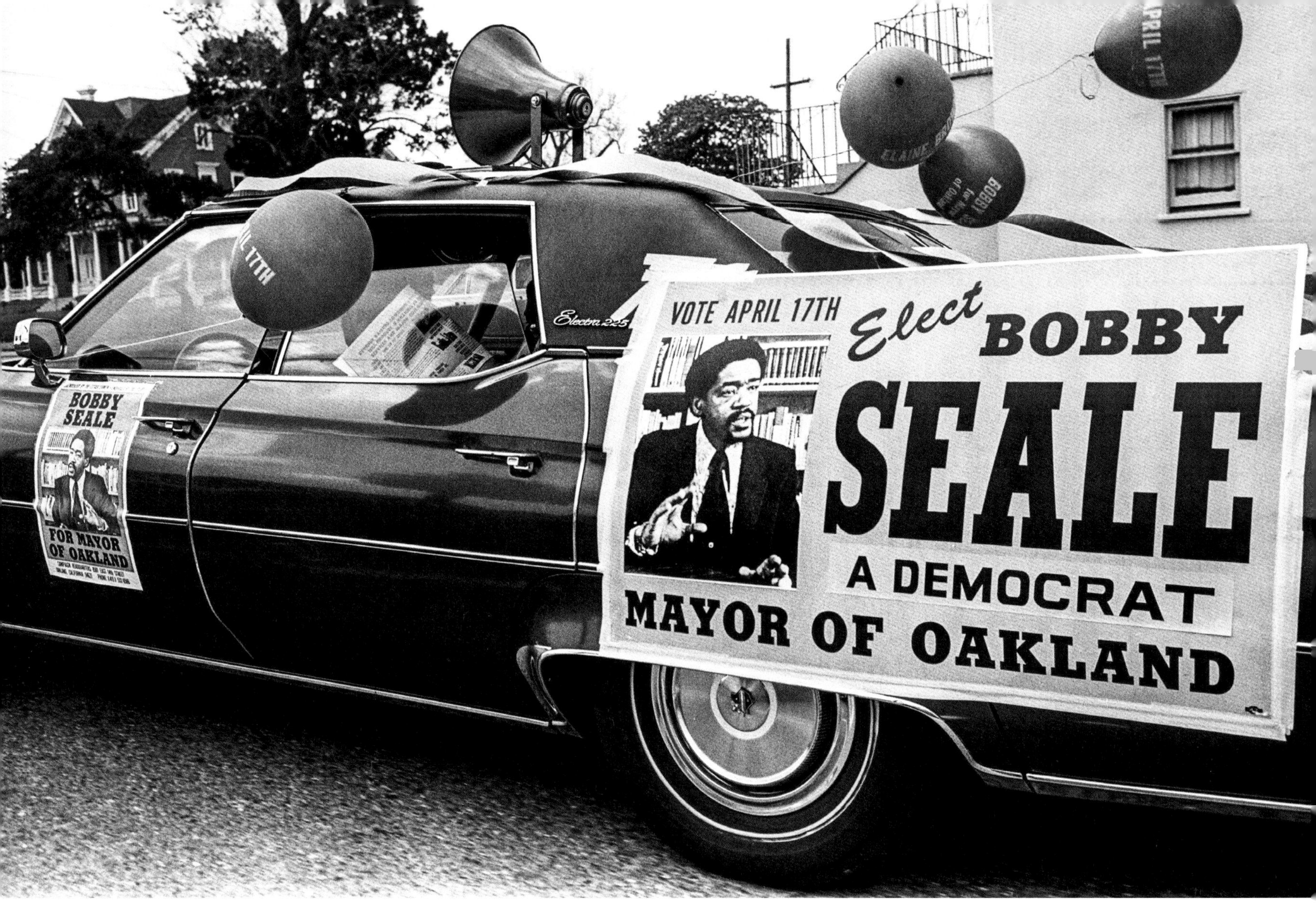

1973 Oakland, California: Bobby Seale for Mayor of Oakland campaign posters, using a Stephen Shames photo of Black Panther Chairman Bobby Seale.

Arlene Clark was family to me. One day, after escorting an elder woman home from shopping at a local grocery store, Arlene called me.

"Mrs. Johnson is like a grandmother to me," she said. "After she opened the door to her house, she invited me in to put groceries away and said, 'sit down, have a little something to eat.' Our seniors are not wealthy men and women. Many raised their grandchildren so that their parents could go to work. Now they are all alone.

"I realize that the S.A.F.E. Program is more than a ride. S.A.F.E. creates relationships with the elders of our community. It is our relationship to each individual senior that is important. We need to find a way to check in with them. *We* are their family."

Though Arlene left this life at a young age, her thoughtfulness led the S.A.F.E. Program to include visits to homes of seniors, for their emotional and social wellbeing. She left a loving legacy through her work in the community with S.A.F.E, educating people about the power of the vote and supporting sickle cell anemia testing. Arlene strengthened countless bonds between her comrades and the members of her community.

Arlene Clark
Oakland Chapter, CA, National Headquarters of the BPP
(a remembrance by Ericka Huggins)

1972 Oakland, California: Women of the Black Panther Party, Arlene Clark and Cheryl Curtis, register people to vote during Bobby Seale's Mayor of Oakland and Elaine Brown's city council campaigns. The Party registered thousands of new voters.

July 1, 1972 *Yes, I'm Against The War!*, artwork by M. Gayle Asali Dickson.

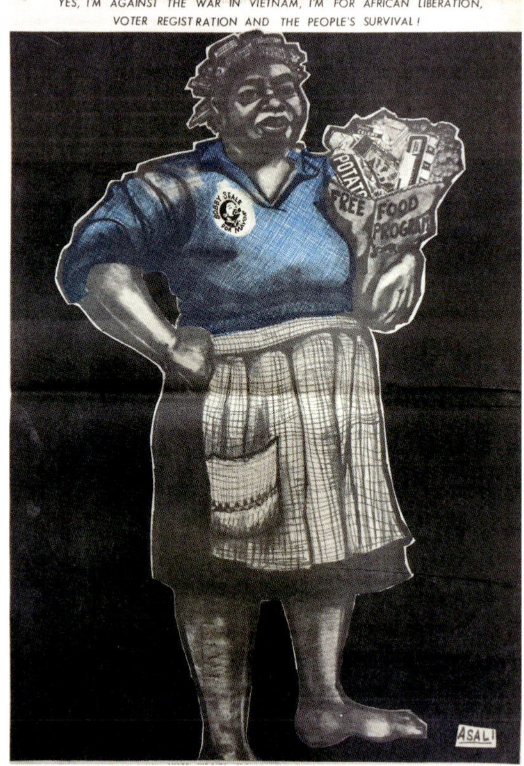

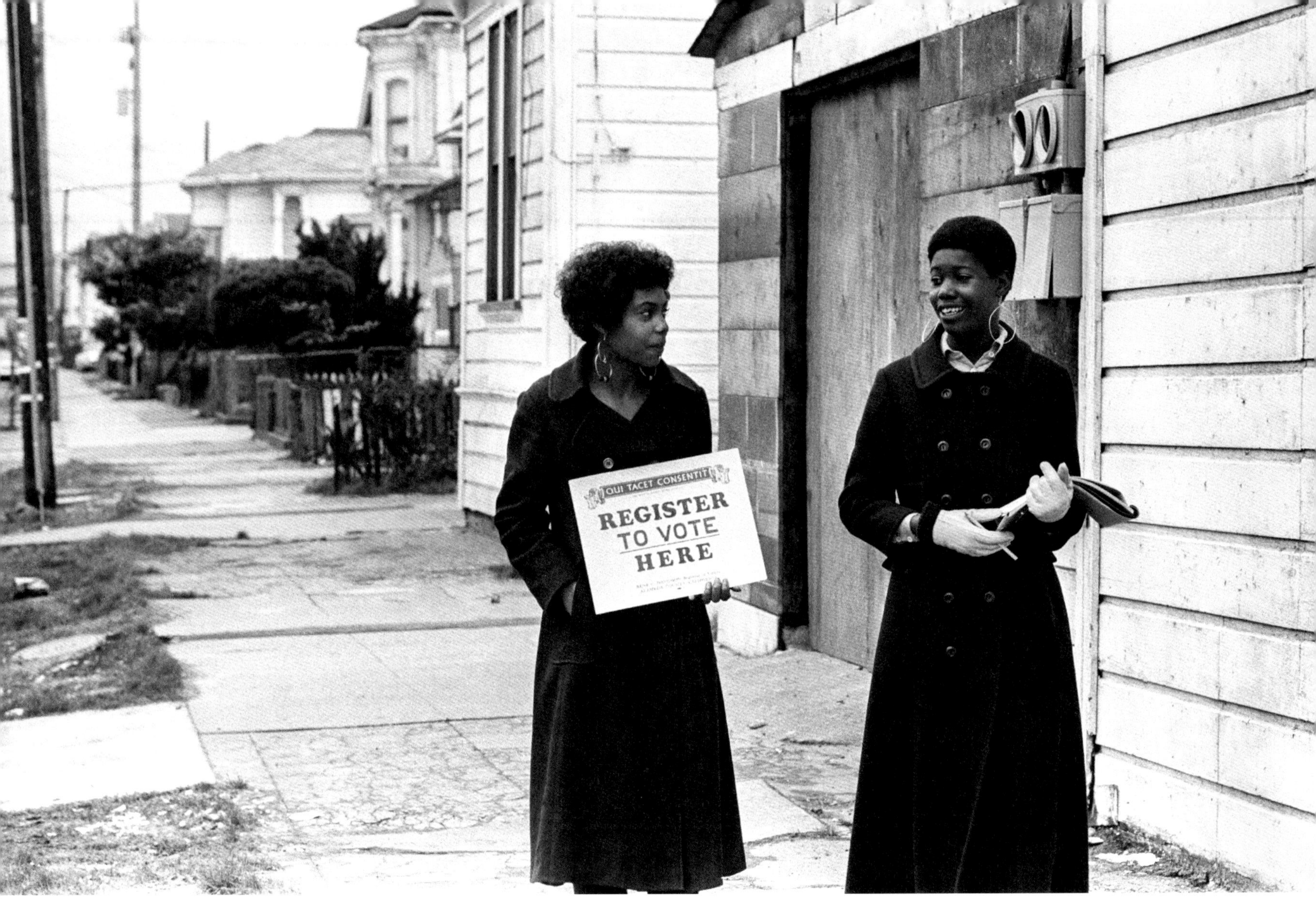
QUI TACET CONSENTIT
REGISTER
TO VOTE
HERE

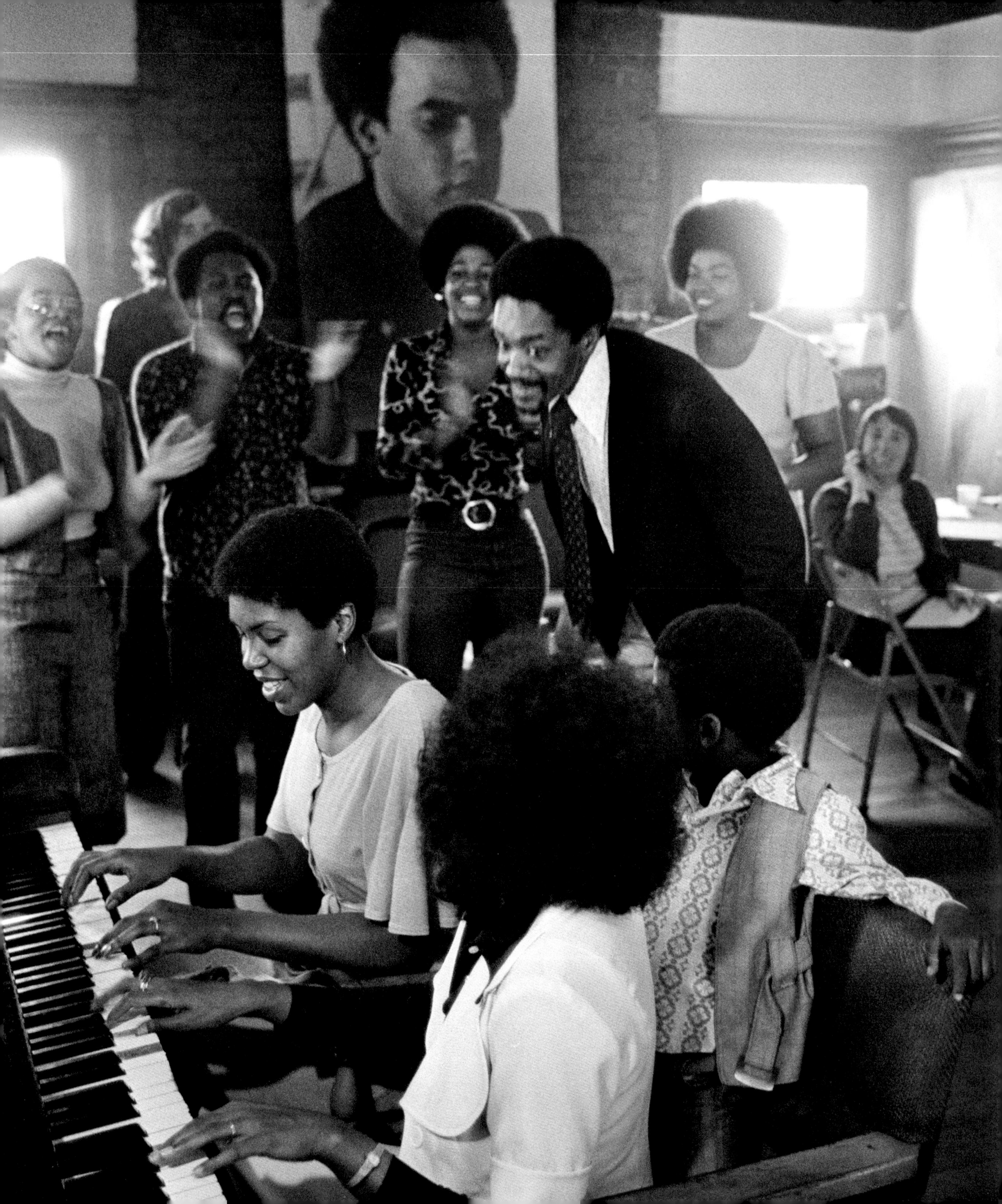

In the '60s, we moved from the Jefferson Projects in Detroit. We later moved to California, first Watts, and then various neighborhoods in Los Angeles, which are now called South Central. I started learning about the Party when, in 1969, John Huggins and Alprentice "Bunchy" Carter were killed. I had lived through the 1965 Watts Riots, and I remember when the Los Angeles SWAT force shot up the Black Panther Chapter office in LA in 1969. These were the times when, in the South, Black children could not go to school; when Blacks were waterhosed when marching for equality, and Black people were being killed. I was able to see how our people were suffering on different levels.

After I graduated high school in 1969 at the age of 16, I moved to Oakland to live with family while I attended Merritt College when it was located in the Flatlands. I was drawn to the political aura of the Bay Area and I joined the Black Student Union, which had Party members in it. I started my involvement with the Party in the Free Breakfast for School Children Program.

That first political education class with Masai Hewitt got me. He went over the Ten Point Program. Each point helped me to understand the real and constant conditions that our people faced in cities across the U.S. These points are still constants. I was assigned to the West Oakland branch. I was the office coordinator. My most memorable moment was during Bobby Seale's campaign for Mayor—I participated in the event to give out 10,000 bags of groceries. Not only did the concept of feeding thousands of people come up, but we did it. And, we got a chicken for every bag. We put the bags together, and people came from all over.

"Serve the people, body and soul" was our motto.

When Bobby was campaigning, Steve McCutchen and I, along with eight other party members, were running for the Model Cities Board and we were all elected. Steve and I ran as "Youth at Large." We went door to door in West Oakland, Campbell Village every single day, getting word of the vote out. We used a door-to-door campaign because people were so receptive to the Black Panther Party. They'd open their doors, invite us in, feed us. At the food giveaway, I saw quite a few people whose doors I'd knocked on. They remembered me.

We were educating the world. It was love that drew us, and that's what kept us.

Millicent Kim Nelson
Los Angeles and Oakland Chapters, CA

October 1972 Oakland, California: Black Panther Party Chairman Bobby Seale watches his wife Artie play the piano. Malik Seale, their son, stands behind his mother.

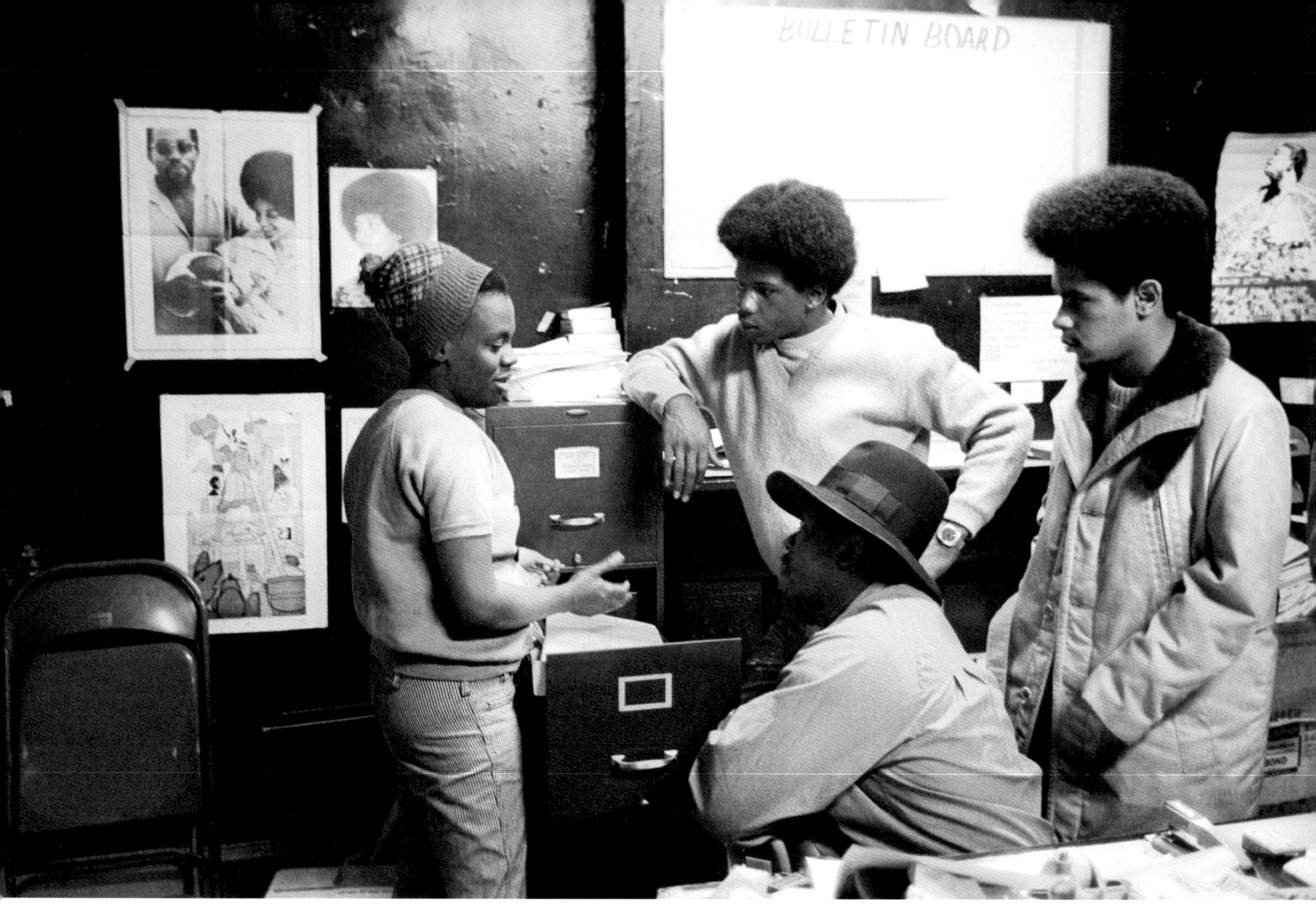

1971 Philadelphia, Pennsylvania:
Barbara Pelson and comrades
inside the Philadelphia Black
Panther office.

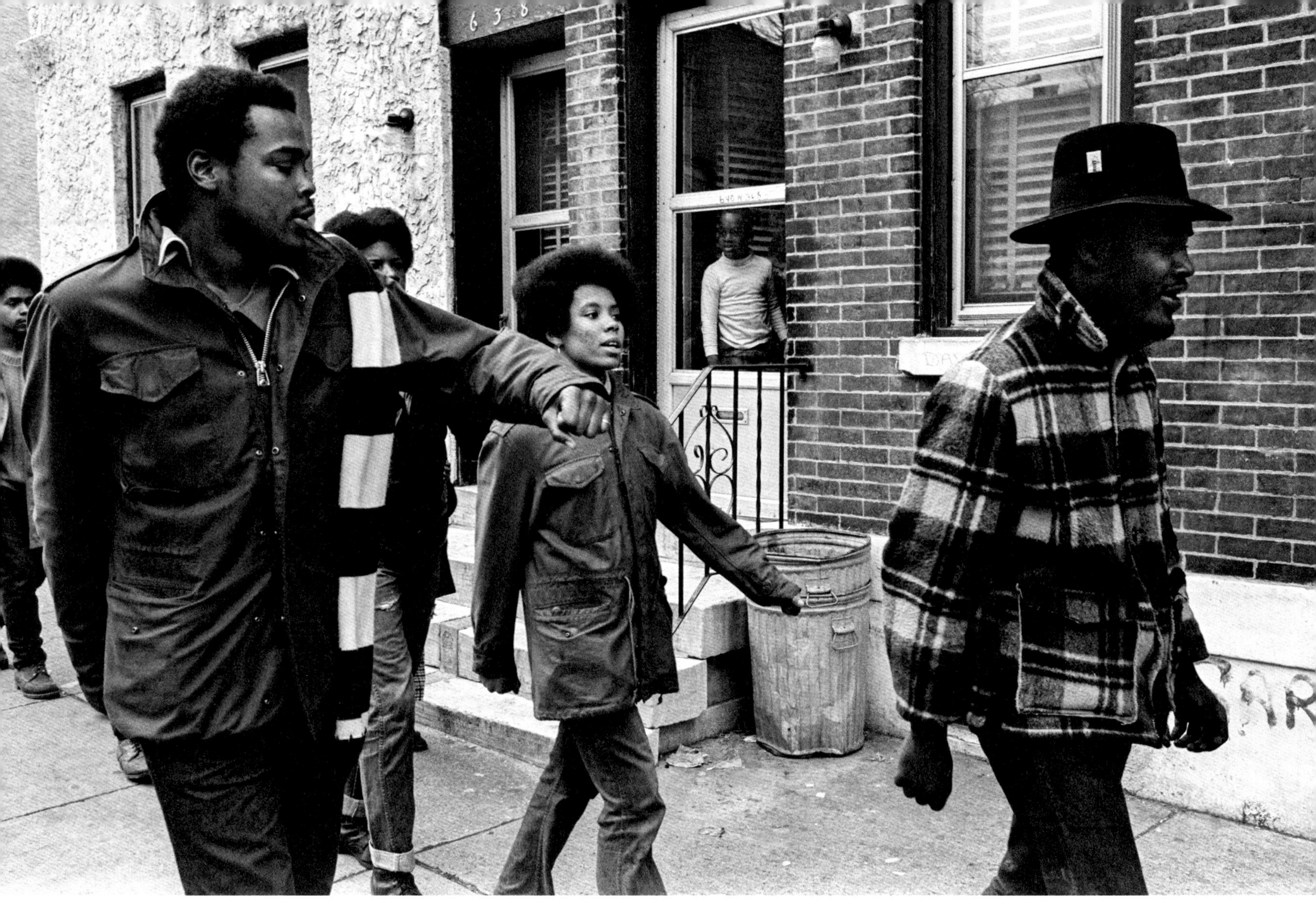

1971 Philadelphia, Pennsylvania:
Black Panthers march through
West Philadelphia.

I was born in Mangakino, in the King Country on the North Island (New Zealand) which is in the middle of nowhere. It was through my brother, Fred Schmidt, that I joined the Polynesian Panthers. He and a group of friends were the founding members of the group in Auckland. On July 16, 1971, a meeting was held at our place in Auckand city. Myself and my school friends, who I treated like sisters, were invited to come along. Melani Anae, a neighbor, was there too. We were invited to listen, to see whether we wanted to be part of the group. They wanted to make sure that the gender balance was there.

I was not really aware of all the atrocities our people had experienced. I realized that we should be there to help our people, so I began helping in different areas. There was so much malnutrition among the young and the old. Miriama Rauhihi, Che Ness's mom, was part of the integral group of people who sourced cheaper prices for fruits and vegetables, a food co-op. We all took turns helping with the food distribution. As a student nurse, I lived five minutes away, and whenever I could help, I would turn up at our headquarters in Ponsonby. We were all so very lucky to have Miriama to hold the office and guide us all to what would be our priority for that day. She was lovely, the heart of our group. She knew where the help was needed most and was always willing to assist. She had fire in her belly. She knew where to drive us.

My most memorable time with the Polynesian Panthers in Auckland was helping local children after school in their home education programs, and our protests against Apartheid. We knew, when it came to Apartheid, how it felt to have fire in our belly, too.

At the end of the day we all should be proud, and our children should be proud of themselves, too. Because of our efforts in the Polynesian Panther Movement, I believe we made a difference in New Zealand society, so that our Polynesian children know where they want to go, what they want to do. They've got to make their choice and make the decision in life—it is up to them.

Etta Gillon Schmidt
Aotearoa (New Zealand)

1970 Berkeley, California: Woman of the Black Panther Party.

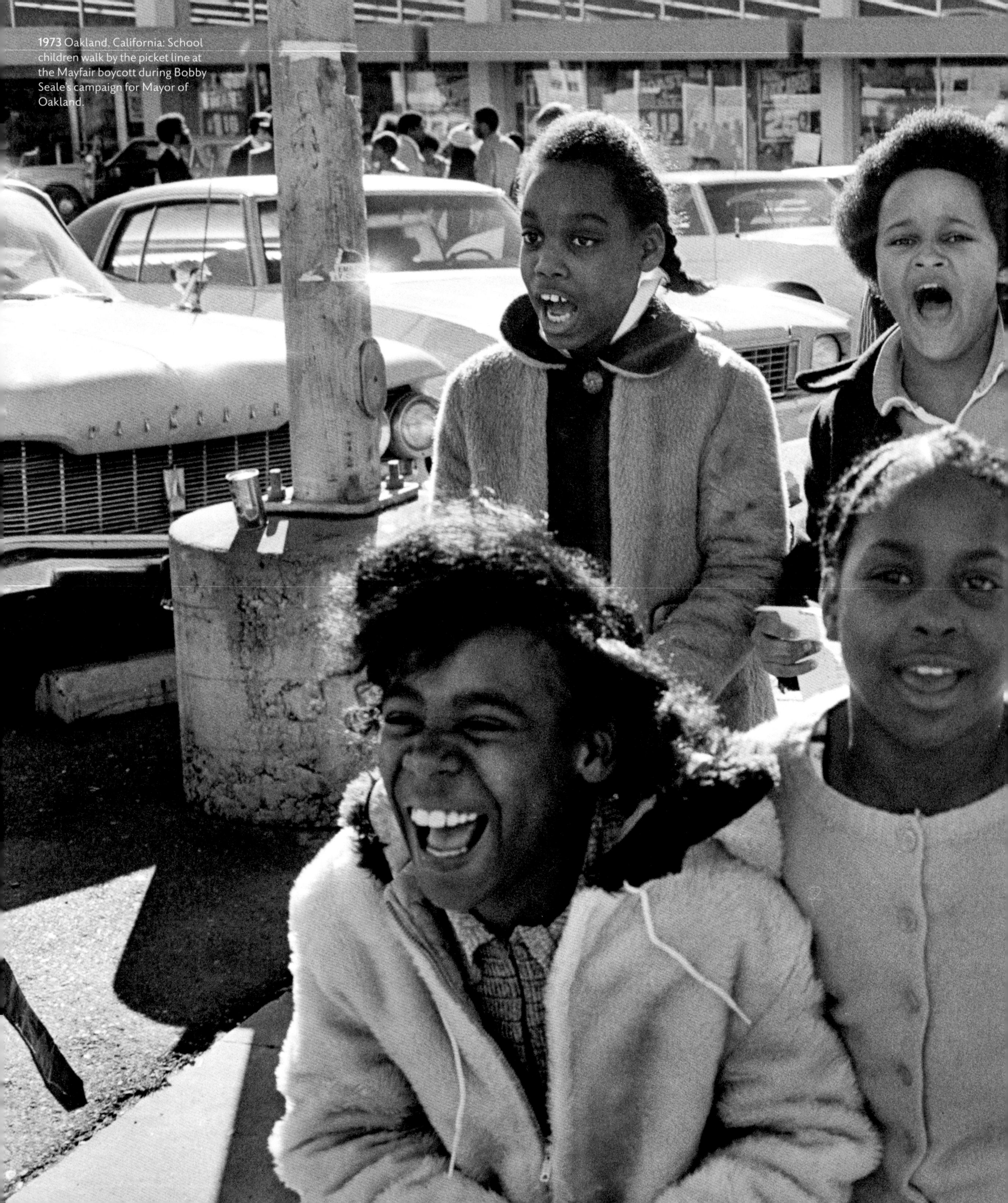

1973 Oakland, California: School children walk by the picket line at the Mayfair boycott during Bobby Seale's campaign for Mayor of Oakland.

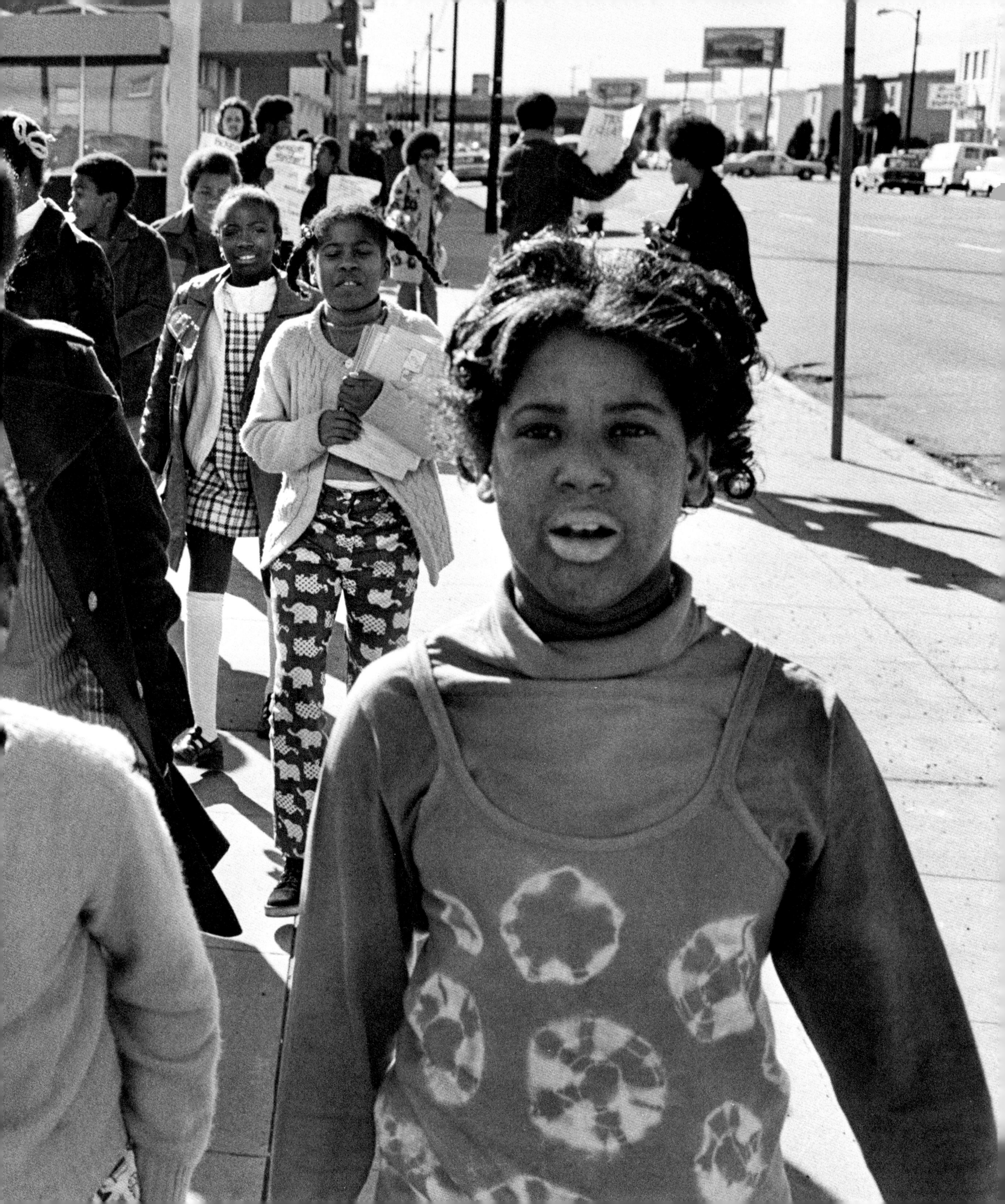

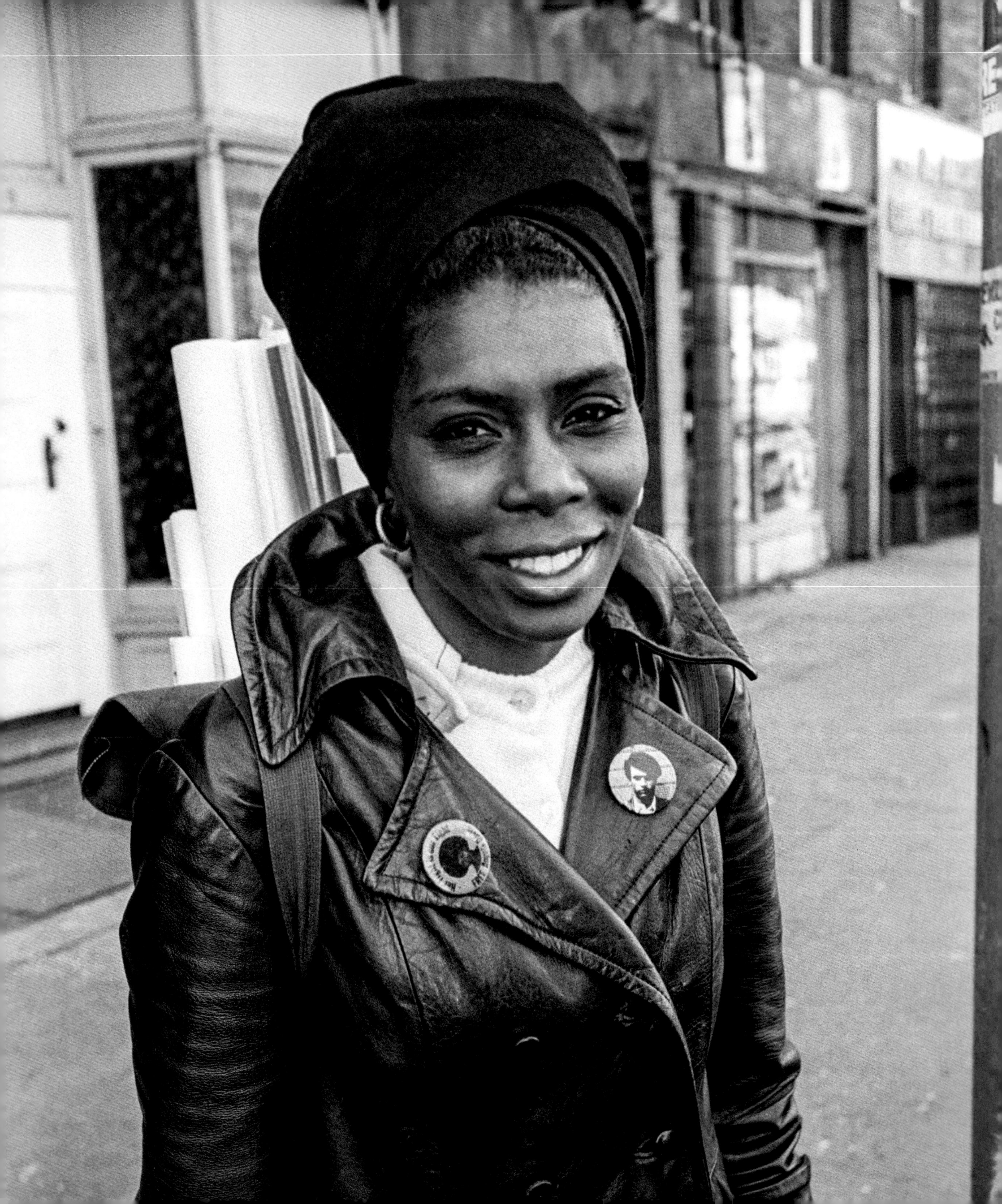

My name is Che Ness. It is a pleasure and an honor to be here. I consider myself a child of the revolution. I am the son of Miriama Rauhihi and Tigilau Ness, both Party members. Everything I know is from being a witness at the coattails of my parents.

Things are a little fresh for me, as my mother passed away in March 2021. No doubt, she would be happy that I'm here to represent. Kia ora.

My mother was about 18 when she joined the Polynesian Panthers. She grew up in rural Aotearoa and drove eight hours from there to Auckland city to work in a sewing factory. After a while, my mom noticed that they were all underpaid and the working conditions were bad. She brought those points to her bosses. They ignored her. She took the story to the union, then she organized a strike. That strike got notoriety in the media, and she was in a story in the local newspaper. From that story, uncle Will Ilolahia approached mom about joining the Party. That was the beginning for her and for me.

My mom loved people. A story that I remember is about how mom's fire and drive took her internationally in the fight for our people. As a member of the Polynesian Panthers, she was asked by the government to go to China to read and give statistics about the Indigenous peoples of New Zealand: per capita-birth rates, those in jail, unemployment rates, and more. She was to speak at a conference and rattle off stats. Someone told her that she shouldn't talk more about the stats because it might be deemed too radical. That was like a red flag to a bull. As she finished her speech, she was escorted from the podium, taken to the airport, and extradited out of the country. She spoke the truth because of the fire inside: her will.

When my mom went to Oakland, California for the 50th Anniversary of the BPP, she loved it. It really meant a lot to her. I can only imagine what it was like, doing all this work for so many years, then to physically see her mentors and tangibly touch them. The reality of being able to meet these people meant a lot to her.

I say a Karakia, a Maorī prayer, to honor my mother. It's a prayer in te reo Maorī, which contains a combination of proverbs that are said when people come together to bless the surroundings, the place, the people, and those who have gone before.

Miriama Rauhihi
Aotearoa (New Zealand) *(a remembrance by her son, Che Ness)*

1970 New York, New York: Black Panther outside the Harlem office.

I'm based at the very bottom of Aotearoa in a place called Aparima. I joined the Panthers at 54 years old. I am very privileged to be invited as an honorary member of the Polynesian Panthers. This was based on the story I wrote for young people about the Dawn Raids and the Polynesian Panthers.

I was a teacher and a university lecturer, and I was really shocked that most of the people that I came across had no knowledge of the dawn raids that happened here in New Zealand to Pacific Island people in 1974 and 1976. They had no knowledge of the Polynesian Panthers and their input. Once I heard these stories, they changed something in me.

I found that I had a choice to do something more to educate all people. The Educate to Liberate program shows that historical knowledge is powerful. Find out what you don't know. Be clear in your intention. This is how the Panthers got the government, the prime minister, to apologize for the awful things that happened 50 years ago.

Pauline Smith
Auckland, Aotearoa (New Zealand)

It was 1971 when I joined the Polynesian Panthers. I was 17. I was there till 1975, and I started my first year of teaching in 1972. We'd all go around the Ponsonby area, working with the co-op to distribute food to communities. We were young, young women then.

One day, we all met up and had a meeting to discuss the attitude of the men. It seems that we always had to do the cooking of the food and the making of cups of tea. We didn't mind that, but the men needed to do that as well.

Women: when opportunities come, whatever they may be, we need to take them on. Whether it's in education or helping within your own community, we can do that. Even if there's opposition from your family, if you know that's what you want to do and believe in it, then you should go ahead and do it. I learned that from my mother, who was involved in a lot of community work. That's what I think women and young girls should do.

Lenora Togalea Noble
Aotearoa (New Zealand)

1971 New York, New York:
Black Panther Party after school
program in Harlem.

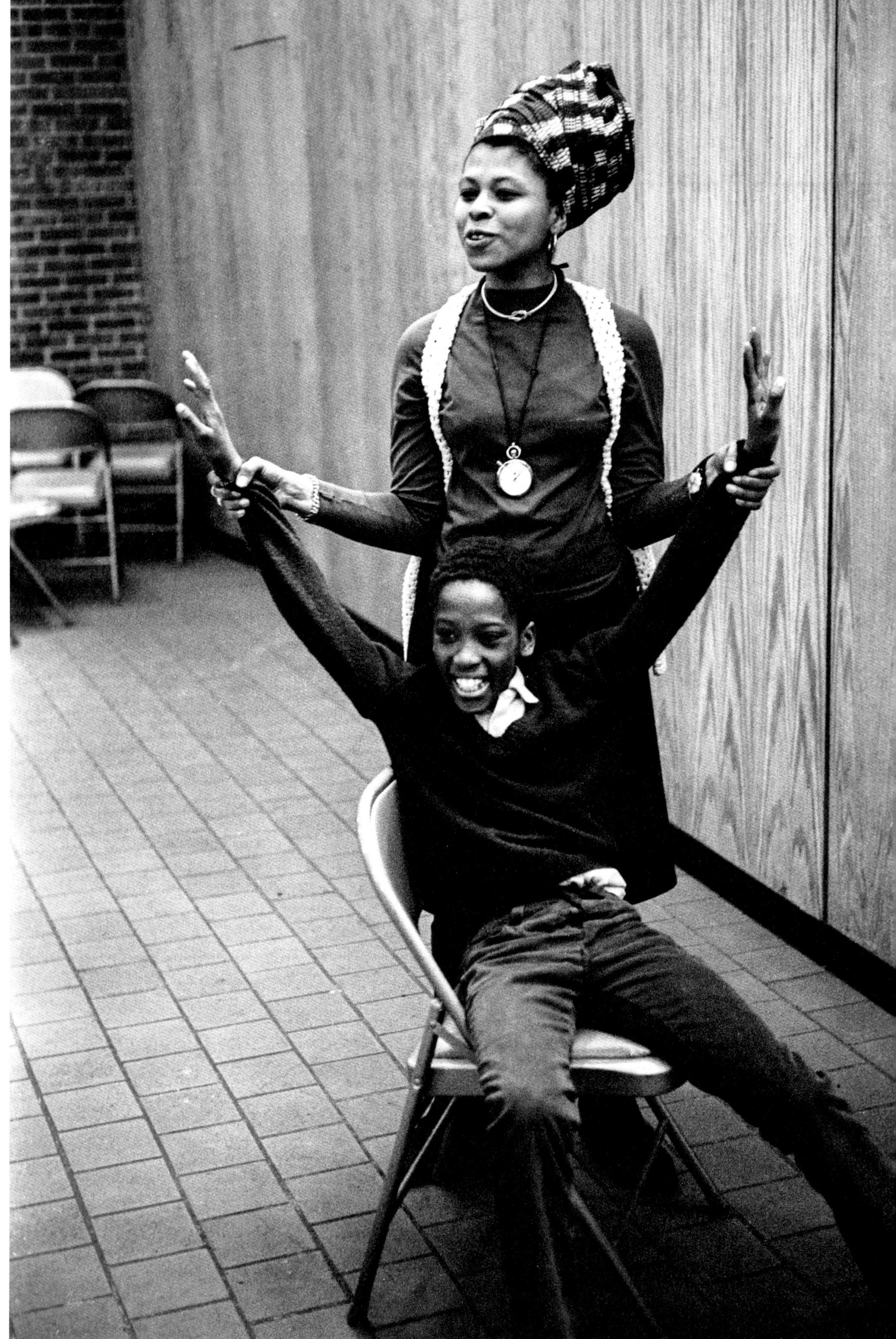

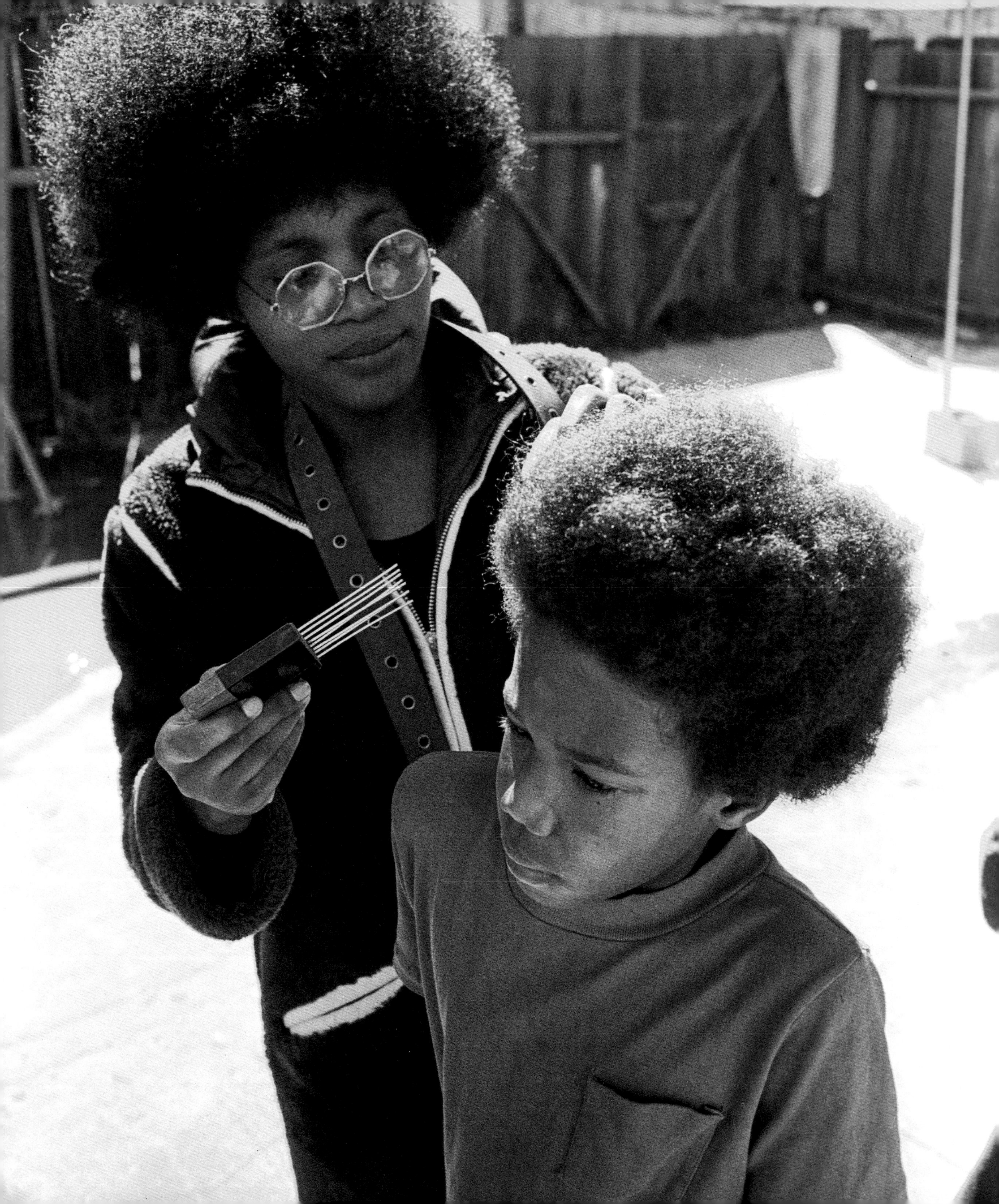

I became involved with the Polynesian Panthers when I worked with Miriama Rauhihi Ness, but I was drawn to the group through the land struggle. We felt strong about what was happening in America, with Black people. The struggles of Indigenous and Black people are alike in some way.

When I think about young women, I want to say to them: Come out, find your places, be inspiring, be fearless. Be dignified, be compassionate. Be daring, be humorous. Be revolutionary in your love. Be aware, be critical. Be proud. Create, meditate, listen, contribute. Be purposeful.

I was young at a time when I could be proud of who I am. I learned to acknowledge our people, my parents, for giving us that kind of head start. It's not often that young Pacific women are given this kind of encouragement.

I am very proud that *you* are including us in this book. I'm so grateful for the connections we have made with the Black Panther Party. Our stories are alike, as are our experiences of racism—the way we look, speak, the color of our skin, our fierceness, our softness; these are things that we are proud of. These very things make us different to the colonizer's expectations of who we should be, and the price for these differences are the sufferings we are challenging everyday… All Power to the People! I'm sending love, strength, and courage.

Betty Siō
Ponsonby, Aotearoa (New Zealand)

Mom was born in Fiji. She worked in the community, in social services. What drew her to the Panthers was their proposal about the injustices against Pacific Island people. From then on, mom formed many groups and helped empower them. After the Panthers, she continued her work for Pacific Island women—especially abused women. She worked with an associate on the street.

I'm glad that with what little I learned from my mom, I can imagine a better world. The Panthers set a moral code for me to follow, and I honor that moral code. Thank you.

Agnes Rose TuiSamoa
Aotearoa (New Zealand) *(a remembrance by her son, Vince TuiSamoa)*

1970 Oakland, California: Majeeda Smith combs Debra Williams' hair at the Intercommunal Youth Institute.

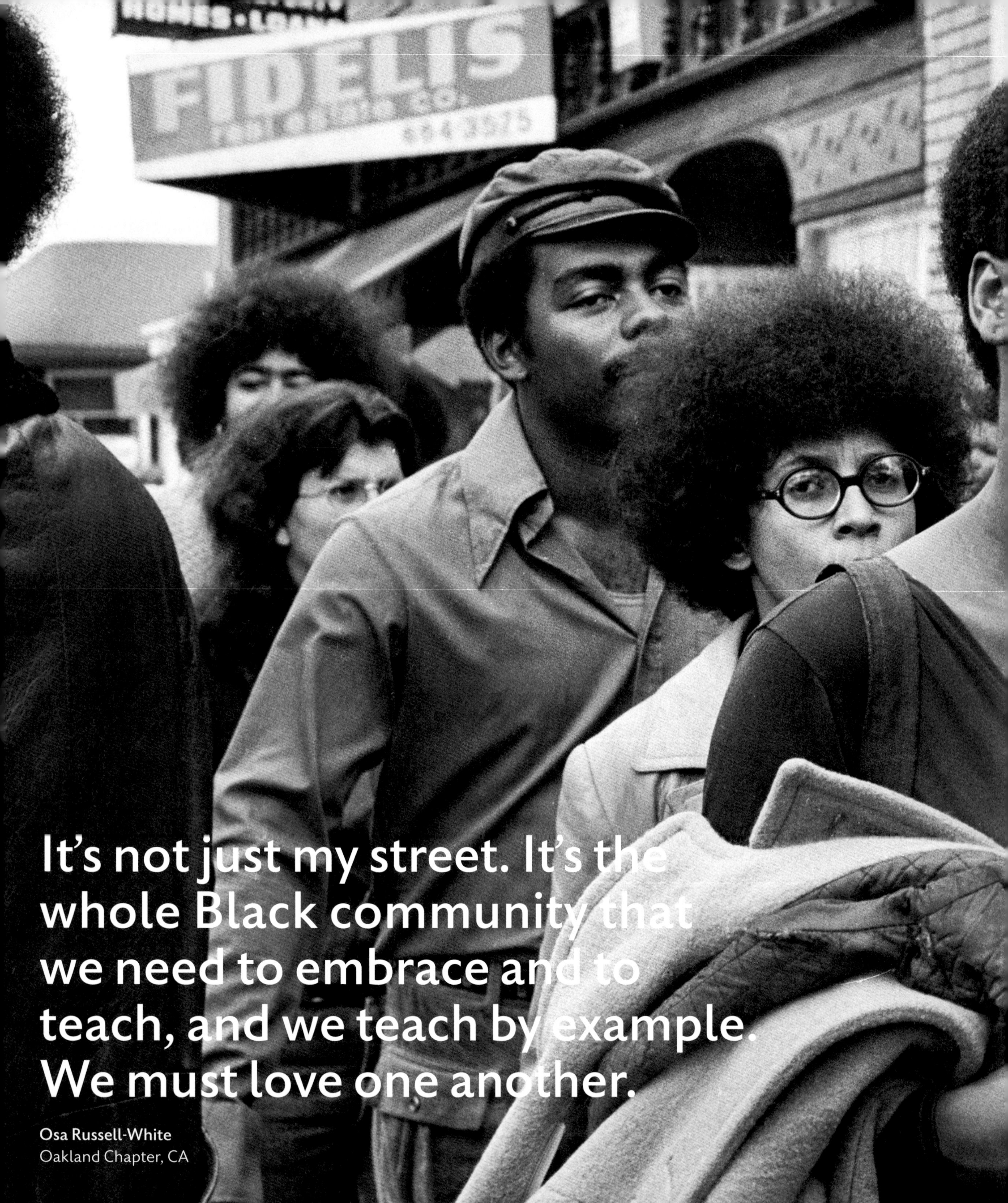

It's not just my street. It's the
whole Black community that
we need to embrace and to
teach, and we teach by example.
We must love one another.
Osa Russell-White
Oakland Chapter, CA

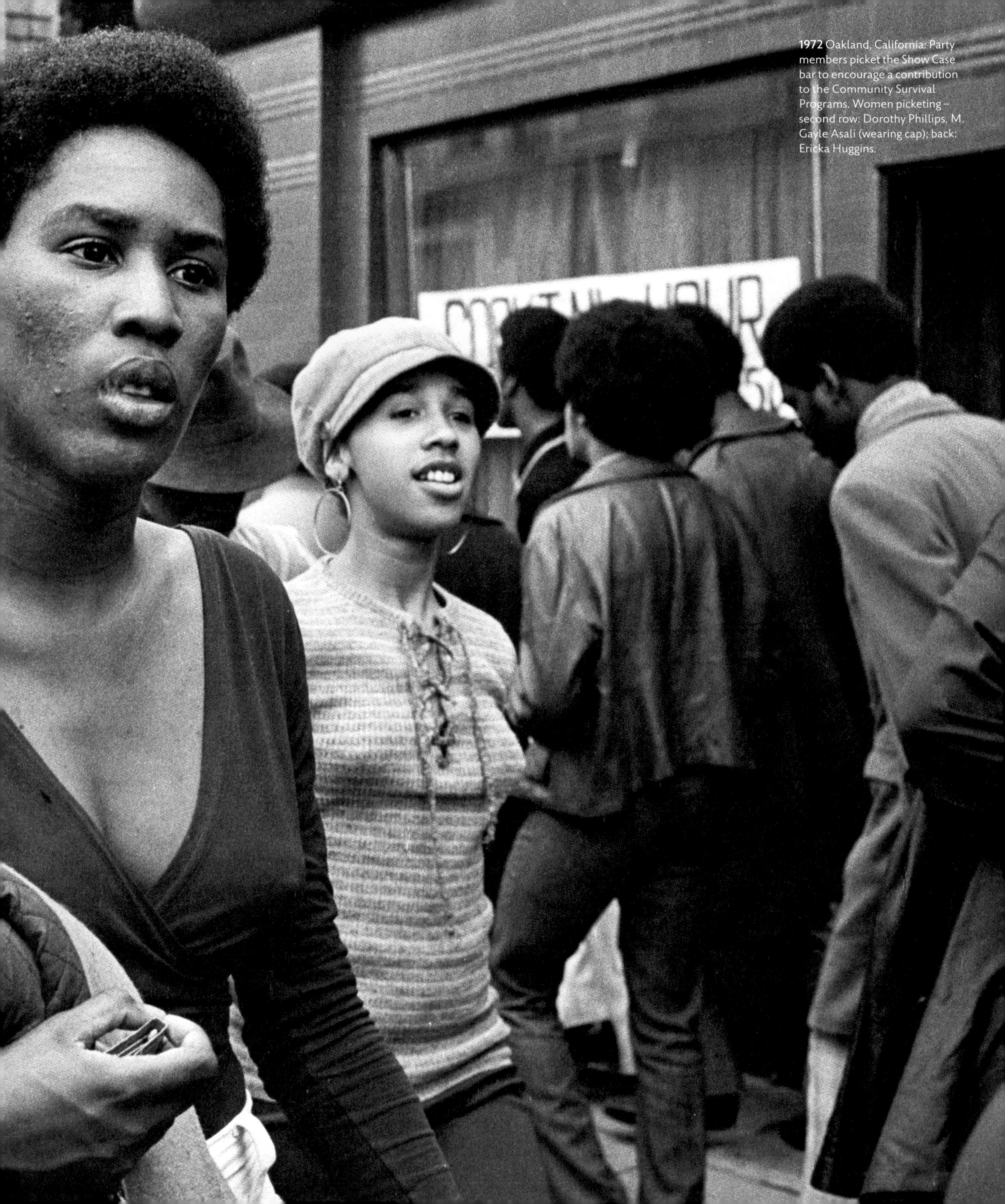

1972 Oakland, California: Party members picket the Show Case bar to encourage a contribution to the Community Survival Programs. Women picketing – second row: Dorothy Phillips, M. Gayle Asali (wearing cap); back: Ericka Huggins.

Afterword

By Alicia Garza

There can never be enough written about the role, leadership, and contributions of women to the Black Panther Party for Self Defense. Much like the many women who hold our communities together, too often our contributions are diminished or erased.

The stories and accounts of the work of the Party are often interwoven with patriarchy, where militancy and boldness and ingenuity are seen as the invention of and purview of men. These accounts are more than unfortunate—they not only strip the contours and texture of this work and who performed it, but they also perpetuate the same rules the Party tried to interrupt, though they may not have always been successful in doing so.

It would be easy to draw the conclusion that women did the caring and emotional work while men did the militant work. But these accounts beg to differ—what is powerful about these narratives is that they demonstrate how care, for ourselves and our communities, was itself a militant, radical act. In neighborhoods across the country, men and women came together to protect, defend, and invest in their communities.

Imagine thousands of militant, radical acts being performed every day, despite surveillance, harassment, and assassination—and imagine half of those militant radical acts being erased simply because we keep telling stories that omit the presence, contributions, and creativity of women.

Imagine women being treated as capable and competent, as the visionaries and architects of our future, but in the present.

Having grown up in the Bay Area, it has been a blessing to see, know, and befriend some of these visionaries. To see them in the grocery store or at the doctor's office. The history of the Black Panther Party for Self Defense is still alive, in our present. They are a part of our neighborhoods and associations, their eyes trained to see the revolutionary potential in all of us, even when we ourselves falter. We have made icons of a select few of these women, but they all deserve their flowers. After all, the seeds they planted continue to bloom, in our communities and also in our freedom dreams.

Their work lives on today. From schools to health clinics to childcare programs, much of their innovation and imagination persists, memorialized in institutions and practices which remain rooted in a deep love for the people, a desire to celebrate and cherish and invest in the present and the potential of us. To meet the needs of our communities ourselves that are cruelly being denied to us. Wherever there was denigration and degradation, the women of the Black Panther Party for Self Defense worked to restore dignity and resilience.

May we continue to be grateful for their contributions, may the memories of those who have left us too soon be a blessing, and may we adopt their strength, their courage, and their revolutionary imagination.

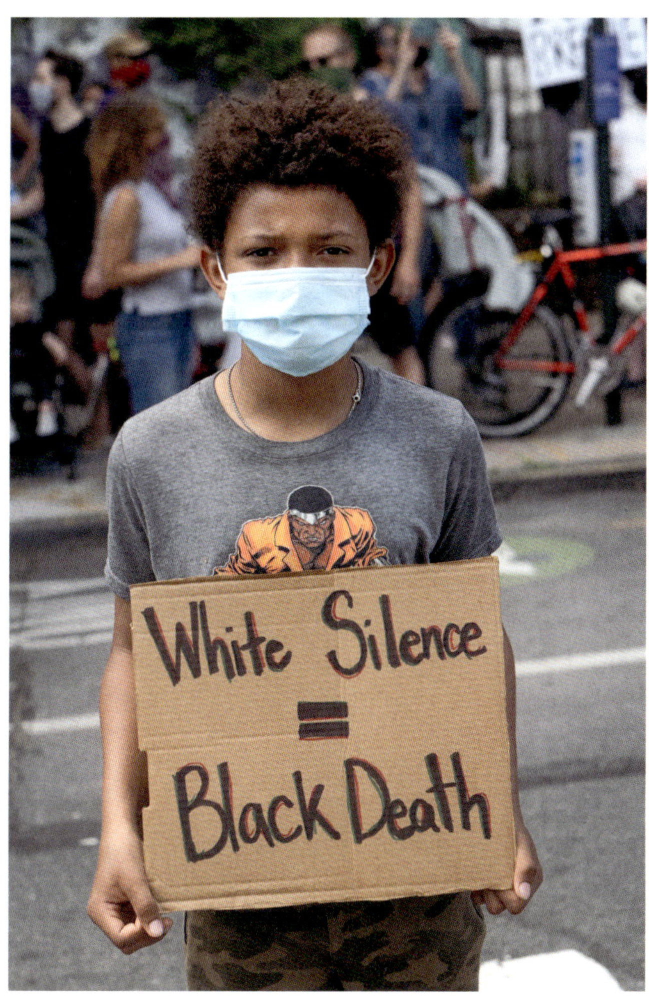

June 7, 2020 Brooklyn, New York: Child holds a sign at the Family March down Prospect Park West from 9th Street to Grand Army Plaza.

ISBN: 978-178884-175-7

British Library Cataloguing-in-Publication Data
A catalogue record for this book is available from the British Library

The author and publisher gratefully acknowledge the permission granted to reproduce the copyright material in this book. Every effort has been made to trace copyright holders and to obtain their permission for the use of copyright material. The publisher apologises for any errors or omissions in the text and would be grateful if notified of any corrections that should be incorporated in future reprints or editions of this book.

Editor: Bryn Porter
Designer: Anna Rieger
Typefaces: Rowton, Redaction

Image credits:
Page 26, Top: Donald Cunningham
Page 26, Bottom: Ducho Dennis
Page 158: Emory Douglas
Page 155: quilt by Rosita Thomas
Pages 48, 54, 124, 131, 138, 146, 151, 172:
artwork by M. Gayle Asali Dickson
Pages 37, 123, 166: Courtesy of Lincoln Cushing and Lisbet Tellefsen.

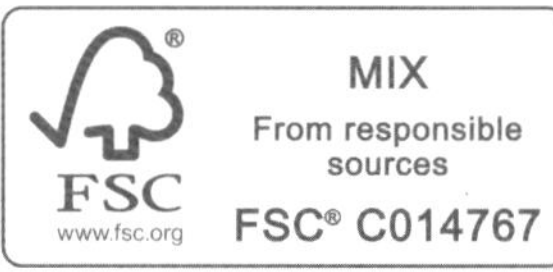

Printed in Belgium
for ACC Art Books Ltd., Woodbridge, Suffolk, UK
www.accartbooks.com

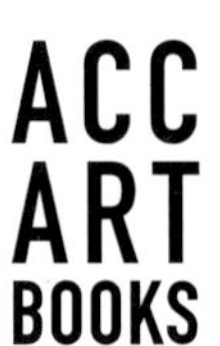

Acknowledgments

Our thanks to: Bobby Seale, for being co-founder of the Black Panther Party, and for always welcoming women to serve the people, body and soul. M. Gayle Asali Dickson, for your inspiring artwork. Rosita Holland Thomas, for your quilt honoring the Black Panther Party. Fredrika Newton, for your assistance with the scanning of photos. Benjamin Stone, for scanning the Huey P. Newton Papers at Stanford University. Jilchristina Vest, for the West Oakland Mural Project, and for compiling the collection of women's names. Angela Darlene LeBlanc-Ernest, for being the pillar of support for the words of each of the women honored in this book. Evelynn Cuautle, for your assistance with the process of transcribing the Comrade Sisters' conversations. Clark Bailey, for encouraging women to participate in this book about their lives. Susan Callender, for your legal support.

Thank you to John "Bunchy" Crear, Donald Cunningham, Dale Rascoe, and Lauryn Williams, Black Panther Party photographers. The family of Ducho Dennis, a Black Panther Party photographer. William Billy Jennings, Black Panther Party Archivist, for your excellent captioning. Lincoln Cushing and Lisbet Tellefsen, for the images of the posters. Thank you for your loving support. Phyllis Stoffman, for your support and for contributing one photo. Ryan Speth, for making the scans perfect. Steven Kasher, Esther Woerdehoff, and François Cheval for your advice and support. Al Quinn and Marty Roysher for opening our eyes. Yadav Jelal Huyler, for encouraging the authenticity of each woman's story and voice. Jade LeBlanc-Ernest, daughter of Angela LeBlanc-Ernest, for the many media consultations that helped us to select appropriate software programs and navigate technology to collect and process all of the Comrade Sisters' conversations. Mary Phillips, for continuing to honor the voices of women through your research and teaching career. Tracye A. Matthews, for your assistance in connecting us with women of the BPP. Don Carleton, director; and Erin Harbour, Aryn Glazier, and Amy Bowman, staff at The Dolph Briscoe Center for American History, at the University of Texas at Austin, for your invaluable assistance with research inquiries and myriad helpful accommodations during LeBlanc-Ernest's photographic archive visits. Bryn Porter, editor, and Mary Albi, director of sales and marketing at ACC Art Books. Anna Rieger, for layout and design. Andrea Smith, publicist at Andrea Smith Public Relations, for your support and love.

Thank you to all of the members of the Black Panther Party, those living and those with the ancestors. All of the children, grandchildren, and great-grandchildren of members of the Black Panther Party, those living and those with the ancestors.

1. We want freedom. We want power to determine the destiny of our Black Community. We believe that Black people will not be free until we are able to determine our destiny.

2. We want full employment for our people. We believe that the federal government is responsible and obligated to give every man employment or a guaranteed income. We believe that if the white American businessmen will not give full employment, then the means of production should be taken from the businessmen and placed in the community so that the people of the community can organize and employ all of its people and give a high standard of living.

3. We want an end to the robbery by the CAPITALIST of our Black Community. We believe that this racist government has robbed us and now we are demanding the overdue debt of forty acres and two mules. Forty acres and two mules was promised 100 years ago as a restitution for slave labor and mass murder of Black people. We will accept the payment in currency which will be distributed to our many communities. The Germans are now aiding the Jews in Israel for the genocide of the Jewish people. The Germans murdered six million Jews. The American racist has taken part in the slaughter of over fifty million Black people; therefore, we feel that this is a modest demand that we make.

4. We want decent housing fit for shelter of human beings. We believe that if the white landlords will not give decent housing to our Black community, then the housing and the land should be made into cooperatives so that our community, with government aid, can build and make decent housing for its people.

5. We want education for our people that exposes the true nature of this decadent American society. We want education that teaches us our true history and our role in the present-day society. We believe in an educational system that will give to our people a knowledge of self. If a man does not have knowledge of himself and his position in society and the world, then he has little chance to relate to anything else.

6. We want all Black men to be exempt from military service. We believe that Black people should not be forced to fight in the military service to defend a racist government that does not protect us. We will not fight and kill other people of color in the world who, like Black people are being victimized by the white racist government of America. We will protect ourselves from the force and violence of the racist police and the racist military, by whatever means necessary.

7. We want an immediate end to POLICE BRUTALITY and MURDER of Black people. We believe we can end police brutality in our Black community by organizing Black self-defense groups that are dedicated to defending our Black community from racist police oppression and brutality. The Second Amendment to the Constitution of the United States gives a right to bear arms. We therefore believe that all Black people should arm themselves for self-defense.